W9-APY-736

MORAL GUIDANCE

MORAL

GUIDANCE

By EDWIN F. HEALY, S.J., *Gregorian University*

Revised by JAMES F. MEARA, S.J., *Saint Louis University*

LOYOLA UNIVERSITY PRESS

Chicago, Illinois

BJ 1249
H 43
rev. ed.

IMPRIMI POTEST:
   Joseph P. Fisher, s.j.
   Provincial of the Missouri Province
   May 17, 1960

NIHIL OBSTAT:
   Austin G. Schmidt, s.j.
   Censor deputatus
   June 2, 1960

IMPRIMATUR:
   ✠ Albert Cardinal Meyer
   Archbishop of Chicago
   June 3, 1960

Preface
to the first
edition

Forty years ago a very large proportion of all non-Catholics in America recognized the authority of the ten commandments and admitted that obedience to the dictates of the Decalogue was necessary for living a righteous life. Those outside the Church agreed in general with Catholic moral teaching in many points. The passing years, however, have brought about a great change. Today the truth of the teaching contained in the ten commandments is often called into question. The Catholic's attitude toward fundamental moral questions is regarded by many as antiquated. Many others, although they do not reject the ten commandments entirely, interpret them so liberally as to deprive them of much of their force. Consequently, there is, at the present time, greater necessity that Catholic laymen know and be able to defend the true, unchanging doctrines of moral conduct. Experience shows that too many Catholics, though well educated in other matters, are regrettably ignorant about some moral questions of not a little importance.

MORAL GUIDANCE has been written as a possible help to the understanding of Christian principles of morality. Perhaps it may serve as a partial antidote to the poisonous notions of proper conduct with which so much of our modern literature is replete. This book is intended, in general, for the use of students, wherever found, who are sufficiently mature to profit from its use. Such students are soon to end the comparatively sheltered life of their school days and will assume before long more serious responsibilities. For the most part they realize this, and consequently they study with greater interest and profit the many problems with which they may soon be confronted. They are as a rule quite mature, and so for them there is little danger that a discussion of the limits of what is licit may lower their ideals.

The student will no doubt be interested in the cases given at the end of most of the chapters. These are meant to illustrate the application of certain moral principles to everyday life. Often enough a person believes that he has a clear understanding of a particular doctrine but, when faced with a concrete case, he may be inclined to judge according to mere feelings and to lose sight of the principles involved.

It will be noticed that no mention is made in MORAL GUIDANCE of the moral aspects of matrimony and other topics of this nature. These have been purposely omitted because in most Catholic colleges today special courses are given on the family and because the subject is adequately treated in the author's MARRIAGE GUIDANCE. Hence these important questions thus receive the attention that they richly deserve.

My thanks are due to all those whose suggestions have helped in my preparation of this textbook. Many fellow Jesuits, both instructors in religion and others, have kindly given me the benefit of their sound advice and honest criticism. I owe a special debt of gratitude to Father Vincent L. Brennan, S.J. and to Father Francis J. O'Boyle, S.J. It was Father Brennan who first discovered the need of a textbook of this kind and who persuaded me to undertake the task of writing MORAL GUIDANCE. Father O'Boyle generously devoted much of his time to a careful reading of the manuscript and called attention to many points that have improved the final copy.

E. F. H.

February 2, 1942

Preface
to the revised
edition

THERE are several reasons why the excellent work of Father Healy was in need of revision. The most obvious is that changes have been made in certain church laws since 1942. A much more important reason is that certain problems have arisen since the time of the original publication (for example, atomic warfare) and that the solution of other problems has changed somewhat because of changes in our society or because of further discoveries. For example, a moral theologian today would approach the problem of the morality of prize fighting with much more caution since the scientific discoveries concerning brain damage resulting from repeated blows to the head. As facts or our knowledge of facts change, there must be a new application of old principles. Incidentally, this is one of the reasons why the study of moral problems is so fascinating and vital.

A third reason is that there has been considerable discussion in the last two decades on the science of moral theology and on the methods of teaching it. Vehement criticism of the traditional approach has forced moral theologians to reconsider their position and either modify it to some extent or at least defend it by explaining the reasons for the traditional approach. There have also been many positive suggestions for the improvement of the presentation of moral principles and problems. An example of a valuable positive suggestion is that more use be made of modern psychological and sociological discoveries. Many of these suggestions have been adopted and are now part of the accepted approach to moral problems.

Finally, there has been a change for the better in the teaching of religion or theology in Catholic colleges. More teachers have received special training for teaching theology in college. The Society of Catholic College Teachers of Sacred Doctrine has been formed and has contributed significantly to the improvement of content and method in the teaching of theology. As a result a college student today is better prepared to deal with theological concepts and to absorb more matter in a given amount of time.

The present revision has been made with these factors in mind. Much of what Father Healy wrote has been left intact. Some material has been dropped and other parts have been changed. A considerable amount of new matter has been added.

Had Father Healy lived, he would of course have been the one to make the revision. On February 22, 1957 he died of a heart attack at the Pontifical Gregorian University in Rome, where he had been lecturing on moral theology during the previous five years. Friends felt that his death was due to the charity which impelled him to accept tasks lying far outside the sphere of duty and to the relentless energy with which he attacked whatever work was to be done. We shall be happy indeed if this revision is not found to fall too far short of what Father Healy would have made it.

MORAL GUIDANCE is not intended to be a complete work on moral theology. Even a four-volume work like *Moral and Pastoral Theology* by Reverend Henry Davis, S.J. does not deal completely with all of moral theology. Consequently teachers and students are expected to use supplementary material in their discussion of the matter presented. The choice of that supplementary matter will depend to some extent on the individual teacher. Some teachers will have a special interest in questions of medical ethics, others in justice in modern business practices or in some other part of the matter covered. Students in turn will develop special interests and will want to go far beyond what is given in MORAL GUIDANCE. The following suggestions may be helpful in guiding them in their study.

Since 1942 *Theological Studies* has been publishing an annual summary and evaluation of the work done in moral theology. In recent years this summary has been divided into two parts and published in two different issues. The summary is entitled "Current Theology: Notes on Moral Theology." Familiarity with such a summary is necessary to get an appreciation of the application of the general principles of moral theology to modern problems. It is suggested that students, at least those who have reached their junior year in college, become familiar with these summaries over a period of five years. Practically all the major problems will be touched on in that length of time and, if they are mentioned only briefly, reference will be made to earlier summaries in which the matter is treated more completely. No other supplementary reading would give the student so broad a knowledge of the whole field. These summaries can also be the source of many valuable references for the writing of papers or the preparation of particular problems to be presented in class.

In addition the student should become familiar with some other general work on moral theology, so that on each problem he will read not only what is contained in MORAL GUIDANCE but also a treatment of the same matter in another book. A certain amount of repetition is necessary to grasp the principles and see their application to problems. Each author will present the matter in a slightly different way, and a comparison of two presentations will help the student to see what is essential. It is sometimes difficult to recognize a truth when it is put in a different way; but once one does recognize it, he has *learned* it. Teachers are well aware that many students can give back what is in the book but cannot recognize a question which asks for the same matter in a different manner. Teachers are free to suggest any work they wish to accomplish this purpose. Here it is suggested that the work used be Father Davis' *Moral and Pastoral Theology*, Volumes 1 and 2.

Some of the matters treated in MORAL GUIDANCE open up whole fields of discussion. They may be covered only briefly, but an attempt has been made to give a short bibliography at the end of each chapter to guide the student who is interested in further reading. These bibliographies are by no means complete, but the works chosen should be in every Catholic library. By going to these works the student can immediately get a much more comprehensive bibliography than could possibly be printed in MORAL GUIDANCE. For example, a premedical student may be interested in pursuing further some problems of medical ethics. The bibliography contains reference to only two books, Father Healy's and Father Kelly's. There are many other excellent books on medical ethics, but with these two as a start the student will quickly become acquainted with others. If possible, a rather large reference or short-term (one-day) reserve shelf should be formed from the books given in the bibliographies. The bibliographies also contain some references to articles in theological publications which will be found in most Catholic libraries. They are not comprehensive, but give at least one reference to each side of a disputed question.

The examples and cases used in the book attempt to bring out only one aspect of a problem or illustrate one principle. In real life the problems are not usually so simple, since several factors may be involved in one case. Teachers and students can use the cases and examples as starting points for more involved cases. Some consideration was given to the possibility of including involved cases in the text, but the idea was rejected because they frequently confuse the main point under consideration. One of the purposes of MORAL GUIDANCE is to help students develop the habit of theological thinking. When a teacher is satisfied that his class is sufficiently advanced, he can then present the students with involved cases.

I would like to express my gratitude to the Reverend Edmund F. Burke, S.J. and the Reverend Mortimer H. Gavin, S.J. for their helpful suggestions. It is hoped that the changes and the additional matter in this revision will make MORAL GUIDANCE a work more suited to the needs of contemporary educated Catholics and will help them in the development of that prudent charity which is the mark of the mature follower of Christ.

J. F. M.

Saint Louis University, May 24, 1960

Contents

CHAPTER I

The purpose
of moral
guidance

THERE are several reasons why an educated Catholic should be familiar with the moral teaching of the Church and the principles on which that teaching is based. The first reason is that the moral teaching of the Church is part of the revelation which God has made to the human race. Part of it can be arrived at by the use of reason, but what we can know about the goodness or badness of human acts from reason is incomplete, often lacks the certainty necessary for practical application, and is in certain areas very difficult of acquisition. If man is to live as he should, revelation is morally necessary. The fact that God has revealed a truth is sufficient reason for a believer to devote his mind to it and make it a part of his thinking.

A second reason for such a study is the need which all men have for guidance in their everyday lives. It is impossible to have a trained theologian at hand to give guidance in all the practical moral decisions which must be made every day. Even if it were possible, it would be inadvisable. A mature Catholic is expected to have some understanding of the reasons why he does things. To be completely passive in carrying out the moral teaching of the Church would be inhuman. Moral acts are vital acts, flowing from intelligent, living human beings, and their meaning should be understood by those who perform them. It is one thing to attend Mass on Sunday out of obedience to the Church; it is quite another to attend Sunday Mass with an understanding of the obligation to worship God and an appreciation of the self-offering essential to proper participation in the Mass. Similarly, there is a great difference between a young Catholic man or woman who practices chastity with an understanding of its beauty and purpose and one who avoids unchastity only because it is forbidden.

A third reason is that we are living in a society which rejects many of the principles on which Catholics base their lives. It does not help a great deal to answer all objections raised by our fellow countrymen, many of whom ask them in good faith, by answering that it is the teaching of the Church. It is true that this is our ultimate reason for accepting these principles; however, many of them are based on the natural law, and the natural law is a form of evidence which men of good faith can appreciate. Others will accept evidence from Scripture. Others simply want to understand why, of two things which seem similar to them, one is allowed by the Church and another is forbidden; for example, they will ask what the difference is between artificial birth control and the use of rhythm. Very few understand the difference between the teaching power of the Church and her power of ruling. They ask why the Church does not change some of her laws on marriage just as she has changed her law in regard to the Communion fast. An ability to explain Catholic morality may not bring others into the Church in many cases, but it will bring respect for the Church and does help to break down prejudice.

ETHICS AND MORAL GUIDANCE

We said above that ethics can never be an adequate guide to reach the perfection demanded of members of the Church. Moral guidance differs from ethics, first of all, in its sources. Ethics is based on reason alone. Moral guidance is based on reason and the teaching of the Church as the divinely constituted authority in matters of faith and morals. The role of the Church is not simply to repeat what is contained in Scripture and tradition but to interpret, explain, and apply the teachings of Scripture and tradition to the contemporary world.

The motive for accepting the conclusions of ethics is the evidence on which these conclusions are based. The motive for accepting the conclusions of moral guidance is the authority of God. This authority may be exercised positively by the infallible teaching of the Church. It may also be exercised negatively. If two groups of theologians differ in their answers to a moral problem, the Church may allow both opinions to be taught; however, the Church in such cases is exercising her authority, for neither group teaches anything contrary to what the Church herself has taught infallibly. In matters which are not taught infallibly the Church allows freedom of discussion and opinion. In these cases the motive for accepting one or the other opinion is the evidence on which it is based.

The spirit of moral guidance differs greatly from that of ethics. It is the spirit of the Gospels. No one can really understand the moral teaching of the Church unless he first has an understanding of the historical Christ both as a teacher and as an example. He summed up His teaching in the twofold love of God and the neighbor; He lived out that teaching by His supreme act of love for the human race on the cross. Moral guidance is permeated by this twofold love. We will say more about this aspect of moral guidance in our treatment of charity in Chapter 3.

Moral guidance and ethics have quite different orientations. Ethics establishes some kind of natural end for man, but the purpose of man is certainly the stumbling block of natural ethics, at least looked at historically; this is especially true of those systems of ethics developed with no reference to divine revelation. Moral guidance begins with the fact that man is in a state of trial but is created to see God face to face in an act of knowledge and love the beauty of which we cannot comprehend. The unending happiness which God has prepared for man is a flowering of the supernatural knowledge (faith), confidence (hope), and love (charity) which man has in this life. It is to be attained by good actions with the grace of God, but can be lost by the free rejection of God (unrepented mortal sin). Revelation gives us certainty about the existence of a future life and about the nature of that life, eternal and supernatural, a life of supreme happiness.

Even pagan antiquity had its ethicians. The work of Aristotle on ethics contains much that is admirable. But how majestic, when compared with the puny stature of human teachers, does not the figure of Christ appear to be! His sublime message surpasses anything that the human mind could conceive. We study the content of that message in moral guidance.

OBLIGATION AND PERFECTION

There has been some criticism of moral theologians in recent years on the ground that they treat only what is of obligation and thereby develop in their students, both clerical and lay, a negative attitude. There is some validity to this criticism, but moral theologians point out that there have been attempts to remedy this defect by including more positive matter in modern treatises and that the teaching of perfection is given in other disciplines and in the sermons, retreats, and other spiritual activities of the faithful. The problem is a difficult one. Our Lord certainly recognized the difference between what is of obligation and what is of counsel. That distinction must be kept and a clear line must be drawn between those things which bind under sin and those which are urged as means to greater perfection. Unless this distinction is kept, there can be no scientific study of moral activity and we are left with somewhat vague general principles which are not sufficient for the solution of complicated moral problems. It sounds very inspiring to say that charity solves all problems, but charity does not tell us which action is a concrete expression of charity in a given situation. Again, if we do not make distinctions, we will be imposing an impossible burden on the faithful, since everything becomes obligatory and they become discouraged because of the magnitude of the task of leading a moral life.

It can also be pointed out that one who lives a life in accordance with the teachings of moral theologians is very pleasing in the eyes of God. If all Catholics kept the commandments and lived according to the precepts of charity imposed upon them by our Lord, the Church would flourish and the glory of God would be increased immeasurably. Let us not look down on those who are fulfilling the essential obligations laid upon them by God; they are most pleasing to Him and deserve the credit due to those who fight the good fight.

On the other hand, care must be taken to see that the faithful do not develop the "it's-only-a-venial-sin" attitude. The Church has always stressed the positive challenge and opportunity for greater perfection held out to us by Christ. She needs men and women who lead a life of perfect submission to God's will. She also reminds those who do less that God ordinarily distributes His graces in accordance with our generosity and that temptations may arise which require the extraordinary help of God. It is almost impossible to adopt the principle of avoiding only mortal sin without putting oneself in danger of falling. One who *de facto* avoids all mortal sin does so because he has done much more than simply avoid mortal sin: he has used the means at his disposal to strengthen himself so that he can resist temptation and adhere to the will of God despite difficulties. In this textbook distinctions are made between mortal and venial sin and between venial sin and imperfection, but enough positive matter is included to counteract the unwholesome negative attitude abhorred both by moral theologians and their critics.

The chief means which should be used to avoid negative attitudes is the development of the virtues. Some of them are treated in Chapter 3; some are treated briefly or developed further in other parts of the book. Since virtues are vital principles of action, it is the task of the individual to develop them in himself. Their meaning and beauty can be presented, but their development comes only with prayer and continual effort in everyday life.

POSTULATES

The postulates of a branch of knowledge are the premises which that branch accepts without demonstration because these facts have already been proved or demonstrated in some other study. The postulates of moral guidance are as follows:

1. God exists and is the rewarder of good and the punisher of evil.
2. God created man and all things.
3. Man has an immortal soul and a free will.
4. Holy Scripture is the word of God.
5. Christ is God.
6. The Catholic Church is the true church of Christ.
7. The pope of Rome, when speaking *ex cathedra*, is infallible.

The subject matter of moral guidance consists of the principal laws which God has given man to guide him in his moral conduct. Before entering into a detailed study of the commandments of God, it is wise first to clarify several general ideas that will frequently recur in this course. A clean-cut understanding of these ideas will help greatly in determining the precise morality of many actions.

Bibliography

Clark, Francis. "The Challenge to Moral Theology." *Clergy Review* 38:214-23, April 1953.

Davis, Henry. *Moral and Pastoral Theology*, seventh edition, edited by L. W. Geddes, Vol. 1, pp. 1-10. 4 vols. New York: Sheed and Ward, 1958.

Doyle, James J. "Ethics and the Faith." *American Catholic Philosophical Proceedings* 31:36-49, 1957.

Ermecke, Gustave. "Catholic Moral Theology Today." *Theology Digest* 2:19-22, Winter 1954.

Ford, John C. and Gerald Kelly. *Contemporary Moral Theology*, Vol. 1, Chapter 1, "The Church and the Moral Law," pp. 3-18; Chapter 4, "Modern Criticisms of Moral Theology," pp. 42-59; Chapter 5, "New Approaches to Moral Theology," pp. 60-79; Chapter 6, "Reflections on the Criticism and New Approaches," pp. 80-103. Westminster: Newman Press, 1958.

Maritain, Jacques. *Science and Wisdom*, translated by Bernard Wall. New York: Charles Scribner's Sons, 1940.

Pinckaers, Servais. "The Revival of Moral Theology." *Cross Currents* 7:56-67, Winter 1957.

Pius XII. *Humani generis*. New York: Paulist Press, 1950.

CHAPTER II

Some
principles
of ethics

IMPUTABLE acts are those whose goodness or badness is attributed to the one performing them. A man who freely and knowingly slanders another is guilty of a morally wrong act. It is his act, not the act of anyone else, and its badness is properly attributed to him. If, however, an individual does not have control over the action which he performs, he cannot be said to be responsible for the action, and its moral badness cannot be imputed to him as something for which he can be held responsible. We must, then, carefully distinguish from other actions those acts which we call inadvertent acts.

An *inadvertent act* (often termed an *act of man*) is an act which, though performed by a human being, does not depend on his free will. Man either has no dominion over such actions or for some reason does not make use of the dominion which he possesses. For example, man has no control of the beating of the heart or of talking in his sleep. He does not exercise dominion over thoughts indulged in during a moment of distraction; nor

7

over things which are done without reflection in such actions as those of walking and eating.

EXAMPLE. A hospital patient under the influence of drugs talks about secret knowledge which he has no right to reveal. He is completely unaware of what he is saying. His action is inadvertent.

THE MORALITY OF HUMAN ACTS

DEFINITION OF A HUMAN ACT

A human act is an act that is deliberately performed by one possessed of the use of reason. *Deliberately performed* means that it is done freely and knowingly.

THE MORALITY OF A HUMAN ACT

Every act derives its morality from three elements: (1) the object of the act, (2) the circumstances surrounding the act, and (3) the purpose which the one performing the act has in mind.

1. The *object* of a human act is that which the one acting sets out to do as distinguished from his ultimate purpose in doing it. For example, the object of a suicide's act is the blowing out of his brains; his *purpose* is to escape evils which he is unwilling to bear. The object of an act places it in a certain category. To take without justification what belongs to another is theft; falsely to impute a crime to another is calumny.

The object is not merely the act considered in its physical make-up. It is the act viewed in its moral nature; that is, the act considered in its relationship to the moral law. Of it the question is asked: Does it conform to the standard of right conduct or is it contrary to this standard? In theft, for example, the physical act of taking money from another is not the object. The object is the *unjust* taking of property belonging to another. It is the taking of another's money considered in the light of the moral law, which forbids one who has no right to do so to take another's money.

If the object of an act is intrinsically evil, the act is *never* allowed. Lying, blasphemy, and stealing, for example, are intrinsically evil.

2. The *circumstances* are elements which are distinct from the act itself but which change or modify its morality. For a Catholic to eat meat is not in itself a sin. If, however, the meat is eaten on Friday, this fact may change the morality of the act.

8

Circumstances are capable of changing:

a) an (ordinarily) indifferent act into a sinful one; for example, to read a novel *while attending Sunday Mass;*

b) an (ordinarily) venially sinful act into a mortal sin; for example, to steal a dollar *from a very poor man;*

c) an (ordinarily) mortally sinful act into a venial sin; for example, to blaspheme *when only half aware of what one is doing;*

d) a sinful action into one doubly sinful; for example, unjustly to strike *a woman who is consecrated to God.*

3. The *purpose* (or end) of a human act is the intention which prompts one to perform such an act; for example, *a boy tells a lie to protect his friend.*

An action is morally good if all three elements (object, circumstances, end) are substantially good. "Substantially" as here used is opposed to accidentally. For example, my attending Sunday Mass may be a substantially good action even though my motive in going to church includes a trace of vanity which makes it accidentally imperfect. The slight sin of vanity that is committed does not change the substance of my act of attending Mass. An action is morally bad if even only one of these three elements—the object, the circumstances, and the purpose—is bad. The reason is that we are always obliged to avoid moral evil. If an action is evil for any one of the three reasons, we cannot avoid that evil part unless we refrain from the whole action. If, then, we perform the act in spite of the substantially evil element in it, we are performing an evil action. These principles make clear the morality involved in the following cases.

EXAMPLE 1. A student in a dormitory plays his hi-fi set at top volume at three in the morning. The circumstances of time and volume make his action bad.

EXAMPLE 2. An employee of a bank embezzles money in order to send his sons to college. The object of his act is evil; his good purpose does not make it moral.

CONDITIONS AFFECTING IMPUTABILITY

One is accountable to God only for his deliberate actions. Deliberate actions are actions performed with the *knowledge* of what one is doing and with the *consent* of the will. In order to gauge the accountability of a particular action one must consider the degree of deliberateness involved. If one's knowledge of the nature of the act or one's consent is diminished, the imputability for the action will be lessened. There are five chief hindrances to full imputability. These are (1) ignorance, (2) emotion, (3) fear, (4) habits, and (5) violence.

IGNORANCE

Ignorance in general is merely a lack of knowledge regarding a certain thing. Since, however, ignorance may be either culpable or inculpable, we must distinguish the various kinds.

1. *Invincible ignorance* is ignorance which cannot be dispelled by diligence in keeping with the object and circumstances. Inability to dispel ignorance may arise from various causes.

a) It may be impossible for the individual to remove his ignorance because he has no way of suspecting that he *is* ignorant.

EXAMPLE. A child baptized in the Church is raised without any religious instruction. He does not know of his baptism nor of his obligation to live according to the laws of the Church.

b) I realize that knowledge on a certain point should be acquired but it is morally impossible for me to acquire it.

EXAMPLE. A policeman knows that certain harmful rackets are flourishing in his district and makes all possible effort to find the criminals. None of the victims will give evidence because of their fear of reprisals. The policeman's ignorance of the criminals is invincible.

No objectively wrong act is culpable if it is performed in invincible ignorance regarding its wrongness. One cannot sin without realizing it. Such an action is not formally sinful, for it is not known as evil. Nor is the state of ignorance regarding the morality of the act culpable, for it is not voluntary.

2. *Vincible ignorance* is ignorance which can be cleared up if one uses sufficient diligence. Vincible ignorance may be one of three kinds: (a) simple, (b) crass, and (c) affected.

a) *Simple vincible ignorance* is ignorance which exists when one uses some, but not sufficient, diligence in an effort to remove his ignorance.

EXAMPLE. A lawyer is in doubt about the advice he should give a client. He consults standard works and does not get an answer. He makes no further effort although he is sure that he could find the answer by some research. The client suffers a serious financial loss as a result of following his advice.

If one performs an objectively evil action in simple vincible ignorance, the action is culpable. However, its culpability is lessened by the presence of that ignorance.

b) *Crass ignorance* is ignorance which, though it is not directly willed, could and should be cleared up, but about which the individual suffering from it does nothing.

EXAMPLE. A hard-working executive suspects that he has a heart condition which may lead to serious trouble. He continues to work at his usual pace and puts off seeing a doctor because he is too busy.

Crass ignorance lessens imputability to a greater or less extent; nevertheless it makes one gravely culpable if it concerns a matter of grave importance.

c) *Affected ignorance* is vincible ignorance which one deliberately fosters in order that he may not be restricted by what investigation might disclose.

EXAMPLE. A woman meets a very attractive man at a party. She suspects that he is married, but goes out with him several times. She deliberately avoids people who could tell whether he is married so that she can continue to go with him.

Affected ignorance in regard to a matter of grave importance is gravely culpable.

EMOTION

Moral theologians often discuss passion as a factor affecting imputability. We prefer to speak of emotion, for passion has so many different meanings for philosophers and psychologists that confusion can result from the use of the term. Moreover, whatever passion may be, it does not affect imputability in and of itself, but only insofar as it results in some emotion.

An emotion is a feeling, such as a feeling of anger, of fear, of joy, or of despair. The tired mother of six children, driven to distraction by their misbehavior, may have a strong feeling of anger. Persons trapped by fire in a theater or school may feel extreme fear. When wars ended with victory for our nation entire cities have gone almost mad with joy. Wealthy men, after losing their entire fortunes in a depression, have suicided as a result of despair. All men, even the good, experience emotions. Christ wept before the tomb of Lazarus. He was angry when He drove the money-changers from the Temple. He feared the approach of His crucifixion and said that His soul was sorrowful even unto death.

He rejoiced because the hour was at hand when He would accomplish the mission given Him by the Father.

The experiences that produce emotions may be chiefly bodily, chiefly mental, or a combination of both. After a long illness a person may have a feeling of discouragement in facing even minor problems. A politician who is convinced that he has rendered faithful service to his constituency may be plunged into sadness because he is overwhelmingly defeated at the polls. An aged man, put in a public institution by his ungrateful children and then never visited by them, suffers both from his illness and because of the lack of love shown by his family.

It is recognized that emotion, particularly fear and anger, may be so intense as to deprive one temporarily of the use of reason. Persons in a panic during a fire, tornado, or shipwreck may fight their way to safety without thinking of how they are injuring others. One may be so angry as to lose awareness of what he is doing. Actions performed while one is influenced to this extent by emotion are not human acts and consequently are not imputable. Such cases, however, are rare. But although emotion may seldom eliminate imputability, it often does lessen it. The extent to which emotion lessens imputability depends upon whether the emotion is antecedent or consequent.

Antecedent emotion is emotion that is antecedent to an act of the will. It is an emotion that occurs spontaneously. For example, somebody does something to injure or interfere with us, and we flare up in anger. The anger is automatic. It begins to exist without our willing that it should exist. Antecedent emotion lessens the guilt of an evil action performed while one is thus influenced, for such emotion arises without one's willing it and beclouds one's reason to a degree. Hence one's action is less free.

Consequent emotion is emotion that results from an act of the will or that is deliberately fostered. It is not altogether unusual for men and women purposely to work themselves up into an emotional state. A timid employee who intends to ask his employer for a raise may believe that he will have a better chance if he thinks of his grievances and allows himself to become angry. A fighter about to enter the ring, a coach who feels that his team needs a tongue-lashing between the halves, a wife who is about to ask a selfish husband for an increase in her spending money, or a teacher who must reprimand an unruly boy may look upon a feeling of anger as helpful for achieving the purpose in mind. For similar reasons one might deliberately foster and seek to intensify an emotion that is already present.

Consequent emotion does not lessen the imputability of actions performed while one is under its influence. The reason is that such emotion results from a free act of the will for which the individual is responsible. One who arouses in himself a feeling of anger or of fear cannot excuse himself on the ground that he "could not help" acting as he did.

FEAR

Fear is one of the emotions, and whatever has been said of emotion in general applies to fear in particular. It is customary, however, to treat fear separately and with more attention to certain details. Matrimonial courts may have to rule upon the validity of marriages said to have been contracted through fear. One who applies for admission to a seminary or to a religious order or congregation should not be accepted if his action was the result of fear. For such reasons it is necessary to say more about degrees in the intensity of fear and the manner in which it affects the one who experiences it.

Fear is mental agitation brought on by the apprehension of some present or imminent danger. This danger may be bodily injury, loss of reputation or of riches, or harm to a friend. The danger may be real or purely imaginary, for as long as something is apprehended as a danger, it can cause fear. Fear can be (1) grave or (2) slight.

1. *Grave fear* is that fear which is aroused by the presence of a danger:

a) that is regarded by most people as serious; for example, fear of death or of the loss of a leg;

b) that is judged to be serious by the one concerned. For example, a certain young girl dreads the thought of receiving a scolding in public, although other girls suffer very little embarrassment from such reprimands.

2. *Slight fear* is that fear which is aroused by:

a) a danger that is not serious; for example, fear of bumping your head on a low ceiling;

b) a grave danger that is not very probable; for example, fear of death when flying a plane on a slightly misty day.

One can be affected by fear in such a way that he is said to act either *through fear* or *with fear*.

One acts *through fear* if it is the fear that induces him so to act.

EXAMPLE 1. A small boy is raiding the pantry for cake. Hearing his mother coming, he runs off through fear of being discovered.

EXAMPLE 2. A student has such a fear of failing an examination that he cheats.

One acts *with fear* if fear merely accompanies one's act but does not cause it.

EXAMPLE. A burglar, while robbing a house, experiences the fear of being caught.

Actions that are performed through fear are voluntary and imputable in most cases. Hence such actions if good are meritorious and if evil are culpable.

EXAMPLE. Through fear of being ridiculed by his companions if he refuses, a young man consents to go to a lewd show.

It is possible for fear to be so overwhelming that it deprives one of the use of reason at the moment. Actions performed while one is so influenced are not human acts, and consequently are not imputable. Such cases are rare.

HABITS

A habit is a constant disposition that tends to influence one to perform repeatedly similar actions. A habit may be good or evil, according to whether it influences to good or evil. If it disposes to evil, it is a vice; if to good, it is a virtue. Some men are habitually honest; others tend to be deceitful. Two general principles may be laid down concerning the effect of habits on the imputability of evil actions:

1. Evil habits do not lessen the imputability of evil actions performed by force of habit if the habit has been recognized as evil and is freely permitted to continue.

EXAMPLE. A secretary has the habit of talking freely about the confidential affairs of clients. She knows that this practice is unjust but makes no attempt to change.

2. Evil habits do lessen the imputability of evil actions performed by force of habit if one is sincerely repentant and is trying to correct the habit.

14

EXAMPLE. An electrician regrets his habit of taking God's name in vain and is trying to eliminate it. One day he bumps his head and immediately includes God's name in his angry exclamations. There may be very little culpability in this habit-produced profanity.

VIOLENCE

Violence as understood by moral theologians is force exerted on a person by another or by others in order to compel him to perform a certain action against his will. In determining the extent to which violence affects imputability three principles must be kept in mind:

1. If one resists the violence as much as possible, the evil act to which one is forced is in nowise culpable.

EXAMPLE. A prisoner in a concentration camp is given an injection of "truth serum" so that he will reveal secret information. He resists as much as possible but cannot prevent the injection. He is not culpable if his revelation of information is entirely due to the injection.

2. If one does not resist the violence as fully as possible, the culpability of the evil act is lessened but not taken away.

EXAMPLE. Another prisoner is deprived of food and sleep so that he will tell the guards what prisoners are trying to escape. His information will lead to the execution of the latter, but he gives it in order to lead a more comfortable life. He is judged to have consented to the evil, but is not so guilty as he would be if no violence were present.

3. If one sees that resistance would be wholly ineffective, there is no obligation to resist, for one is not obliged to do what would be useless. A show of resistance, however, which would not effect a release from the violence might serve either one of two useful purposes: it might *disclose one's lack of consent* to the act to which one is being forced, or it might *aid one in preventing internal consent* to the external act.

EXAMPLE. A man out on a date with a girl parks in a lonely place and begins to take liberties with her. She asks him to stop but he refuses. She can get no help. However, resistance will both show him that she was sincere and help her avoid cooperating with him.

OTHER FACTORS AFFECTING IMPUTABILITY

It is presupposed that students of MORAL GUIDANCE will have some knowledge of modern psychological studies of the freedom of human actions. We do not intend to repeat what is treated in other disciplines, but our discussion of subjective imputability would not be complete without some reference to modern discoveries and theories. Unconscious motivation certainly influences some of our actions. The first reaction of dislike for a person may be due to an association of which we are unaware. Violent emotional reactions to a situation which does not call for them seem to be rooted in some experience which we cannot now recall consciously. Opinions in regard to the influence of the unconscious on conscious activity vary greatly. A Catholic cannot hold the extreme position that "the influence of the dynamic unconscious," to use the current terminology, is such that none of our actions can be called free. On the other hand, it would be insincere and unscholarly to deny that some actions which might be thought to be free may be due totally to the influence of the dynamic unconscious. It would be still more insincere and unscholarly to deny that many of our free actions are influenced by unconscious motivation. However, we must distinguish between unconscious motivation and the rationalizations which almost all of us use to justify some of our actions. Few men are wholly free from the tendency to rationalize.

By a sincere examination of conscience we can usually discover our rationalization or self-deception. We may not have been fully conscious of it when we acted as we did (and therefore imputability was lessened to some extent) but the fact that we can recognize it later shows that we had some awareness at the time. A person is responsible for his conscious motivation and, to a lesser extent, for motivation of which he is only partially aware; he is not responsible for the unconscious motivation as the term is used in modern psychology. The latter is a psychological term and must not be confused with the theological use of the term "motivation." Students should read the excellent treatment of this subject in Volume 1, pages 174-201, of *Contemporary Moral Theology*, by John C. Ford, S.J. and Gerald Kelly, S.J.[1]

THE TWOFOLD EFFECT

It very frequently happens that an action results in more than one effect with moral implications. A city board of health, for example, permanently hospitalized a woman known to be a carrier

---

[1] Westminster: Newman Press, 1958.

of typhoid. One effect of this action was to protect the public against disease and death. Another effect was to deprive a morally innocent individual of her liberty.

It is necessary for us to have a precise knowledge of the conditions under which we may perform an action one effect of which is evil. Before laying down the principle and showing its application certain concepts must be clearly understood.

1. An action may be willed or intended in one of two ways. It may be willed or intended (a) directly or (b) indirectly.

a) To will or intend directly is to will or intend a certain action either as a means to a certain end which one has in view or as the end itself.

EXAMPLE. A gangster deliberately kills a man who refuses to pay for protection. He directly intends his death even though his ultimate purpose may be to scare others into paying.

b) In cases where an effect is willed or intended indirectly, the individual does not will or intend a certain effect (A) in itself, but wills or intends some action (X), knowing that A will result from X. Hence by directly willing X, which is the cause of A, he indirectly wills A. *To will a thing indirectly* is classified by many theologians with *to will a thing in its cause.*

EXAMPLE. A salesman sets out to sell some obscene books. He intends to make these sales only in order to earn money, but he realizes that selling the books will corrupt many. He *directly intends* (1) selling the books as a means and (2) making money as the end. He *indirectly wills* the dissemination of evil literature.

2. In discussing the twofold effect of an action we are not looking upon the action as a mere physical act. We are taking the action considered morally; that is, viewed in its conformity with or difformity from the norm of morality. An action, viewed in the abstract, may be good, bad, or indifferent. For example:

a) The act of praising God is in itself morally good.

b) The act of blaspheming is in itself morally evil.

c) Such acts as walking, eating, writing, or studying are in themselves morally indifferent.

The act of driving a car is in itself directed neither to a good nor to an evil end. Whence, then, the goodness or badness of such an action when it is actually performed? It is true that it is not directed by its very nature either to a good end or to a bad end. However, it can be so directed *by the intention of the one who performs the action.* For example, I am driving my automobile along a certain narrow road. My action of driving along the road is *of its nature* neither good nor bad, but it may be directed toward a good end or toward a bad end through my intention. For example, the action of driving an automobile along the road may be directed to:

a) fleeing from a murder-bent madman (here the act aims at self-preservation);

b) hurrying to the assistance of a sick man (here the act may be a work of mercy);

c) killing a person who is standing in the road (here the act is murder).

If my action is directed toward (a), though of its nature it is indifferent, it becomes good in the concrete; if it is directed toward (c), it is evil.

There are two classes of action that are evil in themselves:

a) Actions that are evil as regards the very substance of the act. Such actions under all circumstances, if knowingly and deliberately performed, are evil. The morality of such actions is absolute, for they are substantially bad. They do not depend on any particular condition for their evil. An example of an action that is substantially bad is hatred of God. Blaspheming is another action that is evil in itself. No circumstance imaginable and no purpose on the part of the one who entertains or expresses hatred of God or who blasphemes could ever make either of these actions other than objectively evil.

b) Actions that are evil because of the lack of the right to perform them in the one acting. In these actions the substance of the act is indifferent; but since the one acting does not have a right to perform them, they become evil. An example of such an action is the taking of another's property. The substance of this action is indifferent. It is illicit if the one taking another's property has no right to do so. In some cases taking another's property is licit; for example, if a destitute, starving man were to take from another's goods what he needs to survive.

THE PRINCIPLE STATED AND EXPLAINED

The principle of the twofold effect may be stated as follows: It is allowable to perform an act that will produce a good and a bad effect, provided (1) the good effect and not the evil effect is *directly intended;* (2) the action itself is good, or at least indifferent; (3) the good effect is not produced *by means of* the evil effect; and (4) there is a proportionate reason for permitting the foreseen evil effect to occur.

1. The good effect and not the evil one must be directly intended and the evil effect must be merely permitted as an unavoidable and undesired consequence. If the one acting directly intends the evil effect, he sins through his evil intention and his entire act is morally wrong. An evil intention always corrupts and makes sinful any action whatsoever. Macbeth performed a corporal work of mercy by extending hospitality to King Duncan, but this good deed became for him a sinful deed because his intention was to murder his guest.

2. The action itself must be good or at least indifferent. If the action itself is evil, it is evidently forbidden. This second condition is verified if the contemplated action is not included in either class of actions that are evil in themselves (for example, blasphemy and stealing).

3. The good effect must not be produced by means of the evil effect. If the evil effect causes the good effect, the evil effect is *directly intended,* at least as a means of producing the good effect. But directly to intend evil is always forbidden, for we are always bound to avoid what is morally bad. If we directly intend evil in our action, an essential part (that is, the intention) of the action is evil. It may be that one's ultimate purpose in performing the action is very praiseworthy, but that ultimate purpose cannot change the evil nature of the bad action which one is now placing. Moreover, Holy Scripture tells us that evil may never be done, even in order that good may come of it (Romans 3:8). One may never tell a lie, even in order to save one's life or to prevent injury to one's own or to another's good name.

4. There must be a proportionate reason for permitting the foreseen evil effect to occur. The law of charity forbids us to risk injuring ourselves or others without necessity. Hence if we had no proportionate reason for allowing the foreseen evil effect to follow from our action, we would be unnecessarily causing injury to our neighbor or to ourselves. What reason would be considered proportionate? If the effect is slight, a slight reason would suffice for allowing it to occur; if the evil effect is grave, the reason for placing the action in question must also be weighty.

19

In the following examples we note how these four conditions are fulfilled.

EXAMPLE 1. A man trapped by fire on the top floor of a forty-story building hurls himself out the window in order to avoid the excruciating torture of death by fire. He is dashed to pieces on the pavement below. He clearly realized that a fall from such a height would certainly be fatal.

Condition 1. He does not wish to be dashed to pieces. He intends merely the avoiding of death by fire.

Condition 2. Flinging himself out the window is in itself an indifferent action. It is merely the act of withdrawing from a place fraught with agonizing torture. He intends only the jumping away from the fire and not jumping to death. He does not wish to be killed. His act is merely an escaping from the present danger with which he is threatened.

Condition 3. The good effect (escaping the flames) is not produced by the evil effect (being dashed to pieces), for even though he were not killed (because, for instance, he landed in a deep pool of water or on the thirty-eighth-floor setback), the good effect would still follow. Hence the evil effect is not the cause of the good effect.

Condition 4. There is a proportionate reason, for he is not putting his life in greater or more immediate jeopardy and he is escaping horrible agony.

EXAMPLE 2. The commander of a submarine torpedoes an armed merchant ship of the enemy, although he foresees that several innocent children on board will be killed by the explosion.

Condition 1. He intends merely to lessen the power of the enemy by destroying an armed merchant ship. He does not wish to kill the innocent children.

Condition 2. His action of torpedoing the ship is not evil in itself.

Condition 3. The evil effect (the death of the children) is not the cause of the good effect (the lessening of the enemy's strength).

Condition 4. There is sufficient reason for permitting the evil effect to follow, and this reason is the administering of a damaging blow to those who are unjustly attacking his country.

On the contrary, the principle of the twofold effect could not be cited to justify the following case, for all the conditions necessary are *not* verified:

EXAMPLE 3. An unmarried woman has an affair with a married man and becomes pregnant. In order to avoid the disgrace of giving birth to an illegitimate child she takes an abortifacient medicine, justifying her action by this, that the potion will have two effects: a good effect (saving her reputation) and an evil effect (causing the abortion).

Condition 1. She drinks the abortifacient for the purpose of procuring an abortion. Hence she directly intends the evil effect. Therefore Condition 1 is not fulfilled.

Condition 2. The good effect (saving her reputation) is produced only if the bad effect (abortion) follows. The bad effect, then, is the cause of the good effect. She will not save her reputation because she drinks the potion, but only because the abortion actually follows. Hence it is clear that her action would be gravely sinful.

Explain the application or nonapplication of the principle of the twofold effect in the following:

1. A child is born blind and crippled. The doctor gives him poison to produce the good effect of removing a heavy burden from the parents and of preventing suffering to the child. The doctor claims that death, the bad effect, is permitted as a means of obtaining the good effect.

2. A sailor in charge of a lifeboat deliberately rows away from several people still in the water. He knows that an attempt to take any more into the boat will result in its being overturned and in the death of most of those already in the boat.

3. Seven sailors were proclaimed heroes of the *Thetis* submarine disaster because they had volunteered to let their bodies serve as buoys to guide rescuers to the sunken British submarine. Captain O'Hara was the first to volunteer to try to get through the escape chamber, though, because of the submarine's position, it was believed a man would be drowned before he could get clear of the hull. If he got the outer hatch open before drowning, his body, floating to the surface with the notation of the *Thetis'* exact position tied to his wrist, would guide the rescue ships. Captain O'Hara got through; the next three were drowned before reaching the outside hatch.

4. Two men are trapped in the debris of a hotel destroyed by a tornado. One finds that, if he pushes up the beam pinning him to the ground, he can struggle out to safety. However, moving the beam would bring half the ceiling crashing down on his companion, who cannot be extricated. He feels justified in pushing up the beam.

5. An aviator agreed to load his plane with high explosives and run it straight into an enemy battleship. He would be blown into bits, but the battleship would be destroyed.

"SINNING FOR A GOOD CAUSE"

One is never justified in performing an evil action even in order that a good may result from it. Let us suppose that in time of war a firing squad is about to execute a number of villagers on mere suspicion of having committed sabotage. A soldier cruelly presses a rifle into a boy's hands and orders him under pain of instant death to shoot down one of the men standing before the wall. Is the boy allowed to kill one of his countrymen whom he knows to be innocent of any wrong? He most assuredly is not allowed to do so, for his action would be murder and nothing can justify murder. The fact that he would be committing murder for the praiseworthy purpose of saving his own life, and even the added fact that the man is doomed to death whether he himself fires the shot or not, does not excuse him.

There are those who would object to the expression "sinning for a good cause." In their philosophy God would be narrow and unreasonable if He considered it a sin painlessly to chloroform a newborn infant whose life could be only a life of pain and deprivation or to tell a "harmless" lie in order to save another from death or injury. But an action that is intrinsically evil is evil under all circumstances. The end does not justify the means. God has not told us that we may commit an action which is of its nature evil in order that we may escape inconvenience or achieve some desirable outcome.

The false principle which we are here condemning would ruin society if generally applied. No man's life, property, or good name would be safe, for each of his neighbors would have the right to use them as he wished if in his own judgment the good results of so doing outweighed the evil which he foresaw would result. Thus the right to sin for a good cause would be against the common good.

LAW

Law in the general sense is a norm of conduct or a guide of action. In the strict sense it is a decree issued by one with authority, aimed at the common good, and properly promulgated. The intellect directs the formation of this decree and the will imparts to it its binding force.

CLASSIFICATION OF LAW

Laws are variously classified according to their nature, their origin, and their binding force.

1. The *eternal law* is the divine, eternal decree which commands that the order of nature be preserved and forbids any violation of that order. This law exists only in God.

2. The *natural law* is the eternal law communicated to rational creatures through the light of reason. This law commands the observance of the duties we have toward God, our neighbor, and ourselves; for example, we must respect our neighbor's good name, we must preserve our health.

The term natural law as here defined excludes the physical laws of nature; that is, the laws of physics, chemistry, astronomy, and other sciences.

3. *Positive law* is a law which proceeds from the free will of the lawgiver and which is promulgated by some sensible sign (for example, the written or spoken word). Positive law may be divided into three kinds: (a) divine, (b) ecclesiastical, and (c) civil. The source of divine law is God, the source of ecclesiastical law is the Church, and the source of the civil law is the state.

a) *Divine positive law* is a law which has God for its immediate author and which is manifested to men through divine revelation. Examples are Christ's precepts regarding baptism, the Eucharist, and marriage.

b) *Ecclesiastical law* is a law which originates from the authority of the Church; for example, the law of Friday abstinence; the laws of a diocese.

c) *Civil law* is a law which proceeds from civil authority, which among us may be municipal, state, or federal. Examples are tax laws, laws governing commerce, and laws concerning the certification of teachers.

Human law, whether civil or ecclesiastical, is divided into (a) morally binding law and (b) merely penal law.

a) A *morally binding law* is one that entails a strict obligation in conscience to do what the law enjoins or to omit what the law forbids; for example, the laws regarding the lenten fast.

b) A *merely penal law* is one that obliges subjects to do what is prescribed, not under pain of sin but under penalty of having to submit to whatever punishment is inflicted for violation. Examples are laws regulating parking or laws limiting the time of the hunting season. One who disobeys a merely penal law does not commit a moral fault, but is bound in conscience not to resist the imposing of the penalty which he has incurred.

The nature of law is a subject which has been widely discussed in recent years by Catholic philosophers and theologians. The existence of such a thing as penal law has been denied and defended, frequently with much emotion. It is a topic which can be discussed with great profit, but a full treatment of the discussion would go far beyond the scope of this book. Practically, the obligation to obey all civil laws under pain of sin cannot be imposed because it is certainly a probable opinion that not all civil laws bind under pain of sin except with respect to the payment of the penalty if we have violated a law and a court has imposed the prescribed penalty. As a matter of fact, however, many of the civil laws do bind in conscience because they simply repeat what is already obligatory from the natural law. Speeding in certain circumstances is morally wrong, while in other circumstances it may be only a violation of a penal law.

INTERPRETATION OF LAW

An authentic interpretation of a law is made by the legislator, his successor, or someone who has received authority from the legislator or his successor. In many cases, however, the interpretation of law is left either to jurists or to custom. Jurists must take into consideration parallel laws, the purpose of the law, and any other factors which might indicate the intention of the legislator. If a law imposes penalties or restricts freedom, it is to be interpreted in the strict sense; that is, in such a way that the individual is given the greatest amount of freedom. Customary interpretation of the law is the best interpretation in the absence of an authentic one.

CONSCIENCE

The moral goodness or badness of our actions depends on their conformity or difformity with the rule of right conduct. Conscience should be our guide in every act.

DEFINITION OF CONSCIENCE

Conscience is the judgment which one makes about the moral goodness or badness of a way of acting that one now faces. It is the conclusion at which reason arrives after applying the principles of morality to some particular action. Conscience pronounces on this action as one that should be done because it is good or as one that should be omitted because it is bad, or marks it as permissible or preferable but not obligatory.

TYPES OF CONSCIENCE

Conscience, from the standpoint of its positiveness and correctness, may be (1) certain, (2) doubtful, (3) correct, or (4) false.

1. A *certain conscience* leaves no doubt about the morality of the way of acting under consideration, but convincingly stamps it either as good or bad.

> EXAMPLE. A businessman is asked by some of his friends to join them in a scheme for making some quick money. After careful investigation he concludes that what they intend to do is unjust. He is certain of the moral obligation not to join them.

2. A *doubtful conscience* leaves the individual undecided as to the morality of the action now before him.

> EXAMPLE. A physician has discovered certain indications for a serious operation. However, the condition of the patient is such that he may not be able to survive the operation. After weighing all the factors he is still doubtful about whether or not he may perform the operation.

3. A *correct conscience* arrives at a judgment that reveals the true morality of the contemplated action as it is objectively.

4. A *false conscience* erroneously tells one that this present evil action is good or this present good action is evil.

> EXAMPLE. An employee learns that his employer has lied to him and now judges that it is not wrong to lie to his employer in turn.

RULES RELATING TO CONSCIENCE

In deciding upon our own course of action and in advising others if it is our responsibility to do so, we should be governed by the following rules:

1. One must always act on the command of a *certain conscience*. Even if this certain conscience is false, it is to be obeyed. The reason is that our conscience is the proximate norm of all our actions and that it is according to the manner in which we conform to this norm that we will be judged by God. Hence if my conscience definitely stigmatizes as evil an action that is objectively good, I am bound to avoid that action. If my conscience definitely tells me that I should perform an action which I consider good but which is in fact evil, I must perform that action.

2. It is never permissible to act with a *doubtful conscience.* An action which conscience does not definitely pronounce to be sinless must not be performed. The reason is that one who acts while doubtful whether his action is against the law or not implicitly wills what is sinful. He says equivalently: "This action *may* be offensive to God, but I am going to do it anyway." He freely and rashly exposes himself to the danger of sinning, since he believes that what he is about to do is either possibly or even probably wrong.

If, then, one is in doubt about the morality of a particular action, one must either make certain that the action is allowed or refrain from performing it. The procedure to be followed in determining that a given action is not sinful is as follows. The individual who is in doubt should first seek information either from approved books on the subject, from his confessor, or from a friend who is reliably known to be well informed. If he is unable to obtain the needed information and his doubt remains, he may settle his conscience according to the doctrine of probabilism.

THE EFFECT OF FALSE CONSCIENCE ON GUILT

One unhappy effect of a false or erroneous conscience is to make its owner guilty of wrongdoing as serious as his false conscience represents his act to be. The following principles apply to such cases:

1. If one commits a venial sin, thinking that it is a mortal sin, one is guilty of a mortal sin.

> EXAMPLE. If a thief thinks that stealing one dollar from anyone at all is a mortal sin and steals it from a wealthy man, he is actually guilty of grave wrongdoing, although such a theft from a rich man would be matter for venial sin only.

2. If one freely commits a sinless act, thinking that it is a mortal or a venial sin, one is guilty of a mortal or a venial sin according to his false evaluation.

> EXAMPLE. If a student thinks that reading a certain book, which is really harmless, is gravely wrong and reads it nevertheless, he is guilty of serious wrongdoing.

3. If one who is unable to act otherwise thinks he is sinning in omitting a certain action, one is not guilty of wrongdoing. In order that an action be imputed to one as a fault, it must be free. The fact that a person erroneously believes that even an action

that is performed without freedom can be sinful does not alter the conditions requisite for imputability.

EXAMPLE. A prisoner who is compelled to remain in his prison cell misses Sunday Mass. In his ignorance he believes that he is guilty of sin because he is not fulfilling the Sunday precept. However, this is no sin on his part, for in order to sin one must act freely, and in this case he could not do otherwise than he actually did.

4. If one is convinced that he will sin if he chooses either of two alternatives, no sin is committed even though the person is subjectively convinced that he did sin.

EXAMPLE. A charitable woman is attending a very sick friend. Sunday morning comes. She realizes that it would be dangerous to leave her sick friend, and no other attendant is available. However, it is Sunday and so she must consider the grave obligation of attending Mass. She believes that if she goes to Mass she will sin against charity in absenting herself from the sickbed. Not sufficiently well informed to understand that such a task of charity excuses one from attending Mass, she is also convinced that if she stays with her friend, she will incur the sin of missing Mass. Nevertheless, she stays with her friend. Here she does not commit any sin in missing Mass (though she thought that her doing so was wrong), because in that particular set of circumstances she could not avoid an imagined wrong, whichever way she acted.

SITUATION ETHICS

Our treatment of human activity would not be complete without some mention of situation ethics, a system, or at least a series of tendencies, stemming from existentialism. It takes several forms, just as existentialism itself has several forms. Atheistic existentialists deny all validity to general principles of morality, holding that man is completely free of all law and of all external agents in making his moral choices. Some Protestant existentialists modify this position by giving value to the principles of morality revealed by God in the Old and New Testament, holding, however, that in a particular situation God can inspire the individual to act in a way contrary to these principles. Man, acting according to the law of love and guided by divine inspiration, must make his choice in each particular situation. The following quotation helps to give some insight into this position:

We might compare such Protestant ethics, as does E. Brunner, to a wagon wheel. The spokes of the wheel are moral norms which all tend to one point, the will of God. However, the moral norms, like the spokes of a wheel, never meet, because at the center is a hole, a vacuum, in which God makes known to me here and now His inscrutable will. Consequently, these moral norms are a general indication of God's will, but in the concrete situation, God indicates to me—as it were independently of these norms—His present will in my regard. Since at times He may even indicate to me a course of action contrary to that prescribed in a general norm, I must look to the actual situation to discover His will.[2]

Some Catholic thinkers have been influenced by situation ethics. The Holy See has put out several warnings about the effect which it would have on the morals of members of the Church. It has had the good effect of making Catholic moralists emphasize the importance of charity and the proper intention in moral acts.

PROBABILISM

Definition of probabilism

Probabilism is a set of practical rules which aid in settling a doubtful conscience. Probabilism as we here use the term is what is known as *pure probabilism*. We shall not enter into a discussion of the various systems of probabilism.

Probabilism is beyond all doubt a safe doctrine to follow. This is clear from (1) the tacit approval of the Church; (2) the fact that the Church herself makes use, in an official way, of theologians who are probabilists; and (3) the fact that the Church herself uses probabilism in deciding cases.

Rules of probabilism

RULE 1

One may follow a solidly probable opinion which favors liberty whenever there is question of a merely doubtful law.

Opinion is the acceptance by the mind of a proposition, but with the realization that the opposite proposition may be true. Thus a man "holds the opinion" that the Republican party is preferable to the Democratic party, but admits that he might conceivably be wrong.

A *solidly probable opinion* is an opinion which is based on reasons that are serious enough to win the assent of a prudent

---

[2] Joseph Fuchs, "Situation Ethics and Theology." *Theology Digest* 2:25, Winter 1954.

man, though they do not rule out the fear that the opposite proposition may be true. The fact that several recognized moral theologians hold an opinion is sufficient to indicate that the opinion is solidly probable.

An opinion *which favors liberty* is an opinion which releases the individual from the obligation concerning which he is in doubt. For example, I am doubtful whether or not the natural law obliges me to reveal certain information to persons in authority. There are good reasons for revealing it and good reasons against revealing it. The opinion which favors liberty is the one that says I am not obliged to reveal the information. This does not mean, of course, that to reveal the information might not be the better thing to do.

A *doubtful law* is one that may not exist at all or that may not apply to the existing situation. If the law is doubtful, an investigation must be made in order to clear up, if possible, all doubt. One must use all reasonable diligence to discover the truth. It is only when, after such investigation, the existence of the law or its application to the present case remains doubtful, that one may use the above rule.

Probabilism may be used only when there is question of a merely doubtful law. This means that the contemplated action must involve no other risk than that of violating some law that may possibly exist. There must be no danger that the action would harm anybody.

PROOF OF RULE 1

If one has solid probability for thinking that a particular law does not exist or does not apply to the present situation, the existence of that law or its application in the existing situation is doubtful. But a doubtful law does not bind. An obligation is either certain or nonexistent. Hence a law, in order to bind, must induce a *certain* obligation. A doubtful law cannot impose upon an individual a certain obligation; for that would mean that the effect (the certain binding) was greater than the cause (the uncertain or doubtful binding force).

The same proof holds for the case where one seriously doubts whether a certain law covers this particular type of action; for example, whether the law of Friday abstinence, which one apprehends as altogether certain, forbids the eating of gelatin.

One may not follow a probable opinion if one's contemplated action would without necessity expose one to the risk of causing harm to oneself or to another.

PROOF OF RULE 2

Here there is question, not merely of a *doubtful law* but rather of a *certain law*. This certain law is either the law of justice or the law of charity, which forbids me unnecessarily to expose either myself or another to the danger of injury. There is certainty, also, that this law include the action in question, for I have reason for believing that danger of injury exists.

Since it is not always easy to apply the above principles to actual cases, we give the following examples of cases in which probabilism may or may not be used. It is taken for granted in these cases that the investigation required for clearing up the doubt has been made.

Probabilism may be used in the following cases:

1. It *seems* to me I have heard that this book is on the *Roman Index of Forbidden Books*. Still, I do not think that this book would be in this good Catholic's library if it were forbidden. I may, as far as church law goes, licitly read the book, for under the circumstances I may conclude that it probably is not forbidden.

2. Does this vegetable soup contain meat? It looks somewhat like meat soup, but one cannot judge too accurately by this. Besides, a restaurant generally avoids using meat, if it can, in order to economize. I may eat the soup.

Probabilism may not be used in the following cases:

1. A baby is dying and the nurse decides that she herself should baptize the baby since there is no priest to be had. She has at hand some liquid that seems to be water. "It is *probably* water," she says, "so I will use it." (She could obtain water without difficulty.) Here, by using a liquid which would make the baptism only *probably* valid, the nurse without necessity risks causing grave harm to the child (that is, the loss of heaven). Hence she may not use a liquid that is only probably water.

2. A workman has means of warning pedestrians that there is a dangerous hole near the sidewalk. When he quits for the day he decides that probably no one will fall into the hole. He puts up

no warning. He thus risks causing injury to someone, and he may not act on the mere probability that no one will be injured.

3. In order to entertain his friends a boy tells an untrue story about a girl. It may or may not hurt her reputation. He risks injury to her good name without a sufficient reason.

Topics for discussion[3]

1 Any system of morality that is not based on belief in God must always prove ineffective.
2 If man does not possess free will, he cannot justly be punished.
3 Are any human acts in the concrete morally indifferent?
4 The study of moral guidance increases the knowledge of one's obligations. Would it not be better to continue without such knowledge? One would not be so restricted.
5 Conscience is an infallible voice within us that clearly tells what is right and what is wrong.

Bibliography

Barbaste, Albert. "Scrupulosity and the Present Data of Psychiatry." *Theology Digest* 1:180-84, Autumn 1953.

Bourke, Vernon J. *Ethics.* New York: The Macmillan Company, 1951.

Cathrein, V. "Ethics." In *Catholic Encyclopedia,* Vol. 5, pp. 556-66.

——— "Law." In *Catholic Encyclopedia,* Vol. 9, pp. 53-56.

Connery, John R. "Current Theology: Notes on Moral Theology." *Theological Studies* 15:594-99, December 1954 (on conscience); 19:533-34, December 1958 (on law).

——— "Shall We Scrap the Purely Penal Law?" *American Ecclesiastical Review* 129:244-54, October 1953.

Davis, Henry. *Moral and Pastoral Theology,* seventh edition, edited by L. W. Geddes, Vol. 1, pp. 11-189. 4 vols. New York: Sheed and Ward, 1958.

Davitt, Thomas E. *The Nature of Law.* St. Louis: B. Herder Book Company, 1951.

Delany, Joseph F. "Ignorance." In *Catholic Encyclopedia,* Vol. 7, pp. 648-49.

Dunn, Edward T. "In Defense of Penal Law." *Theological Studies* 18:41-59, March 1957.

Ford, John C. "Depth Psychology, Morality, and Alcoholism." *Theology Digest* Experimental Issue:46-52, December 1951.

——— and Gerald Kelly. *Contemporary Moral Theology,* Vol. 1, Chapters 10 and 11, pp. 174-247. Westminster: Newman Press, 1958.

---

[3] Not all the assertions contained in the topics are true. The student is to judge the truth of any assertions made and to explain his decision.

Fox, James J. "Natural Law." In *Catholic Encyclopedia*, Vol. 9, pp. 76-79.

Fuchs, Joseph. "Situation Ethics and Theology." *Theology Digest* 2:25-30, Winter 1954.

Gleason, R. W. "Situational Morality." *Thought* 32:533-58, Winter 1957-1958.

Harty, J. M. "Probabilism." In *Catholic Encyclopedia*, Vol. 12, pp. 441-46.

Hildebrand, Dietrich von. *Christian Ethics*. New York: David McKay Company, 1953.

Jone, Heribert. *Moral Theology*, pp. 1-62. Westminster: Newman Press, 1957.

Kelly, Gerald. *Medico-Moral Problems*, pp. 12-16. St. Louis: Catholic Hospital Association, 1958.

Lynch, John J. "Current Theology: Notes on Moral Theology." *Theological Studies* 18:218-20, June 1957.

McGarrigle, Francis J. "It's All Right If You Can Get Away with It." *American Ecclesiastical Review* 127:431-39, December 1952.

Noonan, John P. *General and Special Ethics*. Chicago: Loyola University Press, 1947.

Rickaby, John. "Conscience." In *Catholic Encyclopedia*, Vol. 4, pp. 268-73.

Rickaby, Joseph. "Probabilism." In J. F. Leibell, editor, *Readings in Ethics*, pp. 360-64. Chicago: Loyola University Press, 1926.

Riley, Lawrence J.; Michael Noonan; and Matthew Herron. "Problems of Penal Law." In *Proceedings of the Tenth Annual Convention of the Catholic Theological Society of America*, pp. 259-84. New York: Catholic Theological Society of America, 1955.

Salet, Gaston. "The Law in Our Hearts." *Theology Digest* 7:59-62, Winter 1959.

CHAPTER III

Some
principles
of Christian morality

O NE of the complaints made against modern theological writings is that many of the words used have ceased to have their original meaning and are bound to be misunderstood by a modern reader. Even the critics, however, admit that it is practically impossible to invent a new terminology and that the only solution is to revive certain terms, to make them significant again. Among those terms is "virtue," which carries with it today the connotation of prudishness and lack of virility. Virtue is considered to be somewhat dull and uninteresting; actually the word itself means power and implies manliness, strength, and courage.

THE MORAL VIRTUES

In a more technical sense a virtue is a habit or disposition which inclines a man to do good actions. Hence we speak of many virtues because man can be inclined to many different good actions, such as acts of justice and charity. To understand fully what is meant by virtue in Christian theological writings we must go back to Christ Himself and see the virtues in the concrete. Such a knowledge of the life of Christ must be presupposed here. If it is lacking, it should be supplied by reading and study of the Scriptures and lives of Christ.

St. Thomas organizes his treatment of the moral life around the virtues, and some modern theological writers follow the same plan. Others think that one or other of the virtues should be taken as the point of departure. In MORAL GUIDANCE we are following another system—the organization of the moral life under the commandments; but it would be impossible to explain the commandments in all their fullness without first arriving at a clear understanding of what is meant by the virtues.

Man has within him certain basic powers or faculties which enable him to act. Chief among these powers are the intellect and the will. These powers or faculties can be further modified or perfected so that they incline an individual to act in a certain way. When these modifications or perfections dispose him to good actions, they are called virtues or good habits. These can be divided in several ways.

A virtue can be formally in the intellect; that is, the proper act of the virtue can be in the intellect rather than in the will. This does not mean that there may not be some dependence on the will. Among these virtues are science, wisdom, faith, and prudence. Science pertains to particular areas such as mathematics, history, or physics. Wisdom pertains to the whole field of knowledge and considers it in relation to the First Cause. Faith gives us knowledge of truths revealed by God. Prudence pertains to practical judgments about things to be done. Other virtues—charity, for example—are principally in the will, but there is a dependence of these virtues on those of the intellect, for the will does not act until the intellect has presented something to it as good.

Virtues can be natural—that is, acquired by man through his natural powers and actions; or they can be supernatural—that is, produced in man by God. The latter differ from the former in that they give the *ability* to act in a certain way which man would not have unless God communicated it to him. The moral virtues are both natural and supernatural; the theological virtues are supernatural only. Virtues can be speculative or practical: wisdom is speculative, prudence is practical. The theological virtues concern actions directly pertaining to God; the moral virtues concern actions directly pertaining to created things.

THE VIRTUE OF PRUDENCE

Holding the central place among the virtues is prudence, the supernatural virtue which inclines one to perform actions which are morally good and lead one to one's supernatural end. It presupposes the theological virtues and the other moral virtues. Without faith I will be lacking in the principles on which to make a proper judgment in regard to means. Without charity I will not be inclined to perform actions which further union with God. Without hope I will also fail to choose to do such good actions, for I will not see their usefulness. Similarly, if I do not have the moral virtues of justice, temperance, and fortitude, I will be incapable of making proper decisions because my mind will be swayed by prejudice or emotion. Looked at from the opposite viewpoint, all the other virtues require prudence. Charity which is imprudent is not really charity; it is only when I properly judge an action in relation to my supernatural end that it can be truly charitable. A father who feared to correct his children and who refused them nothing might appear to be charitable, but he would be failing in charity by not directing them to their supernatural end. Similarly, courage which is imprudent is not courage but rashness.

Although the proper act of the virtue of prudence is a command of the intellect telling us to do the prudent thing, this act must be preceded by deliberation and judgment. If we fail to deliberate, the command is likely to be based on insufficient evidence. If we fail to make a judgment, we will never arrive at the act of command. Hence we find people who are rash because they act without thought and others who are overcautious because they can never make up their minds. We find still others who deliberate and make the proper judgment but who vacillate and never make the final decision to "do this." It is only when we take this final step that we can be said to be prudent. Prudence is an absolutely essential virtue for leading a moral life.

It should be clear from what has been said that the supernatural virtue of prudence presupposes the natural virtue of prudence. The supernatural virtue orders man to his supernatural end and inclines us to judge according to the principles given to us in revelation. It is more perfect than the natural virtue both by reason of the cause (God working in us) and by reason of the acts to which it leads (supernatural acts). The natural virtue of prudence, of course, should not be identified with the prudence of the world which is condemned by our Lord.

The following examples illustrate some of the principles in regard to the virtue of prudence:

EXAMPLE 1. A superior believes without further investigation certain damaging statements about one of his subjects. He summons the latter and punishes him for his alleged misconduct. The superior has failed to deliberate properly and is imprudent.

EXAMPLE 2. A student spends half an hour trying to decide whether he will take some recreation or study during the next hour. He has failed in the second step by not reaching a judgment soon enough in relation to the importance of the matter.

EXAMPLE 3. A very generous husband gives so much to charity that he is unable to take care of the needs of his family. His wife serves on so many committees that she does not have time to train her children properly. Both are imprudent.

There are degrees of prudence, and one should not be discouraged by failures. All who are trying to serve Christ have essential prudence because they ordinarily decide correctly in matters which involve serious obligations. This essential prudence can be perfected more and more through union with Christ by prayer, the proper use of the sacraments, and the practice of the other virtues. There is a mutual causality between prudence and the other virtues. They all grow together in those who generously determine to become like to Christ and who use the means to carry out that determination.

All should pray for this virtue which is so necessary for leading a good Christian life. "Show, O Lord, thy ways to me and teach me thy paths" (Psalms 24:4).

THE VIRTUE OF JUSTICE

Justice is a virtue that inclines the will to give to each one his rights. A right is the moral power to own, to use, or to exact something. It gives me a title by which I can justly claim a thing as my own. For example, I have a right to my good name, to own my own house, to my bodily integrity. I am entitled to (have a title to) these things. Rights have their origin in the natural law or in positive law that conforms with the natural or divine law. The state is not the fountainhead of rights. Moreover, the adage

"Might makes right" is obviously false, for it concedes rights only to those who possess the power to enforce their claims.

DIVISIONS OF JUSTICE

Since there are different kinds of rights, there are also different kinds of justice. Justice is ordinarily classified according to the following divisions:

1. *Commutative justice* is a virtue that regulates those actions that involve the rights that exist between one individual and another individual. If A steals B's book, he violates commutative justice. Any violation of commutative justice imposes on the guilty person the duty of restitution (that is, the duty of repairing the harm caused). It is important to note that only violations of commutative justice give rise to this duty of making restitution. Nations, cities, and business corporations are looked upon as individuals in certain relations. Hence if I unjustly take goods (for example, a typewriter) that belong to the state, I sin against commutative justice.

2. *Distributive justice* is a virtue that regulates those actions that involve the rights which an individual may claim from society. According to distributive justice the state must distribute the common burdens and privileges equitably and must make it possible for each citizen to exercise his rights and for all citizens to live together peacefully. If, for example, a governor gives a position to a relative who is clearly undeserving, distributive justice is violated.

3. *Legal justice* is a virtue that regulates those actions which society may justly require of the individual for the common good. According to legal justice the state may institute just laws and may perform such acts as further the common good. The state, for example, may make laws concerning imports, and if a traveler smuggles contraband goods into a country, his action is a violation of legal justice.

SOCIAL JUSTICE

Father Drummond begins his discussion of the meaning of social justice with the statement that the "number of opinions with regard to the nature of social justice is legion."[1] He also notes in

---

[1] William F. Drummond, *Social Justice,* p. 19. Milwaukee: Bruce Publishing Company, 1955.

the same place that each opinion has contributed something to the clarification of the concept. We will try to explain the term as it seems to be used in the papal encyclicals and then add some further meanings attached to it by various writers.

Social justice is the virtue which inclines one to work for the reform of the economic order by group action in order to make the institutions of society serve the common good. The obligation, it is true, falls upon the individual; but the individual as such is not capable of reforming institutions and must therefore work as a member of a group. The aim of social justice is to change these institutions, whether they be public or private, so that all the members of a community receive a just share of the community good and other benefits both material and spiritual. Perhaps the best example of the type of thing with which social justice is concerned is the just wage. This right of the worker has received special attention in the writings of the Holy See on social justice. It is very difficult for an individual to influence an economic factor such as wages, but many individuals can bring about a gradual change so that workers receive at least more of the economic goods to which they have a right. The history of the labor movement in our country has shown what can be done by group action for the reform of institutions.

Some writers widen the meaning of social justice to include the use of one's talents for the common good, not only in the economic field but in anything which creates a real benefit for the community.[2] An example might be that of a doctor who works for better medical practices through a medical society such as the American Medical Association. Without entering into a discussion as to whether this type of activity should be called social justice, we can say that individuals have an obligation to use their talents for the promotion of the common good. All of us have received many benefits from the community and have a corresponding obligation to contribute to the welfare of others. Our Lord Himself said that we would be judged on the use or misuse of the talents God gave us. It is impossible for us to develop our talents without at the same time making a contribution to the common good. Even (perhaps we should say "especially") a man who spends his

---

[2] See Bernard W. Dempsey, "The Range of Social Justice." *Social Order* 7:20-24, January 1957.

whole life in doing research without any direct contact with others is contributing to the common good by advancing the knowledge on which our civilization is based. Incidentally, the English word "talent" has a fine ambivalence: it recalls the parable of our Lord which refers to the use of material things (money) and it also means abilities. Thus it combines both aspects of social justice in the wider sense of the term.

Although social justice imposes real obligations, a failure in social justice does not require restitution. A man is responsible for failing to contribute to the common good and will be held accountable before God, but he is not obliged to make restitution for failing to do his share. Moral theologians, therefore, sometimes discuss whether a thing binds in commutative justice or in social justice. This is not an idle question, for on the answer to it depends the obligation to make or not make restitution.

Since Leo XIII the popes have been stressing the need for Catholics to be more active in promoting the common good. In our own country we have sometimes been suspicious and wary of institutions because they were controlled by people who did not agree with much of what we hold as true. Catholics have sometimes stayed out of politics because of the difficulties of reconciling certain practices with their principles. They have been somewhat afraid of intellectual groups dominated by freethinkers or subjectivists. There has been some basis for their fears, and one should make a prudent judgment on the good he can do by joining and trying to influence groups which are predominately non-Catholic. One who is not sufficiently prepared may suffer harm and accomplish little good. However, those with ability and training should be encouraged to join social groups which are not specifically Catholic but which are working for some legitimate good. They should not join them with the pious purpose of making them Catholic; this is doomed to failure and makes others rightly suspicious. Their intention in joining such groups should be to enable them to accomplish their purposes more perfectly. A Catholic who joins a union or an intellectual group should do so in order to help the group accomplish its legitimate aims.

THE VIRTUE OF TEMPERANCE

Temperance is a virtue which regulates the carnal appetite for the pleasures experienced through the senses, particularly the sense of taste and the sense of touch. Hence it inclines one to act in accord with reason in partaking of food and drink or in regard to venereal pleasure.

Eating or drinking, if done wholly for the mere pleasure involved, is counter to the intentions of nature. Nature established pleasure, not as an end in itself, but as a means to attract one to perform some useful or necessary action. Hence eating or drinking for pleasure alone is against the virtue of temperance.

> EXAMPLE. A man who has for serious reasons been put on a diet by his physician sits down to a Thanksgiving Day dinner and deliberately eats many things which, though they are very palatable, are sure to injure his health. He violates temperance.

To indulge in venereal pleasure outside the state of matrimony is against the prescription of nature, for nature offers this pleasure as an inducement to and a reward for accepting the burdens of married life. Temperance prohibits any indulgence in venereal pleasure to the unmarried and urges the married to show moderation in the use of this pleasure.

> EXAMPLE. A young man goes about, idly giving free rein to his eyes, though he knows that he will probably see many unchaste sights. He is violating the virtue of temperance.

Sobriety and chastity are species of the virtue of temperance.

THE VIRTUE OF FORTITUDE

Fortitude is a virtue which inclines us to perform a good action or to refuse to perform a bad action despite temporal evils, even that of death. It enables us to overcome fear and it offsets the special difficulties that render obedience to the dictates of right reason hard on such occasions. One who lacks this virtue flees from the threatening evil and so leaves undone the contemplated act.

> EXAMPLE 1. Catholics who practice justice in business and as a result must be satisfied with a lower standard of living show fortitude in acting against human respect.
>
> EXAMPLE 2. St. Lawrence displayed fortitude in an eminent degree when he was being burned alive by his persecutors. Martyrdom is the most excellent of the acts of this virtue.
>
> EXAMPLE 3. A gangster, while robbing a bank, subdues the fear he experiences of being shot by a vigilant watchman. This bandit is not, however, practicing the virtue of fortitude, for the action that he is performing is not a good one.

40

Fortitude also moderates the spirit of rashness and temerity which prompts one needlessly to rush into danger. Cowardice is opposed to fortitude. Cowardice is the weakness of not facing dangers or difficulties when reason dictates that they should be faced. Pontius Pilate, for example, showed cowardice in not releasing Jesus, whom he knew to be innocent (Mark 15:2-15). Those Catholics are cowardly who are afraid to defend their Church against the unjust attacks of an acquaintance when it is clear that they should do so.

Many practical applications of the moral virtues can be made by one who is studying the commandments. It is an ignoble thing for one to study the commandments for no other purpose than to learn what must be done or avoided under pain of damnation.

THE THEOLOGICAL VIRTUES

The theological virtues are faith, hope, and charity. They are so called because their direct object is God *(theos)*. By faith we believe in God, by hope we trust God, by charity we love God and our fellow men for God's sake.

THE VIRTUE OF FAITH

Faith is the virtue by which we believe what God has revealed because God has revealed it. An explanation of the definition and a discussion of the necessity of faith is presupposed from other courses in theology. Here we are interested in the obligation of eliciting acts of faith.

Since faith is the basis for the whole supernatural life, we are bound to make acts of faith regularly during our lives. Unless we do so, supernatural principles of conduct will become inoperative in our lives. Natural motivation will take the place of supernatural and will not suffice in time of crisis. On the other hand, the more frequently we elicit acts of faith, the more influence these supernatural principles will have on our daily lives. Through frequent acts of faith we grow in all the other virtues. Frequent acts of faith give us an appreciation of the value of supernatural things. There is a great deal of difference between a Catholic who simply believes revealed truths and one who has a vital appreciation of their value; this vital appreciation comes from frequent acts of faith. For instance, two Catholics attend Sunday

Mass: one of them believes in the Mass but remains more or less passive during it; the other not only believes but realizes the importance of the Mass and exercises his faith continually during it. Both get something out of their participation in the Mass, but the latter goes away from it inspired and motivated to imitate Christ more perfectly in his everyday life, whereas the former may be little changed by his participation.

The obligation to elicit acts of faith is fulfilled by one who leads a good Catholic life even though he does not make explicit acts of faith regularly. In special circumstances one would be obliged to make explicit acts of faith; for instance, an act of faith might be necessary to overcome a temptation, or failure to make an act of faith might imply a denial of faith.

It is wrong to deny one's faith either directly or indirectly. One would deny his faith directly by apostasy (total rejection of the faith) or by heresy (the obstinate denial of a particular truth revealed by God and taught by the Church). If one suspends his assent to a truth revealed by God and taught by the Church, he sins against faith but is not a heretic. Difficulties which arise against faith are not doubts. There are bound to be difficulties when we are trying to get some understanding of mysteries. One would deny his faith indirectly by participating in public non-Catholic worship. This is discussed under the First Commandment, pages 70-71.

One must believe at least implicitly all truths revealed by God and taught by the Church. It is obligatory, however, to believe certain ones explicitly. This obligation would extend to the substance of the Apostles' Creed, the necessary sacraments, and the commandments of God. Parents have an obligation to see that their children are taught these rudiments of the faith.

THE VIRTUE OF HOPE

Hope is a theological virtue by which we trust in God because of His goodness and omnipotence. This trust is a confident expectation that God will bring us to eternal salvation by giving us the means necessary to attain it. Hope in regard to the means is absolutely certain because we know God gives all men the grace necessary for salvation. Hope in regard to the attaining of the end is conditional: the actual attaining of the end depends on our free cooperation, and therefore we cannot be absolutely certain of salvation. However, those who are doing whatever they are able can have moral certainty of salvation. Hope, like fortitude, is a virtue somewhat neglected by most Christians. Yet it is a very important virtue for the development of perfection. One has only to read the epistles of St. Paul to realize the certainty with which early Christians looked forward to final union with God. We live in a society which has questioned all forms of certainty and we have been affected by its spirit of doubt. We need to counteract this spirit with hope.

One can fail in the virtue of hope simply by not making acts of hope when such acts are necessary for salvation; for example, after one had despaired or when an act of hope is necessary to overcome temptation. The practice of a good Christian life includes the exercise of the virtue of hope and fulfills the obligation; however, it is an excellent practice to make frequent explicit acts of hope in order to increase one's appreciation of the supernatural end for which we are striving and in order to motivate ourselves for a more perfect practice of all the virtues. We sin against hope by despair (not to be confused with weariness or the feeling that God has abandoned us) and by presumption. Despair is an act of the will by which we give up hope of salvation or the means of salvation. Presumption is an act of the will by which we trust too much in our own strength (and thereby deny the need of God's grace) or expect to be saved in a way contrary to God's attributes or free determinations; for example, one who knew of the obligation to be baptized could not be saved if he deliberately willed not to be baptized.

THE VIRTUE OF CHARITY

There has never been any hesitation among Catholic theologians in asserting that charity is the greatest of the virtues. Even if man had been left in a purely natural state, his purpose in life would have been to learn of the First Cause and to strive for union with Him through love. In the present supernatural order man finds his perfection in knowing God through faith and in loving Him through charity, an infused supernatural power by which we love God above all things. Charity is the greatest of the virtues because it unites us with God above all things and moves us to unite ourselves ever more perfectly with Him by acts of love. It is a dynamic virtue because one who has charity seeks to do the will of God in all things: "If you love me, keep my commandments" (John 14:15). Theologians express the dynamic nature of charity by saying that it informs all the other virtues, so that an act of justice is at the same time an act of charity. The corollary of this principle is that there can be no perfect virtue without charity. An act of justice performed without charity is imperfect because it does not further supernatural union with God.

Although God is the primary object of the virtue of charity, we know from revelation that our supernatural love must extend to ourselves and to all our fellow men. Our Lord summarized His teaching by pointing out this twofold obligation of love of God and of men. This love of our neighbor and ourselves consists first of all in the desire to work out our own salvation and to assist our neighbor in working out his salvation. The two are not incompatible: if I work for my own salvation (that is, if I do the will of God), I am at the same time assisting my neighbor, at least by my prayer and good example. Prudence is required to determine precisely what the will of God is for me in certain situations. For example, I might find it hard to determine whether the better thing in a particular situation would be to devote some time to prayer or to spend the time in instructing my neighbor or in relieving the temporal necessities of the poor. These particular decisions may at times be difficult, but it is certain that prudent activity for the salvation of my neighbor is one of the most efficacious means of working out my own salvation. Imprudent activity—for example, the spending of all available time in charitable activities to the neglect of prayer and my own spiritual development—not only hinders my own growth in perfection but also renders work for my neighbor inefficacious.

THE OBLIGATION OF ASSISTING OUR NEIGHBOR

What follows concerns only what is of obligation in regard to assisting our neighbor. One who had the determination to do only what is outlined here would be in danger of failing in essentials and would certainly not be striving for the perfection of charity. God distributes His grace according to our dispositions, and a spirit of generous charity toward our neighbor is among the most pleasing dispositions in the eyes of God.

The law of charity obliges us to assist our neighbor when he is in need. The greater his need, the greater the sacrifice we must make for him. It is therefore necessary for us to have a clear understanding of the types and degrees of need that may exist.

One is said to be in *extreme spiritual necessity* when he is in immediate danger of losing his soul unless given assistance. In another's extreme spiritual necessity we are obliged to sacrifice any temporal good (for example, our life or our property), provided our hope of saving him is proportionate to the risk of losing the temporal good that we are endangering. Situations might arise in which even a layman would be obliged to go into a place of danger in order to administer baptism or possibly to assist a dying person to make an act of contrition. Priests, however, are the ones who are most frequently called upon to risk their lives in order to baptize, to absolve, or to administer extreme unction.

One is said to be in *grave spiritual necessity* if he can overcome the danger of losing his faith or his virtue—and ultimately his soul—to which he is exposed, but only with great difficulty. In such a contingency we are not obliged to go to the assistance of our neighbor if to do so would cause us grave inconvenience.

Extreme temporal necessity is the imminent danger of losing one's life or of being subjected to lifelong invalidism or servitude unless assistance comes. Charity requires us to assist our neighbor in his extreme temporal necessity, even at the cost of grave inconvenience, for our neighbor's *life* is preferable to our *convenience*.

Grave temporal necessity is the imminent danger of losing temporal goods (for example, wealth or authority) of great value but of lesser value than life itself. Charity does not require us to assist our neighbor in his grave temporal necessity if to do so would cause us grave inconvenience.

Those who are more closely related to us by blood, religion, nationality, or friendship should be helped first. Moreover, although charity may not impose an obligation upon us, justice, piety, or duty may do so, as in the case of pastor and parishioner, son and mother, or policeman and citizen.

COOPERATION

In everyday life it is necessary for us to work together with our fellow human beings. Most of the things which they do are legitimate and good, and it is through working with them that we find our salvation. We were created social beings, with an

45

obligation of living with others and of cooperating with others. Cooperation in the good works of others raises little moral problem except in certain cases in which one neglects one's own obligations as spouse, parent, or citizen in order to help others. This point was mentioned under charity.

The chief moral problems in regard to cooperation arise in regard to sinful actions of others, and it is in this sense that the word is ordinarily used by moral theologians. The latter do not always agree in the precise meaning which they attach to the word. In general, however, we can say that cooperation means the concurrence with another person in a sinful action. This concurrence may be accomplished in various ways: (1) by acting with another in the same sin, as would happen if one person joined another in a serious act of vandalism; (2) by supplying him what is helpful in performing a sinful action (for example, by providing a person with a gun with which to commit a robbery); (3) by commanding or suggesting that he do something sinful, by encouraging him to do it, or by suggesting means of doing it. A very important distinction is that between formal and merely material cooperation. Formal cooperation is always sinful; material cooperation may be licit.]

[FORMAL COOPERATION

To cooperate formally is to assist in some way in the sinful act and at the same time to desire that it be performed. This type of cooperation is always sinful: it is at least a sin against charity because by it we will do spiritual harm to our neighbor; frequently it is also a sin against some other virtue such as justice. The types of cooperation mentioned above in (1) and (3) are necessarily formal. This type of cooperation is obviously immoral and therefore always forbidden.]

People sometimes wonder about the morality of rejoicing over the good effects of someone's sinful action. Such rejoicing does not necessarily mean approval of the sinful action. For example, if a man who has done great harm to the common good is murdered, I can be glad that a benefit has come about for the common good without approving of the sin itself. However, we must be careful that we do limit our rejoicing to the good effect; in such cases it is easy to rationalize and extend our approval to the sin itself.

It would likewise be wrong to hope and desire that someone may assassinate a man who is a persecutor of Christians or in some other way a menace to society. One should content oneself with praying that God may remove the evil in a manner that is conformable with His infinite wisdom and goodness.

MATERIAL COOPERATION

[Material cooperation is that in which, without approving of another's wrongdoing, I help him to perform his sinful action by an act that is not of its nature sinful. For example, because forced to do so, I supply a burglar with tools for his robbery, or I provide him with some information regarding the location of certain gems, and so forth. *)rewrite*

Material cooperation with another's evil act is allowed when one has a proportionate reason for so acting. To have a proportionate reason means that, in this particular case, the good effects balance the evil effects that result from the cooperation. Why is cooperation in such circumstances licit? First of all, the action of the one who thus cooperates is not in itself sinful. It is not sinful in itself, for example, to give tools to another. Secondly, the one who cooperates materially by providing tools or in some other way need not desire or approve the sinful use to which the tools are to be put. He foresees that, through his material cooperation, a sinful act will be performed, but his obligation of preventing this sin is an obligation of charity, not an obligation of justice. But charity does not impose an obligation when the cost or burden is out of proportion to the good that will result. It therefore follows in general that there may be circumstances in which material cooperation is permissible.]

[PRINCIPLES APPLYING TO MATERIAL COOPERATION

The following principles apply to material cooperation under the several conditions that may exist:

Principle 1. Material cooperation is never licit when it would help in the performance of an action that is gravely injurious to the common good. The reason is that the lesser or private good must yield to the greater or common good.]

> EXAMPLE. If a communist was running for the presidency of the United States, my cooperative action of voting for him would help on an action that is gravely injurious to the state, and so it would not be allowed.

Principle 2. When my cooperative action would render easier the performance of an action that is gravely injurious to an innocent third party, my material cooperation is allowed only when exacted from me through fear that refusal will bring me injury equal to that of the third party. If my neighbor is threatened with grave injury, charity requires me to prevent that injury if I am able. If, however, my attempt to avert harm from him would cause me similar injury, charity allows me first to provide for my own safety.

> EXAMPLE. A rejected suitor forces his way into a residence and threatens to kill the housewife unless she gives him a kitchen knife, with which he declares that he intends to kill his rival. She has a sufficiently grave reason (the saving of her life) for permitting the misuse of her knife by the rejected suitor.

Principle 3. In cases in which material cooperation is neither clearly illicit because of serious injury to the common good nor clearly illicit because of injury to an innocent third party, but where the action involved is gravely sinful, it is necessary to consider how closely the cooperative act is connected with the principal act. We may distinguish in the following manner:

a) If the cooperative action is very proximate, only an *extremely* grave reason makes cooperation permissible. The reason is that charity forbids cooperation of this kind without a proportionate reason.

> EXAMPLE. An intern in a public hospital is assigned to assist at an illicit operation. Refusal to do so would jeopardize his position and his career. It would also make it impossible for him to carry on work which he has been doing for the spiritual good of other patients. If no scandal is given, he would have a sufficient reason for assisting. In no case, of course, could he perform the operation itself.

b) If the cooperation is less proximate, a grave reason would allow one to cooperate.

> EXAMPLE. A linotyper is employed in a printing establishment where both good and bad books are produced. His cooperation in the printing of the bad books is less proximate, and so a grave reason (for example, great need of money) would allow him to keep his job. A similar example is that of a clerk in a drugstore who is called upon to sell objectionable magazines and contraceptives. If he is in real need of the money he earns and if to give up his position would expose him to the danger of not being able to find other employment, he may remain in his present position. He should, however, keep his eyes open for a position in which he would not have to sell such articles.

c) If the cooperation is remote, a slight reason would suffice to permit one to cooperate.

EXAMPLE. In the printing establishment where both good and bad books are produced a man not in special need of money may work as watchman.

SCANDAL

Scandal is some word or act that tends to tempt or incite another to sin. It is sufficient if the word or act *may* induce others to sin, even though the sin does not follow. If one realizes that he is giving scandal, he is accountable for it, even though the scandal does not actually occasion a sin.

EXAMPLE. I give another a lascivious book, but he, because of his virtue, does not sin.

Scandal is not given (1) if the other would commit the sin independently of the bad example, and hence is not influenced by it (X blasphemes in the presence of Y, who blasphemes habitually), or (2) if the other could not be at all incited to the same sin by the bad example (an atheist blasphemes in the presence of a nun).

THOSE WHO TAKE SCANDAL

Besides those who are scandalized by the action of another which of its nature tends to incite to evil-doing, there are some persons who, because of their abnormal disposition or because of their hypocrisy, find occasions of sin in the innocent actions of others. We may classify them as follows:

1. Those who are pharisaically scandalized. A person is said to take pharisaical scandal if he maliciously misconstrues another's good or indifferent action.

EXAMPLE. A puritanical old maid is "scandalized" at the sight of a Catholic playing an innocent game of cards. The Catholic may continue his game of cards even though he foresees that his action will be an occasion for someone's being pharisaically scandalized. One need pay no attention at all to scandal of this kind.

2. Those who are scandalized because weak. In this case one finds occasion to evil in another's good or indifferent act because he himself is either weak in virtue or lacking in knowledge (that is, ignorant). When we speak of weakness and ignorance, we

mean weakness or ignorance notably greater than that which is commonly found in the average adult.

EXAMPLE 1. A man has such a weakness for drink that the sight of others drinking sometimes starts him on another spree. His weakness, however, need not prevent others from enjoying an innocent drink in his presence if they have a proportionate reason for acting as they do.

EXAMPLE 2. A freshman in college entertains deliberate doubts concerning his faith because of matter in his textbooks which would cause no difficulty for a reasonably well-informed person. In his case the taking of scandal is due to a lack of knowledge.

Circumstances must determine to what extent we are obliged in charity to avoid giving scandal to the weak. Physicians, for example, may licitly discuss among themselves topics that would scandalize the young or the uneducated. Charity, however, forbids them to discuss such things where the young or ignorant may hear if they can omit the discussion without serious inconvenience. A sick man who badly needs this particular kind of food may eat meat on Friday, but doing so may scandalize a pious Catholic who knows of no exception to the law. Charity would prompt the sick man to inform the pious Catholic of the lawful exception to Friday abstinence if circumstances are such that he can do so.

One may licitly refrain from fulfilling even a grave positive precept that is not necessary for salvation in order to prevent serious scandal of the weak. Thus, a wife who knows that her husband makes her observance of the abstinence required on ember days an occasion for blaspheming may (but need not) refrain from observing this ecclesiastical precept.

THOSE WHO GIVE SCANDAL

Those who are guilty of words or deeds that are an occasion of sin to others may desire to lead others into sin or they may be entirely uninterested in or even regret the spiritual injury which their action will occasion. We must, then, carefully distinguish between two kinds of scandal: (1) direct scandal and (2) indirect scandal.

1. *Direct scandal* is that in which the sin of the other is desired or intended.

EXAMPLE. I indulge in impure talk which I realize some youngsters will overhear, and I intend to allure them to sin.

Direct scandal involves a twofold sin: a sin against charity and a sin against that virtue which the scandalizer attacks.

2. *Indirect scandal* is that in which the other's sin is foreseen but not wished.

> EXAMPLE. A social worker calls a spade a spade in describing immoral conditions in a tavern in order to arouse his audience to put an end to the evil. He foresees that some present will be incited to sin by his words and will yield to the temptation.

Indirect scandal may be either illicit or licit. It is illicit under two circumstances:

a) Indirect scandal is illicit if my action itself is bad; for example, I steal, lie, adore a pagan idol.

b) Indirect scandal is illicit if my action is good or indifferent but if I do not have sufficient reason for doing it in circumstances where I see that others will thereby be incited to evil.

> EXAMPLE. A college professor when requested by the bishop to report on an article in an off-color magazine reads the magazine in the presence of youngsters who will thus be led to follow his example. He could without much inconvenience read the magazine in his room.

There are circumstances under which indirect scandal is licit. It is licit to perform a good or indifferent act if a sufficient reason exists, even though it is foreseen that some will be scandalized. Life would be intolerable if we were obliged to avoid even virtuous actions because of the malice or weakness of others. The mother of a seriously sick child, for example, may miss Mass on Sunday, even though she is certain that busybodies in the neighborhood will commit the sin of rash judgment or stay away from Mass themselves without adequate reason.

DEGREES OF GUILT IN SCANDAL

Scandal is a grave or a slight sin according to the nature of the sin to which the one scandalized is incited. If, for example, I scandalize another so that he tells a lie, the scandal is ordinarily a venial sin; if I scandalize him so that he commits adultery, the scandal is a mortal sin.

REPARATION FOR SINFUL SCANDAL COMMITTED

There is no doubt that a person who has given scandal, especially in serious matters, has an obligation to make reparation insofar as it is possible. A businessman who has taught younger men in the firm how to cheat customers certainly has an obligation to try to undo the harm by explaining to them that he now realizes that his practices were wrong and that he is sorry that he led them astray. If he knows that it will do no good to try to change their minds, at least he has the obligation to make it clear that he no longer approves of such practices.

In many cases it will be impossible to make reparation because the parties who took scandal may be unknown. A girl who has performed in indecent shows could not possibly find out who had attended and to what extent they were scandalized. In such cases the best she can do is lead a good life and let it be known that she is sorry for her past actions. Each case of scandal will be different and the means of making reparation for it will depend on the circumstances and the nature of the scandal given. A prudent judgment in an individual case could probably be made only with the help of a confessor who can weigh all the elements and the usefulness of attempted reparation.

Lest our treatment of the influence of our actions on others seem too negative, we should recall here that the most powerful means that we have for the salvation of our neighbor is good example. The high standards of morality of the Catholic laity, their devotion to the Mass and the sacraments, and their practice of charity to those in need keep the Church alive and flourishing and win over to her many who would be left cold by rational argumentation in proof of her divine authority. Just as we are to be blamed for the foreseen harm to our neighbor involved in scandal, so we are to be praised for the foreseen good which comes to our neighbor from our good actions. And just as love for our neighbor is the most powerful motive for the avoidance of scandal, so it is the most powerful motive for helping him by our good actions to attain the supernatural end for which he was created by God.

OCCASIONS OF SIN

An occasion of sin is whatever presents a danger (exterior to us) of violating the law. By saying *whatever* we included everything: things (for example, a book), places (for example, a tavern), and persons (for example, a bad companion). By saying *presents a danger* we restrict an occasion of sin to one which is of such a nature that temptation and consent are possible. An occasion of sin is something that may arouse an impulse to sin. By saying that an occasion of sin presents a danger of *violating the law* we mean that there is danger of consenting to the impulse (danger of sinning) and not merely danger of experiencing the temptation.

KINDS OF OCCASIONS OF SIN

An occasion of sin may either be remote or proximate and either voluntary or necessary.

A *remote occasion* means either (1) circumstances in which sin for any ordinary individual is possible but not at all probable or (2) circumstances in which the individual in question has shown that he does not as a rule sin. Remote occasions exist everywhere. To avoid them one would have to leave this world. Such occasions are, for example, listening to the broadcasting of an ordinary musical program; attending a decent movie; the commingling of the two sexes in work and recreation.

A *proximate occasion* means either (1) circumstances in which any ordinary individual is almost morally certain to sin (for example, attending a burlesque show) or (2) circumstances in which the individual in question as a rule sins. Some circumstances are such that they provide a proximate occasion of sinning for practically anybody who faces them; for example, an obscene book. Confronted with these severe temptations, the normal individual would sin. Even in these circumstances, however, there are some who would not be incited to sin as would the average person; for example, a very virtuous person who is so constituted that certain things make no impression on him, or a mature person who has become accustomed to disregarding occasions of sin through long exposure to them. Everyone must take it for granted that he will react to temptation as the ordinary individual does unless he is sure that he is an exception. Other circumstances are such that they provide a proximate occasion of sin for some, but not for all. Occasions of sin looked upon as proximate for all men are known to be such from the study of the ways and nature of men in general. Occasions of sin that are proximate only for certain individuals are known to be such as a result of one's own experience or of knowledge of one's own moral frailty.

A *voluntary occasion* of sin is that which can easily be removed or avoided by the person involved. Under ordinary circumstances one can abstain, for example, from dancing, drinking, or certain kinds of reading which for him are occasions of sin. Failing to do this, he makes the occasion of sin a voluntary one. A *necessary occasion* of sin is one which cannot be removed at all, or, at least, only with great difficulty.

EXAMPLE 1. One is imprisoned in the same cell with an evil companion whose seductive influence is known to be a constant source of grave moral danger. In this case it is physically impossible to remove the occasion of sin.

EXAMPLE 2. A newspaper reporter may meet with many occasions of sinning in the assignments given him which he is not at liberty to refuse. He cannot without serious loss give up his work, for both he and his family depend on it for a livelihood. It is morally impossible for him to remove such occasions.

PRINCIPLES APPLICABLE TO OCCASIONS OF SIN

The following principles indicate our obligations in regard to the avoidance of the occasions of sin:

Principle 1. We are not obliged to avoid the remote occasions of sinning. Two reasons can be alleged in support of this principle: (a) the danger of sin is slight and can easily be overcome; (b) if we were obliged to avoid the remote occasions of sin, it would be impossible to live, for we could not avoid all such occasions and continue to discharge our normal functions in society.

Principle 2. We are obliged to avoid all voluntary proximate occasions of sinning. As we have seen, a proximate occasion of sin for an individual is one in which *as a rule* he sins. The fact that sin will follow under the circumstances that exist may therefore be either (a) morally certain or (b) merely probable.

a) When we are morally certain that such an occasion will end in our sinning, we *must* avoid it, since our duty to avoid sin entails the obligation to avoid whatever will inevitably lead us into sin.

EXAMPLE. An alcoholic knows that every time he visits a certain barroom he becomes completely intoxicated. In spite of this knowledge he again deliberately drops in there for a drink. Since the proximate occasion in question is an occasion of sinning grievously, he is obliged under pain of mortal sin to avoid the barroom where he knows he will certainly become intoxicated.

b) When we have only probability that a certain set of circumstances would be an occasion of our sinning grievously, we do not have a serious obligation of avoiding it, since here we do not choose what will inevitably lead us into sin. However, a venial sin would be committed in seeking such an occasion, for we would thus be guilty of imprudence in regard to our spiritual welfare.

> EXAMPLE. A man who realizes that a certain companion has frequently led him into serious sin associates with this companion without sufficient reason. He justifies this action on the ground that he is not certain to sin. He is guilty of venial sin, more or less serious according to the probability of serious sin in the circumstances.

The distinction between occasions of sin which are morally certain to lead us into sin and those where only probability of sin exists is a valid distinction, but it should not lead us to conclude that all cases will clearly come under one or the other. There are degrees of moral certainty and of probability. The judgment as to whether it is seriously wrong to put oneself into a certain set of circumstances must be based on all the factors involved. Much harm can be done by exaggerating the obligation to avoid occasions of sin, for such exaggeration may lead people to conclude that it is impossible to fulfill the obligation, to become very discouraged, and often to fail to avoid occasions which are undoubtedly sinful. On the other hand, the unqualified statement that it is only venially sinful to put oneself in circumstances in which sin is probable but not morally certain may lead to laxity. It is imprudent to try to lay down general principles for all men or even for a special group such as teen-agers, since people differ greatly and should be advised as individuals.

Principle 3. If we are in a necessary proximate occasion of sinning, we are obliged to make it remote.

The occasion of sinning is not in itself a sin and does not entail the necessity of sinning. One in such an occasion through necessity (that is, he cannot avoid it at all, or can avoid it only at the cost of grave inconvenience) is in the danger but does not love the danger, provided he is in the occasion unwillingly. No one lives in the circumstances that necessitate sinning. Everyone can make a proximate occasion remote. This is effected by such means as prayer, the sacraments, and the custody of the eyes.

> EXAMPLE. A medical student for whom certain courses have proved to be a proximate occasion of sin may continue with his study of medicine provided he uses the means necessary to minimize the temptations and to enable him to resist them.

It should be pointed out here that people who are living in a necessary occasion of sin are very much in need of regular advice. Many of them will not succeed in overcoming the temptations that arise and may easily become discouraged after several failures. The first attitude which the confessor or adviser will attempt to form in them is the resolve to overcome the difficulty in spite of occasional failures. For them discouragement is the greatest enemy. Second, he will point out to them that they are exercising certain virtues despite their failures. The humility which is required to admit again and again that we have failed is certainly pleasing to God. The acts of contrition and love of God made after failure are sincere and meritorious. Finally, he will point out to them that on many occasions in the past great sinners have become great saints, that for some people the path to sanctity is devious. The experience of Alcoholics Anonymous certainly has been valuable. The humility, self-sacrifice, and charity of those who have gone through the required steps is admitted by all who know them. Many of them have become holy only because they were forced to admit their own weakness and have thrown themselves upon the mercy and love of God.

Some particular applications of the principles on occasions of sin are treated in Chapter 9 (the Legion of Decency and steady dating) and Chapter 13 (reading).

DEGREES OF GUILT IN SIN

Sin is a violation of the eternal law. Every law, human or divine, has its origin in and receives its binding force from the eternal law. Whatever violates a human law, unless it be merely penal, indirectly at least violates the eternal law, since the eternal law commands obedience to human law.

An *imperfection* is different from sin, and can be either negative or positive.

A *negative imperfection* is a lack of greater perfection in a human act.

EXAMPLE. I give a poor man alms. Giving him more than I actually give would ordinarily be a greater perfection; hence my alms may be considered negatively imperfect.

A *positive imperfection* may be an action or omission that is contrary to a counsel (for example, to omit a higher good, as when one does not follow a clear vocation to the priesthood; or to violate laws that are not binding under pain of sin, as when one drives twenty-seven miles per hour instead of the twenty-five allowed by the law).

FORMAL SIN AND MATERIAL SIN

Formal (realized) sin is the act of freely and knowingly violating the law of God. A formal (or realized) sin always entails knowledge of the wrongness of the action that is being performed and freedom to do or to omit that action. Sin is essentially an act of the will and so is internal. There is never a sin unless man acts knowingly and freely.

EXAMPLE. I know that this is Friday and that I am forbidden to eat meat today; yet I eat it anyway, realizing that I am sinning.

Formal sin entails only the sinfulness that is apprehended in the act itself or in the cause, for there is no sin without knowledge. Hence if I steal five dollars from a poor man who I think is wealthy, I incur only the guilt of robbing a rich man. If I steal money from a man and I do not know that this money belongs to the Church, I incur only the guilt of an ordinary theft, not of sacrilege.

Material (unsuspected) sin is the act of unknowingly violating the law; for example, I forget that today is Friday and I eat meat. Material sin is not really a sin in the ordinary sense at all, for there is no moral guilt involved in this type of action. Hence it should not be mentioned in confession.

EXAMPLE. A 10-year-old boy repeats a blasphemous sentence, not knowing its evilness. He need not confess this should someone tell him the meaning of what he said.

Since formal sin is in the will, it might be asked what the external act adds to the internal act. The external act first of all indicates a continuation of the will act. It also frequently adds to the malice of the sin.

MORTAL SIN AND VENIAL SIN

Mortal sin is a deliberate violation of the law of God in a serious matter.

EXAMPLE. Without excuse I deliberately omit Sunday Mass, fully realizing the gravity of the offense.

Venial sin is a violation of the law of God (1) in a relatively light matter or (2) without full consent of the will.

EXAMPLES. (1) One tells a slight lie. (2) One half consents to an impure desire.

DISTINGUISHING BETWEEN MORTAL SIN AND VENIAL SIN

How is one to determine whether the subject matter of a sin is serious or light? Our sources of knowledge on this point are (1) Holy Scripture, (2) the pronouncements of the Church, (3) the teachings of the fathers and theologians, and (4) the nature of the action itself.

1. Holy Scripture calls some sins abominable, worthy of eternal punishment, hated by God, or such as will exclude from the kingdom of heaven. These terms identify sins as mortal.

2. A sin is mortal if the Church explicitly brands it as such or if the Church imposes grave punishment for it (for example, excommunication or deprival of Christian burial).

3. The fathers and theologians, especially the moral theologians, have discussed the gravity of sins of different kinds. To contradict the opinion which is commonly held by these authorities, who are trained specialists in this field of knowledge, would be temerarious.

4. The nature of the action itself may clearly indicate the gravity of a sin. That sin must be considered serious matter which causes grave injury to God, to the Church, to the state, to our neighbor, or to ourselves.

REQUISITES FOR MORTAL SIN

Three things are necessary in order that an action be a mortal sin: (1) grave matter, (2) full advertence, and (3) full consent.

1. The action itself must be a serious violation of God's law; for example, murder, bank robbery, adultery. We can know which actions would constitute a serious violation of God's law from Holy Scripture, the Church, the fathers and theologians, or from the nature of the thing itself, as has been explained above.

2. Full advertence means that the person is aware of the moral character of the act and of his serious obligation to perform or avoid it. A person who is half-asleep, or in a daydream, or partially distracted has some awareness of his actions (if interrupted, he could tell you what he had been doing), but he is not usually

fully aware of the moral character of his actions and would not ordinarily have full advertence. A person who is aware of his obligation to perform or avoid a certain action but who does not realize that he has a serious obligation to avoid it would be lacking in full advertence.

EXAMPLE. A thief steals a valuable painting but thinks that it is a cheap imitation. He does not have full advertence.

It is sufficient for full advertence to realize the grave malice only in a general sort of way.

EXAMPLE. An inveterate sinner commits crime after crime with little reflection on each occasion. His sins would be grave.

3. Finally there must be full consent. The will must freely choose what is fully understood.

DEGREES OF GRAVITY IN MORTAL SINS

All mortal sins are not equally evil. This is evident from several considerations.

1. Holy Scripture refers to some serious sins as more grievous than others; for example, "He who betrayed me to thee has the greater sin" (John 19:11).

2. Mortal sins differ because of the nature of the act. Hatred of God is a greater sin than simony or perjury. Murder is worse than a grave theft.

3. Mortal sins differ because of the strength and duration of the act of the will. One who desires a serious evil and carries out the desire sins more gravely than one who merely desires but does not act on the desire. One who carefully plans and executes a murder sins more gravely than one who commits such a crime in a sudden burst of anger.

DEGREES OF GRAVITY IN VENIAL SINS

Venial sins, like mortal sins, are not equally evil. The greater or lesser evil may be due to (1) the subject matter or (2) the amount of deliberation.

1. Venial sin may differ in malice because of the subject matter. There is a difference between stealing five cents and stealing fifty cents; between drinking just a little too much and stopping just this side of getting thoroughly intoxicated; between not avoiding an occasion of sin when the danger of sinning is very

slight and not avoiding an occasion of sin when the danger of sinning is notably greater.

2. Slightly evil actions may be performed with full deliberation or with only imperfect deliberation.

Sometimes one hears of indeliberate venial sins. This is a contradiction in terms because, if there is no deliberation, there is no sin. The term, however, usually means "slightly sinful offenses against God, the malice of which is lessened because they are committed with only imperfect deliberation."

THE DECALOGUE

God did not lay down the ten commandments in order to make life harder for His rational creatures. He proclaimed the Decalogue in order to call man's attention more vividly to the dictates of the natural law and to give him a divinely inspired, infallibly sound code of morals. These precepts, then, are not tyrannous restrictions placed on our liberty. They are intended for our benefit; that is, they were given to protect us against ourselves and against our neighbor, to safeguard and keep sacred human rights and liberty.

All races of men, however uncivilized and ungodly, have had a code of morality drawn up for their self-protection. Many of these codes failed partially in their object because they did not coincide with the teaching of the ten commandments. Superstitious practices, for example, branded as sinful by our First Commandment were allowed among many barbarous tribes, and with devastating results. Again, we notice that in some codes of morals abortion and infanticide were not prohibited, and so the lives of thousands of innocent victims were mercilessly snuffed out. Without respect for authority, taught by the Fourth Commandment, dire consequences would follow. The Sixth and Ninth Commandments protect family life. And so it is with the rest of the Decalogue. Each precept enunciates some dictate of the natural law. Disobedience to these commandments brings injury to ourselves and to the human race. Disobedience results in abject slavery to vice and not in liberty of spirit.

The commandments, then, are a positive help to man in the work of saving his soul. However, because of the wording "Thou shalt not" many see in them only the negative side. But they are equivalent to the two great commandments which Christ emphasized: "Thou shalt love the Lord thy God with thy whole heart" and "Thou shalt love thy neighbor as thyself." The ten commandments, therefore, clearly indicate to man his duty to love God with his whole being by adoration, by praise of His name, and by public worship, and to love his neighbor by respecting his person, property, and rights.

The ten commandments form an epitome of what man is morally obliged to do or to omit doing. They comprised the first written law directly promulgated by God, though this promulgation occurred many centuries after the fall of Adam. When Cain slew Abel he was bound by the restrictions of the ten commandments insofar as the ten commandments are substantially the teachings of the natural law. Hence the Decalogue always bound men in conscience. It bound even those who lived before the time of Moses, through whom the ten commandments were given to all the people of Israel. Hence, too, the ten commandments bind all men today whether they are Protestants, Jews, Mohammedans, Catholics, or pagans. Moreover, Christ renewed the precepts of the Decalogue in a special manner (Matthew 19:17). One should not forget that it was not the whole of the Mosaic law that was abolished at the coming of Christ, but only that special system of religion and external form of government which Moses inaugurated. The special system of religion that was divinely prescribed for the Israelites prefigured the mysteries of the Christian religion. Since, then, the purpose of that ritual was to foreshadow the sacrifice of the Mass, there is today no obligation to observe the Mosaic ceremonial law with its once-obligatory abstinences, ablutions, and various kinds of sacrifice. The moral precepts contained in the Decalogue, on the contrary, concerned all nations and all times, and so they still bind all men.

Cases to be analyzed[3]

1 A Catholic who is nationally prominent has been excused by his pastor from the Friday abstinence obligation because his doctors insist on his eating a certain kind of meat every day. However, Friday often finds him eating in the dining car of a train. If he eats meat on such occa-

---

[3] In discussing these cases analyze the morality involved and substantiate your decision by reference to principles that have been explained.

sions, he will undoubtedly scandalize many of his fellow travelers. If he abstains from the meat, his health will suffer. He is worried about how he should act.

2 As a salesman stopped for a traffic light, his automobile was boarded by a dangerous gangster. The gangster, hotly pursued by the police, put a gun at the salesman's back and ordered him to speed up as fast as possible. The salesman obeyed the gangster's command, but wondered afterwards whether this cooperation in effecting the gangster's escape from the police was not gravely sinful.

3 "The morals of the Middle Ages do not fit today's conditions," says a young woman. "Modern economic conditions and knowledge have changed the old double standard for men and women."

4 "Everybody has a right to be happy; and a Catholic, burdened with the obligations of the commandments, finds little joy in life. Moreover, his strictness makes him a 'wet blanket' on the good times of others," complains the same young woman.

5 A public official is unfair in portioning out the legally prescribed mothers' pensions. In confession he accuses himself of a violation of commutative justice.

6 A man with a grudge against the administration deliberately breaks five large windows in City Hall. He tells his confessor that he was guilty of a sin against legal justice.

7 A dejected and ill-clad man approaches a pedestrian on the street and asks for money for a meal. "I haven't eaten in three days," he says, "and I am dying on my feet." The man accosted refuses to help this man, though he could spare a dollar.

8 A Catholic sells rosaries to natives who he knows will wear them as ornaments and not use them as helps in prayer.

9 An office worker lends his fountain pen to his friend at the next desk, who needs it to write a letter. He knows that his friend's letter will be very lewd and will probably seduce the reader to sin.

10 When a beggar meets a lawyer on the street and there in front of several acquaintances earnestly begs for money, the lawyer gives it to him. He knows that the beggar will put the money to bad use, but it would cause him great embarrassment to refuse the request.

11 Unless a passenger tips a taxi driver generously, he is sure that the driver will utter much profanity. The passenger, however, because he has not much money to spare now, pays the man only the required fare.

12 A Catholic college graduate frequently tunes in on the radio sermons of a clever and eloquent Protestant minister. "I know that much of his teaching is false," says he, "and so listening to this preaching won't hurt me."

13 A binder works in a printing shop that turns out many obscene books. Since he has a family to support and cannot find a job elsewhere, he believes that he is justified in remaining at this plant.

14 A bartender often has occasion to wait on customers who, though they are already partially intoxicated, wish to keep on drinking. Because a re-

fusal would mean a quarrel and loss of trade, he serves such customers the liquor they demand, although he knows that they will become wholly intoxicated.

Topics for discussion[4]

1 A Catholic is always a marked man, and so his public actions can readily help or harm the Church.
2 Is direct scandal the same thing as cooperation in another's sin? Explain your answer.
3 Explain the malice of mortal sin, of venial sin.
4 A venial sin does not become a mortal sin though often repeated, but frequent repetition of the same kind of venial sin prepares the way for grave sin.
5 Name some ancient nations that permitted or prescribed practices in their social or religious life that were at variance with the teaching of the ten commandments.

Bibliography

Aumann, Jordon. "The Theology of Venial Sin." In *Proceedings of the Tenth Annual Convention of the Catholic Theological Society of America,* pp. 74-96. New York: Catholic Theological Society of America, 1955.

Connery, John R. "Current Theology: Notes on Moral Theology." *Theological Studies* 18:575, December 1957 (on social justice); 19:542, December 1958 (on cooperation).

———— "Prudence and Morality." *Theological Studies* 13:564-82, December 1952.

Cronin, John Francis. *Catholic Social Principles.* Milwaukee: Bruce Publishing Company, 1955.

Davis, Henry. *Moral and Pastoral Theology,* seventh edition, edited by L. W. Geddes, Vol. 1, pp. 203-361. 4 vols. New York: Sheed and Ward, 1958.

Dempsey, Bernard W. "The Range of Social Justice." *Social Order* 7:20-24, January 1957.

Devine, Arthur. "The Passions." In J. F. Leibell, editor, *Readings in Ethics,* pp. 207-10. Chicago: Loyola University Press, 1926.

Drummond, William F. *Social Justice.* Milwaukee: Bruce Publishing Company, 1955.

Ford, John C. "Reply to Father Vann." *Homiletic and Pastoral Review* 57:124-27, November 1956 (on virtue and pseudovirtue).

Gilleman, Gerard. "Moral Theology and Charity." *Theology Digest* 2:15-18, Winter 1954.

---

[4] Not all the assertions contained in the topics are true. The student is to judge the truth of any assertions made and to explain his decision.

Harvery, John. "The Nature of the Infused Moral Virtues." In *Proceedings of the Tenth Annual Convention of the Catholic Theological Society of America,* pp. 172-221. New York: Catholic Theological Society of America, 1955.

Humbert, Alphonse. "The Notion of 'Scandal' in the Synoptics." *Theology Digest* 3:108-12, Spring 1955.

Jone, Heribert. *Moral Theology,* pp. 63-91. Westminster: Newman Press, 1957.

Leclercq, Jacques. "Can a Layman Be a Saint?" *Theology Digest* 4:3-8, Winter 1956.

Morrison, Bakewell. *Character Formation in College.* Milwaukee: Bruce Publishing Company, 1938.

Newman, Jeremiah. "Theology of Social Action." *Theology Digest* 3:145-59, Autumn 1955.

O'Doherty, E. F. "Religion and Mental Health." *Theology Digest* 5:97-102, Spring 1957.

Olivier, Bernard. "The Meaning of Christian Hope." *Theology Digest* 3:89-92, Spring 1955.

Rickaby, Joseph. "The Cardinal Virtues." In J. F. Leibell, editor, *Readings in Ethics,* pp. 236-41. Chicago: Loyola University Press, 1926.

Rondet, Henri. "Towards a Theology of Sin." *Theology Digest* 4:171-76, Autumn 1956.

Ryan, John A. "Charity and Charities." In *Catholic Encyclopedia,* Vol. 3, pp. 592-604.

Shields, Leo W. *The History and Meaning of the Term Social Justice.* Notre Dame: University of Notre Dame Press, 1941.

Vann, Gerald. "Unconscious Motivation and Pseudo-Virtue." *Homiletic and Pastoral Review* 57:115-23, November 1956.

Waldron, Augustine. "Virtue." In *Catholic Encyclopedia,* Vol. 15, pp. 472-75.

CHAPTER IV

The

"I am the Lord thy God, . . . Thou **first**
shalt not have strange gods before me."
Exodus 20:2-3

commandment

GOD is our Lord and Master, and as such He alone is worthy of divine worship. This First Commandment reminds us of the duty we have of recognizing our dependence on Him and of acknowledging His perfections. This warning which the Creator has deigned to give to His rational creatures is intended to protect man against the evils of idolatry, superstition, atheism, and other degrading practices which are opposed to the proper worship of God.

The First Commandment is both *affirmative* and *negative*.[1] It is affirmative insofar as it prescribes acts of the virtue of religion; it is negative insofar as it prohibits acts contrary to the virtue of religion. The virtue of religion is a moral virtue which inclines one

---

[1] Protestants make two commandments out of this commandment. Hence their numbering of the remaining commandments is different from that used by Catholics. Their Third Commandment is the Catholic Second; their Seventh is the Catholic Sixth. Protestants combine the Catholic Ninth and Tenth Commandments into one commandment: "Thou shalt not covet."

to give due worship to God as Creator and Master of all things. Acts of other virtues are sometimes spoken of as acts of religion. For example, a man who teaches catechism to children is said to be performing a religious act. Strictly speaking, his action is an act of charity and is called an act of religion because he does it for the honor and glory of God. We are using the word only in the strict sense; that is, as referring only to acts of worship.

THE WORSHIP OF GOD

The worship of God is essentially the acknowledgment of God's excellence and of our dependence on Him. The worship that is prescribed by the First Commandment must be not only internal (that is, performed through acts of the intellect and will), but it must also be external (that is, expressed by outward acts). The reasons for this are as follows:

1. Worship with the soul alone is not complete service, for God is Lord of man's body as well as of his soul. The soul is not the whole man.

2. Man is naturally inclined to give external expression to his thoughts and desires.

3. External reverence (shown by the acts of kneeling, joining one's hands, and so forth) helps to foster internal devotion and to prevent distractions.

4. Through external reverence we give that public evidence of our submission to God which is due to Him and which contributes to our neighbor's edification.

The most perfect act of worship is sacrifice. A sacrifice is the offering of an external gift to God to symbolize our internal dispositions. By offering sacrifice we dedicate ourselves and all we have to the service of God. Christ left us the perfect sacrifice in the Mass. At the Last Supper He dedicated Himself to His death on the cross, submitted Himself perfectly to the will of the Father. He symbolized His complete dedication in the twofold consecration of the bread and wine at the Last Supper and gave to the apostles and their successors the power to repeat this offering of Himself. In the Mass, however, it is not just Christ who offers Himself. As members of the mystical body we are empowered to offer Christ to the Father, and thus we have a perfect gift. As participators in the sacrifice of Christ we also offer ourselves with

Him. Some self-offering is necessary for participation in the Mass. Even one not in the state of grace can offer oneself by asking God for the grace to repent. The most perfect offering, of course, is the complete submission of our will to the will of God with the resolution not to offend Him even in slight matters.

Further development of the value and necessity of sacrifice is to be found in treatises on dogmatic theology. The requirements for fulfillment of the obligation to offer sacrifice will be taken under the Third Commandment.

PRAYER

When we talk of prayer we are usually thinking of the prayer of petition. For many centuries the word was actually limited to this meaning. St. John Damascene defined prayer as "the petition of fitting things from God," and it is this definition which St. Thomas uses in his discussion of prayer in the *Summa theologica.* In modern terminology prayer includes acts other than petition. Chief among those acts is the prayer of adoration. Much of the official prayer of the Church consists of such acts; for example, parts of the Gloria of the Mass. Prayer of adoration is certainly the most perfect form and is obligatory for all men. Our Lord's own prayer, the Our Father, begins with it and proceeds to the prayer of petition. It is impossible to say a prayer of petition as it should be said without including, at least implicitly, the prayer of adoration. Thanksgiving follows naturally from adoration: in it we recognize God's goodness as a source of benefit to us. It too is obligatory and is presupposed as a disposition in the prayer of petition. Prayer of contrition is obligatory only on the presupposition of sin. Our Lord and Mary did not practice such prayer, but it is necessary for all of us because we know that all adults do sin unless they have received a special privilege from God.

PRAYER OF PETITION

Our Lord told us that, unless we prayed, we would perish. The Council of Trent admonishes us to do what we are able and to pray for what we are not able, implying that, unless we pray, we will not overcome the temptation and difficulties of our lives. The first thing for which we ask is eternal salvation, and we ask for all other things in relation to it. Chief among those things, of course, are the graces which we need in our everyday lives.

It is somewhat difficult to put the obligation to pray in concrete terms. Must we pray every day? Several times a day? Once a week? Since we are always in need of God's help, it would seem that there is an obligation to pray every day. How much is hard to determine. It would depend to some extent on the individual. Certainly we have an obligation to pray when prayer is necessary to overcome a serious temptation or when we have offended God seriously. Beyond this it is hard to impose any definite obligation. However, it should be remembered that God ordinarily distributes His grace according to our dispositions and that we do not know when we shall be in need of His special help. Spiritual advisers know that the first step in the process of withdrawing from God is usually the neglect of prayer.

CONDUCT DURING PRAYER

Since prayer is a "conversation" with God, one must conduct himself with proper respect when praying. This applies both to obligatory prayers and to prayers which are said out of devotion. Since the latter are begun freely, some have argued that we need not worry about distractions during them. This principle, however, is not universally true, nor can it be applied to prayer. If we were to approach any individual, even one inferior in status to ourselves, and ask him to consider a request that we wished to make, we would be looked upon as extremely rude were we to walk away as he was bending his ear to listen to us. If we owe such courtesy to men, we undoubtedly owe far greater reverence to the infinite majesty of God.

For this reason theologians hold that, even though our prayer be freely undertaken and is not a matter of obligation, we may not engage in any actions which are incompatible with thinking of what we are doing. For example, to chat, to read, or to write would prevent one from giving thought to any prayer attempted during these actions. On the other hand, one could pray and at the same time engage in washing one's hands, dressing, or driving an automobile, provided one could give sufficient thought to the act of praying.

Our prayer should also be characterized by humility, earnestness, confidence in God, and other attitudes befitting a sinful creature who is addressing his Maker. If we pray at home, it will help to kneel respectfully before a crucifix or a holy picture. The best place for prayer, however, is before the Blessed Sacrament in a church or chapel. One who spends fifteen or thirty minutes every day in prayer of this kind is in little danger of losing his soul. He will also find that he receives strength to rise superior to his temptations and trials, from which so many continue to suffer because they will not use the means that God has provided for overcoming them.

KINDS OF PRAYER

There are two kinds of prayer: (1) mental prayer and (2) vocal prayer.

1. *Mental prayer* engages only the three powers of the soul. These are (a) the *memory,* which offers a pious truth or some event to the mind for reflection; (b) the *intellect,* which ponders over the meaning and application of this truth; and (c) the *will,* which forms aspirations and good resolutions as a result of the truths made known by the memory and the intellect.

2. *Vocal prayer* is a "conversation" with God (or the saints) which is expressed in words. In vocal prayer one does not merely think of the words of the prayer, but forms them with the tongue. Vocal prayer is prescribed for the gaining of various indulgences; for example, the indulgences of the rosary, of the prayer before a crucifix after Holy Communion. Aspirations, however, such as "My Jesus, mercy!" need only be made mentally in order to gain the indulgences attached. Mutes can gain all indulgences by mere mental recitation.

FOR WHOM MAY WE PRAY?

We may pray not only for ourselves but for any other living person (even though he is excommunicated), for the souls in purgatory, and (provided there is no scandal) for the excommunicated who have died. Hence we may pray for deceased Protestants and may have Mass offered for them privately.

FORBIDDEN FORMS OF WORSHIP

The First Commandment forbids us to sin against religion by excess or defect. Of course, we cannot worship God too much, but worship can be wrong by excess if we use false or unbecoming forms of worship or if we worship an object that is not deserving of worship. Worship can be wrong by defect if in what we offer God as an act of worship there is irreverence toward God or some sacred person or thing.

Worshiping God in an unbecoming manner is forbidden both by the natural law and the Church. A man who handles poisonous snakes to show that he has trust in God is acting in an unbecoming way because he is putting the worship of God on the same level as a side show. The orgies with which some of the pagan religions attempted to express worship were certainly objectively unbecoming. It is obvious that a Catholic is forbidden to engage in such worship.

A type of worship which contains heretical matter either implicitly or explicitly would also be clearly forbidden. A Catholic would never be allowed to say a prayer, whether he did so in private or publicly, that contained heresy. For instance, he could not pray that God bring someone to salvation even if the one concerned did not repent. To do so would be to deny that salvation depends on the free cooperation of man with the grace of God, and this is heretical doctrine.

JOINING IN NON-CATHOLIC WORSHIP

A more difficult problem is that of joining in worship which is not unbecoming and does not contain heretical matter, but which is offered by people who are not members of the Church. A distinction must be made between private and public worship before we can solve this problem. Private worship is that offered by an individual or a group independently of their association with a particular church. Prayers said before meals in the home are private in most cases. Public worship is that offered by a group acting as members of a particular church; for example, the prayers and ceremonies of a Protestant service. Public worship need not be offered in a church.

A Catholic could join with others in private worship which did not contain heresy and was not unbecoming. For instance, he could say the Our Father with non-Catholics at a nonreligious public gathering. He could be present at public worship of non-Catholic groups for a sufficient reason; for example, he could attend a wedding or a funeral as an act of courtesy. To sit or stand with the others present at such a function is allowable. Catholic nurses or maids who must accompany their charges to Protestant services commit no sin, provided they are present in the capacity of servant and not as worshipers, and provided too that there is no proximate danger to their faith through listening to heretical sermons. The same may be said of Catholic husbands who take their non-Catholic wives to Protestant services.

To act as best man or as bridesmaid at a Protestant church wedding may be allowed provided there is a good reason (for example, fear of offending a close friend) and it is prudently thought that no scandal will be given. The bishop of the diocese is the judge of whether scandal would be given, and so his permission is necessary.

In no case can a Catholic participate actively in the public worship of another religious group. He could not join in the prayers or sing hymns as part of the religious service. Such participation is not forbidden by church law only; independently of any positive law of the Church it would be wrong. The chief reason why it is wrong is that it contains an implicit admission that God has given authority to some other group to determine how He is to be publicly worshiped. When Christ established the Church He left it a public worship by instituting the holy sacrifice of the Mass and the sacraments. He also gave the Church authority to add ceremonies and prayers to the Mass and the sacraments and to institute or approve other forms of worship such as Benediction or the Stations of the Cross. She alone has authority to determine how God is to be worshiped publicly.

Although active participation in the public worship of non-Catholics is forbidden, the Church does not say that such worship is evil. The sacrifice of the Mass offered by a validly ordained Greek Orthodox priest is valid and good in itself because it is Christ who offers it. Valid baptism by members of any group has the power to give grace. The psalms recited by a group of Protestants are still prayers approved by God. Those who participate in such prayers in good faith and with the intention of pleasing God are doing something subjectively good and often derive great profit from them.

MORAL REARMAMENT

The need of cooperation between men of good will is recognized both by Catholics and other religious groups. There are many areas in which methods for correcting social abuses or for promoting public morality can be agreed upon. However, a Catholic who cooperates with others for the common good must not lose sight of the fact that such cooperation must be limited by the principles which he holds to be revealed by God. He must not give the impression that he accepts the principle that one religion is as good as another or that the Church possesses no authority to condemn as morally wrong certain methods that may be proposed for establishing a better social order or for the improvement of public morals.

The moral-rearmament movement known as Moral Rearmament is American in origin but has had greater success in Europe than in our own country. Its founder, Frank Buchman, is a former Lutheran turned evangelist. He insists on the direct working of the Holy Spirit in each individual who has been "changed" or converted. Despite the fact that its leaders deny that it is a religion, there can be no doubt that it has all the elements of one and that it attempts to determine thought and action in all spheres of a person's life. In addition, it has been used by some as a means of preserving the *status quo,* especially in the economic sphere, a fact which has induced a number of labor leaders to criticize it severely.

A Catholic may not hold a position in Moral Rearmament. Some bishops have forbidden Catholics to attend its meetings. Others have allowed participation as long as no scandal is involved and it is understood that Catholics cooperate as Catholics with no compromise on doctrinal matters.

FALSE OR UNBECOMING FORMS OF WORSHIP

We have already mentioned a few examples of unbecoming worship, but they were not the type to attract a modern Catholic. However, there are individuals in the Church who mistakenly attribute infallible effects to a prayer or action repeated a certain number of times or in a certain place. One occasionally finds cards in the back of churches telling one to say a prayer for so many days and to make out a number of similar cards to be distributed among others. If one refuses, he is threatened with dire punishments with which God will afflict him. Such attitudes are superstitious and serve only to bring the Church into disrepute. Because of their ignorance those who indulge in such practices probably are not guilty of serious sin.

Much more serious are false claims to special revelations from God or to visions and miracles. Some who make such claims are impostors; others are deluded. Catholics should adopt the attitude of the Church. She is very reluctant to give such alleged revelations any recognition unless there is evidence that they actually occurred. Even then she does not propose them for belief to the faithful but simply recognizes that there is sufficient evidence for a prudent judgment that a miracle has occurred or that someone has had a revelation or a vision. Any devotion that originates in an alleged vision or revelation is tested by the Church according to the public revelation of which she is the custodian. Her approval of such devotions means that they do not contain anything contrary to faith or morals and that they are a fitting way of honoring God.

It has happened that people who were otherwise very holy have been deluded by false visions or imagined revelations. Simple souls, psychopathic personalities, and publicity seekers have on more than one occasion within our own times claimed to have received revelations from God or to have been visited by the Blessed Virgin. Catholics should be slow to believe and especially to publicize alleged visions, revelations, or miracles, since great harm can come to the Church if it is proved that they are false. Nor should such things become a substitute for the public teaching of the Church. Some have gone so far as to say that people would be damned for not accepting a certain private revelation— or worse, interpretations of private revelations.

These cautions should not lead us to the opposite extreme of denying that there are authentic visions, revelations, and miracles in our own day. God is free and omnipotent to do what He wills; but as intelligent beings we have the obligation not to accept something as from God without evidence.

We also sin by excess against religion by worshiping an object that is not deserving of worship. This can be done by (1) idolatry, (2) divination, and (3) vain observance.

Idolatry

Idolatry is the worship of idols or mere creatures in the place of God. Idolatry is always gravely sinful. Even if one practices idolatry in the privacy of his own room, he is guilty of mortal sin. Were he to perform this same action in public, his sin would be greater. What if a man under threat of death goes through the external actions of worshiping an idol, but without believing interiorly in the false deity? Even in this case he would be guilty of grave sin, for he would be violating his duty of professing his faith.

Divination

Divination is the attempt to learn hidden things, particularly things that are to happen in the future, by express or tacit appeal to the devil for aid. Many things that are to happen in the future can be foretold by science or conjectured with considerable probability by informed observers. We know when eclipses are to occur, when comets are to appear. Meteorologists are perfecting their methods of foretelling the weather. Physicians foretell the progress of a disease and are often quite accurate in stating how long a patient will live. Sociologists know reasonably well in what percentage of cases parole will prove successful. In everyday life men are constantly asking those who are wise and experienced what can be expected to happen if a certain investment is made or a certain plan followed.

When, therefore, we speak of "learning hidden things," we are speaking primarily of things that are unpredictable because they are due purely to chance or the free acts of men, which only God knows with certainty. But we also include things that are hidden because effective methods of arriving at the answer are not employed. One might use divination, for example, to attempt to learn when the next total eclipse of the sun is to occur in a certain part of the world. Just as one might use divination in an attempt to learn what astronomers could tell him, so he might use divination in an attempt to learn things ascertainable in many other natural ways.

Divination was widely practiced in the past by numerous nations. History tells us little if anything of men who appealed directly and explicitly to Satan, although it is thought that there have been persons who "sold their souls to the devil" for the sake of gaining wealth, power, or something else that they desired. In former days the direct appeal in divination was to a witch, a wizard, an augur, an oracle, or a soothsayer. Today, at least among the civilized nations, the appeal is ordinarily to a fortuneteller of one kind or another.

The persons from whom information concerning the future is sought do not claim to possess it of themselves. They supposedly obtain the information from some intelligence outside themselves by using some device (such as a crystal ball) or going through some ritual. This intelligence cannot be God, since He has severely condemned all such attempts to acquire knowledge of what will happen in the future (Deuteronomy 18:10-12). The only other possible source of information is the devil or the evil spirits in general. One's appeal is therefore tacitly or implicitly to Satan if one is not aware that one must be appealing to Satan. If one knows that one is appealing to Satan, the appeal would be explicit and not tacit.

To appeal to the devil for information is a very great act of irreverence toward God, who does not wish us to become suppliants of His worst enemy. Furthermore, knowledge of the future free acts of men is a strictly divine attribute (Isaias 41:23) implying infinite perfection and hence carrying in its train all the other divine attributes. To practice divination is consequently equivalent to treating the devil as if he were divine. It is an act of idolatry and of its nature a serious sin.

MENTAL TELEPATHY, CLAIRVOYANCE, AND EXTRASENSORY PERCEPTION

Mental telepathy is the communication of ideas from one mind to another without words, signs, gestures, or any other ordinary means of communicating thought. Clairvoyance is the seeing or knowing of events occurring at a distance, as when a mother becomes aware that her son, now at the other end of the world, has been killed in an accident. Extrasensory perception includes such things as the ability to read a sealed letter or to give the name of a playing card lying face down on a table. It is doubtful whether all recorded instances of these three phenomena can be ascribed to fraud, delusion, or coincidence. The human mind may be capable of a sort of "mental radio" resulting in knowledge with sources that we are not as yet prepared to explain. Just as a musical or mathematical genius with amazing powers appears only in a million or more individuals, so the power of transferring or acquiring knowledge by mental telepathy, clairvoyance, or extrasensory perception may be very rare. The use of these powers by one who possesses them cannot be called divination, nor does their use pose any special moral problems. Their use should be governed by the general principles applicable to the ends, objects, and circumstances of human acts.

GUIDES REGARDING KNOWLEDGE OF DOUBTFUL ORIGIN

There have apparently been cases in which hidden events, past, present, or future, were made known after recourse to some one of the means of divination about to be discussed. Some such cases can no doubt be ascribed to fraud, others to coincidence, others to guesses that happened to be correct. Some may possibly have been due to powers of communicating and receiving thought possessed by man and not yet fully understood.

The following principles may safely be accepted as our guides in regard to knowledge of this kind:

1. In case of doubt attribute the effect to natural causes and not to Satan. We are, we realize, still ignorant of many of nature's hidden powers, and we should not have recourse to the preternatural for an explanation without necessity. The fact that any given event is an exception to the physical law of nature should be proved before being accepted as such.

2. If after prudent investigation it is quite certain that natural causes cannot explain a particular effect, then, if doubtful about its source, ascribe the effect to Satan and not to God. If it were God who produced the effect, His hand in it would be clearly indicated by the attendant circumstances (for example, by the holiness of the person through whom the effect is produced, by the dignified manner in which it is performed, and so forth).

KINDS OF DIVINATION

Among the various forms of divination that are of special interest today are (1) fortunetelling, including palmistry, phrenology, and crystal gazing; (2) astrology; (3) dream omens; and (4) the ouija board.

FORTUNETELLING

Fortunetelling is the art of manifesting to another the fortune (luck), good or bad, which the future has in store for him. The real objective of fortunetelling is the disclosure of future events, though frequently, in order to inspire confidence in her secret powers, the fortuneteller will communicate to her client bits of his past that would naturally be unknown to her. Fortunetellers make use of various approaches to their secret store of knowledge. As a help in peering into the world of hidden events they employ, for example, tea leaves, a crystal sphere, or a small pool of blood. We know that many such fortunetellers exercise their art without any pretense at doing more than guessing the future, and they guess the future for their clients in order to amuse them. Other fortunetellers believe in their own (supposed) preternatural powers and take their art very seriously.

What of the morality of having one's fortune told? That depends entirely on the particular circumstances of the fortunetelling. We may distinguish and estimate the sinfulness of the various cases as follows:

1. If I consult a fortuneteller and she, I know, is serious about it, I am guilty of a grave sin of cooperation.

2. If *she* is not serious about it but I am, then I am committing a grave sin of irreverence toward God, for I am attributing to this creature knowledge which God alone has.

3. If the fortuneteller is not serious about it and I put only slight faith in it, I am guilty of a venial sin. Generally speaking, this is the case. Most fortunetellers are in the business only for the money, and the fraud is apparent. The customers visit them out of idle curiosity but with some faith in their power to foretell the future.

4. If the fortuneteller is not serious about it and I put no credence in her powers at all, but visit her merely as a pastime, there is no sin. This is the case at places like church bazaars. Even here, however, there is danger, as experience has shown that when in such circumstances one is told something (about a large inheritance of money, a great misfortune, and so forth) that actually happens, faith in fortunetelling is enkindled, at least to a certain degree. The fortunetelling done through cards issued from slot machines, scales, and the like is merely harmless amusement.

PALMISTRY

Palmistry is the art of divining by studying the lines of the hand. According to these fortunetellers, there exists a current of unseen life which enters the palm through the index finger and distributes a subtile force throughout the hand. Lines and mounts on the palm, they say, indicate the subject's wealth, power, success in marriage, and so forth.

If palmistry attempts to foretell the free future, it is to be ranked in sinfulness with fortunetelling in the manner just indicated. If palmistry merely aims at analyzing one's character, it may not accomplish the desired effect, but it is not sinful. Our temperament and inclinations have some relation to our organic make-up, and it may be that the palmist can obtain some knowledge of them from the study of the lines of the palm of the hand. If palmistry is done merely for amusement and neither reader nor subject takes it seriously, it is quite permissible and sinless.

PHRENOLOGY

Phrenology is the science of reading intellectual or sensual tendencies or dispositions by means of the undulations on the cranium. The data thus gathered, though at times true, are not reliable. The findings of phrenology may show tendencies but will not cause or invariably lead to the predicted good or bad events. It would be sinful to suppose that these physical signs of the cranium doom one to what phrenology indicates. It would not be sinful to believe that the bumps, or bodily conditions of which the bumps are indications, may incline one in the way claimed by phrenology.

CRYSTAL GAZING

In crystal gazing the fortuneteller or seer uses a crystal globe, a mirror, a pool of ink (or blood) in his palm, or something similar for conjuring up pictures of his client's future. One may gauge its morality according to that of fortunetelling in general.

HYPNOTISM

In 1778 Franz Anton Mesmer began to effect wonderful cures by means of hypnotism, then known as animal magnetism. Before long charlatans began to use hypnotism for the purpose of discovering secret and future events. Hypnotism as a result came to be discussed by moralists as a type of divination, and through convention is ordinarily kept under that heading even today. The principal moral issue involved, however, is the licitness of depriving another, or of permitting oneself to be deprived, of the exercise of his free will. For this reason hypnotism falls more properly under the Fifth Commandment, which forbids in general any violence done to the physical integrity of the individual, but we may follow the conventional order and discuss it at this point.

Hypnotism is a kind of artificially induced sleep in which one's mind, though in a passive state, is alert to the suggestions and directions of the hypnotist. This sleep or trance may be produced (1) by an intense act of the will; (2) by staring steadily for a certain period of time at some shining object (for example, a mirror) or at the hypnotist; or (3) by listening in a relaxed state of mind to the regular, unvaried tones of some dreamy chant or simple instrument.

Hypnotism produces in the subject a sort of sleep coupled with the suspension of control over his will, and with both it brings a ready receptiveness to the hypnotist's suggestions and a prompt obedience to his commands. The subject is in the hypnotist's power but the extent of his subjection is disputed. Some research has indicated that those in a hypnotic trance will refuse to execute commands which in their normal state they would consider immoral. Other research, however, has indicated the opposite, and the extent to which the hypnotized person obeys would seem to depend upon the depth of the trance. Whatever further research may show the facts to be, it is *certain* in all cases that the exercise of free will is impaired, and *probable* that it may be completely lost during the trance.

Since hypnotism is not wrong in itself, its use under certain circumstances may be without fault. Repeated hypnotism has effects which would not result from a single hypnotism and must therefore be used with greater caution. Since hypnotism, however, violently deprives the subject of the full use of reason and free will, a justifying cause is necessary for allowing it to be practiced. Moreover, because hypnotism puts the subject's will in the power of the hypnotist, certain precautions are necessary to safeguard the subject's virtue and to protect him and others against the danger of his being guilty of any injurious action. For a grave reason (for example, to cure an alcoholic or one with a suicide complex) it is licit to exercise hypnotism, given the precaution that it is done in the presence of a trustworthy witness by a competent and upright hypnotist. The consent (at least presumed) of the subject must be had.

There is disagreement in medical circles on the psychological effects of the use of hypnotism. However, there is general agreement that it can have harmful effects, especially when the one employing it is not fully qualified. There is not a sufficient reason, therefore, to use hypnotism merely for entertainment. It would also be wrong for one not qualified to use it for a good purpose. It is quite easy to induce hypnotism, but its effects can be controlled only by an expert. Even the experts insist that it should be used only in carefully selected cases. Amateurs who are tempted to use hypnotism should read the careful statement of the American Medical Association's Council of Mental Health; it was submitted to the annual convention at San Francisco in 1958 and printed in the *Journal of the American Medical Association*, Volume 168, pages 186-89, September 13, 1958.

ASTROLOGY

Astrology is the so-called science of foretelling the future through a study of the influence which is supposedly exercised by the stars. It is divided into (1) natural astrology and (2) judicial astrology.

Natural astrology is the science of predicting the weather through a study of the stars. Weather forecasts issued by the United States Weather Bureau depend upon a study of existing atmospheric conditions, not upon a study of the position of the moon and other heavenly bodies. It is not improbable, however, that the influence of the sun, the moon, and the planets on atmospheric conditions is great. Since natural astrology is a physical science, there is no question of sinfulness in connection with its use, except insofar as the astrologist is bound to be objective and truthful and to have a right intention.

Judicial astrology endeavors to foretell one's future according to the relative position of the sun, the moon, the planets, and certain constellations at the time of one's birth. The Egyptians, the Babylonians, the Assyrians, the Hindus, and the Hellenistic Jews were believers in astrology. This older school of astrology was deterministic, holding that the stars actually controlled the course of man's life. To hold this was to deny the existence of free will in man; hence the Church was stern in her condemnations of astrology when it appeared in Europe after the Crusades had opened the way to penetration by Arabic learning.

Astrology is far from being a dead issue today. At the time of this writing at least one magazine devoted to astrology was being published in the United States. Astrology has been proposed quite recently as a means of giving vocational guidance in our schools. Says Luntz: "Disregarding the conclusions of the vocational specialists, some of which undoubtedly have merit, we return the unequivocal answer, which does not necessarily conflict with these conclusions, that success is found where the obvious trends of the natal horoscope have been followed; failure, where they have been disregarded."[2]

A horoscope is a diagram showing the relative positions of the planets and the signs of the zodiac for the "twelve houses of heaven" for a given longitude and latitude at the moment of birth of an individual. After the diagram has been made it must be studied and interpreted. A thorough interpretation of a horoscope requires long experience. A horoscope is not supposed to reveal only a single fact or a number of facts that are similar in nature— for example, that the native (this is the word used for the individual born with a certain horoscope) will be inflexible, tenacious, persevering, independent, and fearless. A horoscope can be expected to contain a mixture of good and bad elements. Even if a native is born under the influence of Saturn, which of itself is productive of hardship, ill health, and poverty, other elements in his horoscope may give hope of some measure of better things. One born under the influence of Jupiter cannot be certain of enjoying nothing but good fortune, despite the fact that "Jupiter governs all things into which the element of abundance enters. Being the great benefic, it bestows abundance of good in all departments, physical, mental, spiritual."[3]

A natal horoscope does more than reveal what life has in store for the native; it can be used to learn at what time it is best to undertake a project or disastrous to begin it. "When is 'exactly the right time' to apply for that position, launch that business, open that store? The progressed or 'directed' horoscope furnishes the answer. . . . He must compare the transiting $\odot$ and $\mathbb{D}$ with his own natal positions and then, having arrived at a satisfactory hour, narrow it down to an exact minute by transiting MidHeaven

---

[2] Charles E. Luntz, *Vocational Guidance by Astrology*, p. 17. Philadelphia: David McKay Company, 1942.
[3] *Ibid.*, p. 33.

and Ascendant positions."[4] It may be noted that Adolf Hitler made constant use of astrology in deciding when to act or not to act.

While there may be astrologists today who hold that man is not free to act contrary to his horoscope, this opinion is certainly not universal and is probably the less common one. "Planetary and sidereal 'influences,' so called, merely chart the course. They do not force anyone to follow it. . . . Man does have free will."[5]

A few of the many considerations that may be kept in mind when forming a judgment of the morality of judicial astrology are as follows:

1. While some astrologists insist upon the existence of free will in man, it is doubtful whether they can hold what they do and still leave man free. Moreover, judicial astrology claims to be able to foretell the free future, knowledge of which is possessed by God alone and by those to whom He chooses to reveal it. For example, judicial astrology claims to be able to make known the year, the day, and even the hour at which a store can advantageously be opened. Now, to predict success for a store because it is well managed, well stocked, and located in the right neighborhood is something that can be done on the basis of experience; but to predict success independently of all factors of this kind is to assume that customers will come freely. In this case the astrologer does not predict success because he knows what the store will be like; he predicts it because he knows what customers are going to do.

2. Judicial astrology runs counter to certain established facts. We know that an individual's powers are due partly to nature and partly to nurture. By nature he receives from his parents certain genes determining the constitution of body and mind. By nurture these gifts are developed and perfected—or degraded and even lost if nurture is harmful rather than beneficial. At all times God's grace is operative to assist the individual to make good use of what he has received. For these facts there is a massive array of proofs supplied by education, psychology, sociology, and revealed religion. Judicial astrology at least implicitly denies the influence of all these things. No matter what one's nature and nurture may be and no matter what the help of God may bring to pass, the

---

[4] *Ibid.*, pp. 32, 104.   [5] *Ibid.*, pp. 17-18.

position of the stars may doom one to a life of comparative failure or may lead to achievement impossible in the light of the meager gifts that are actually possessed. Jupiter could make a world figure out of a child who was born a half-wit. Saturn could make a failure out of a genius.

3. Climate, the nature of available food supplies, and other similar factors do influence health, behavior, and even character. But this influence is exerted according to certain known laws and is ordinarily exerted slowly. The supposed influence of the stars is exerted instantaneously at the moment of birth. It is a permanent influence affecting one's entire life. It also affects the reactions of others to the individual in question. Such an uncanny influence is at variance with known physical laws, particularly the general law that there must be a relationship of proportion between a cause and its effect.

4. Various causes may hasten or delay the birth of a child. An unborn child with a certain natural endowment could therefore have an entirely different life prospect because born a day earlier or a day later than might have been anticipated.

5. In a large city many infants are born the same day or even the same minute. The infants born the same day or the same minute have different abilities, temperaments, and tendencies. It is unreasonable to claim that the same horoscope fits all of them.

6. Astrologists claim that their theories have been proved true. Luntz speaks of "the proven teachings as they came down the years."[6] The alleged proof to which he refers consists principally in reiterated affirmations unsupported by any evidence and to a lesser extent in a study of the horoscopes of certain leaders such as John D. Rockefeller, Adolf Hitler, and Winston Churchill, in whose cases it is affirmed that what their horoscopes foretold did actually come to pass. But such conformity between the prediction of a horoscope and reality must be shown to exist in a very large number of cases, including cases both of successful men and of failures, before any conclusion can be drawn. Chance would result in conformity in many cases. We might, for example, propound the theory that males born on Saturday could become All-American football players and that males born on Sunday could, if they made good use of their gifts, become bishops, cardi-

---

[6] *Ibid.*, p. 24.

nals, and popes. Merely by chance one seventh of all good football players would be born on Saturday and one seventh of all prominent churchmen would be born on Sunday. The fact that they were born on Saturday or Sunday would have no influence on the outcome. Moreover, thousands of others born on the same days lacked any desire or ability to succeed as athletes or churchmen. The number of cases that would have to be studied to prove (or disprove) the existence of a causal connection between the stars and the course of men's lives would be extremely large. Astrology has never offered proof of this kind.

The moral guilt of one who believes in astrology depends both upon the seriousness of his belief and upon the kind of astrology in which he does believe. "In the long history of its development and application," says Margaret Morrell, "astrology has been variously defined as a science, a pseudo science, an astral theology, and an art, and it is still so defined *by the conflicting branches of its advocates.*"[7]

DREAM OMENS

An omen is a sign by which some future event can be foretold. If the sign is learned by means of a dream, it is called a dream omen. Moralists devote special attention to dreams that are omens because the certain knowledge of future events due to chance or the free acts of men is something that only God possesses. It should be noted, however, that the question is whether we are free to believe in a dream, whether it refers to the past, the present, or the future. St. Joseph was told in a dream[8] that the child whom Mary was to bear had been conceived of the Holy Spirit (Matthew 1:20-21). The Magi were warned in a dream not to return home by way of Jerusalem (Matthew 2:12). Pilate's wife suffered many things in a dream on the day of the crucifixion, and sent word to her husband to have nothing to do "with that just man" (Matthew 27:19). Whether a dream reveals something about the past, gives orders for the present, or foretells the future, the question is whether we are free to believe in the dream.

---

[7] Margaret Morrell, "Astrology," in *Collier's Encyclopedia*, Vol. 2, p. 392. Italics added.

[8] While the passage in St. Matthew might be interpreted as meaning that Joseph was roused from sleep to receive the message of the angel, it was nevertheless possible for the entire thing to have occurred during a dream.

Dreams may be caused in various ways. They may, and ordinarily do, arise from altogether natural sources. Though there is much doubt about their exact origin, dreams are thought to be caused by such things as some recent occurrence, a coming event of importance with which one is preoccupied during one's waking hours, haunting worries, frayed nerves, an overburdened stomach, or the like. Since the devil can influence our phantasms, it may be that at times God allows him to do so. Hence one may believe that the origin of some dreams is found in Satan. Again, dreams may be sent directly by God Himself. This we know from the lives and letters of the saints, but more especially from Holy Scripture. For example, "He [God] said to them: . . . if there be among you a prophet of the Lord, . . . I will speak to him in a dream" (Numbers 12:6). See also Nabuchodonosor's dream that was interpreted for him by the prophet Daniel (Daniel 4:1-24).

What is to be said of omens that are attributed to dreams that arise from these various sources? First of all, dreams that arise from natural causes (for example, from overeating) can of course give us no certain knowledge of free future events, and to believe in the omens of such dreams would be mere superstition. Second, Satan has no share in that uniquely divine knowledge of the free future, and so he cannot predict with certainty events that depend entirely on man's use of his free will. Hence we are not allowed to believe in dream omens that have Satan as their author, for that would be to attribute to him a divine perfection. We must conclude, therefore, that we are not permitted to accept as omens dreams that we think arise either from natural causes or from satanic influence.

If, then, a dream is not of divine origin, we should ignore its predictions. But how shall we determine whether this particular dream of ours is from God or not? We may, in general, rest assured that, if God makes use of such extraordinary methods to communicate with us, He can undoubtedly see to it that we realize clearly that it was He who sent us the dream. To deny this would be to deny the omnipotence of God. If He chooses to do so, God may give some sign, as when Mary was told that her cousin Elizabeth was soon to become a mother (Luke 1:36-37) or when the shepherds were told on the night of Christ's birth that they would find the child wrapped in swaddling clothes and lying in a manger (Luke 2:12). Some negative signs that will help prevent delusion in this matter are as follows. We know that the dream is not from God:

1. If it does not influence one toward some good action; for example, a person involved in an embarrassing situation dreams of a lie that will solve his problem if used.

2. If what is suggested is not something worthy of God; for example, if one dreams that one should unfailingly manicure one's nails every Sunday.

3. If it affects one so that one is not disposed to serve God; for example, if one dreamed that one was buried in hell, and now despairs of ever being saved.

We may accept the following principles concerning the licitness of giving credence to dreams:

1. It is a mortal sin habitually to guide one's life by dreams that are clearly not from God. So to act would be an indication of either serious credence in a superstitious practice (that is, in the case of dreams of natural origin), or implicit worship of Satan (that is, in the case of dreams coming from him).

2. It is a venial sin to be influenced at times in little things by dreams that are not from God; for example, to avoid a road that was pictured to me in a dream as dangerous.

3. It is no sin, of course, to believe in a dream that is clearly from God, and it would be at least praiseworthy to act according to its suggestions.

THE OUIJA BOARD

The ouija board or planchette, widely used as a fad some years ago, consists of a plain, flat board that is marked along its edges with the letters of the alphabet and all the digits. At this board one or two (usually two) sitters take their places and rest their fingers lightly on a small three-legged, heart-shaped table that is called a planchette. The third leg of this planchette forms a pointer, and as the planchette moves about it points out the various letters or numbers of the ouija board. A bystander or nonsitter asks the ouija board a question and then the answer is spelled out by the planchette's pointer. The use of the ouija board is sinful under the following circumstances: (1) When the answers to be given pertain to the secret past of anyone except that of the sitters. By "secret past" is meant all those things that an individual has good reason for wishing kept secret. (2) When the answers to be given pertain to the free future. (3) When the answers to be given are expected to come from the spirits of the departed or from demons.

SPIRITISM

Spiritism is the practice of attempted communication with the spirits of another world. Every educated Catholic should know something about the morality of spiritism, for since spiritism is so much in vogue today, we are bound to meet many who believe in it and practice it. To stigmatize all spiritistic phenomena as fraudulent is to arouse the pitying contempt of many a sincere devotee of spiritism.

Though spiritism is nearly as old as the human race, it was only about a hundred years ago that the modern cult appeared. In 1848 at Hydesville, New York, two young girls by the name of Fox heard mysterious rappings one day in the farmhouse where they lived. Curious, they arranged a code with the mysterious "rapper" who was, in their opinion, the ghost of a man who had been murdered in that very house years before. Their alleged communications with the departed marked the beginning of our modern spiritism, which has continued to grow more and more popular, until today its practice is very widespread.

Displays of "magic" are quite common at spiritistic seances. Pictures on the walls fall down with a loud noise, move mysteriously about the room, and then return to their places; a human head or hands or feet appear luminously in the darkened room; at times a spirit in a flowing robe of white walks among the sitters and chats with them, often nonsensically, making such inane remarks as: "Spirit So-and-So has a new tooth," "The supply of tobacco and whisky is plentiful in the spirit world." During these conversations secrets are revealed and truths are mixed with falsehoods. It seems that the answers given by the "spirits" to questions asked are generally accommodated to the audience, so that to devout sitters nothing is said against religion (at least, in the beginning), while in the presence of the impious or immoral, heresy or lasciviousness is approved.

The possible explanations of these various spiritistic phenomena are as follows:

1. Fraud. Quite frequently these spiritistic seances have been investigated by competent, impartial men and very often have

been found to be fraudulent. Some investigators assert that all spiritistic phenomena can be duplicated, without any pretense of preternatural influence, by a magician who is skilled in all the tricks of his trade. Nevertheless, it seems quite certain that not all such phenomena can be so easily explained away. Some of these strange happenings, we must confess, seem to postulate preternatural powers.

2. God. These phenomena are not produced through divine power, for God could not encourage any practice that leads to error. God, the source of all truth, could not stand sponsor for falsehoods, could not give reason for causing contradictory replies to be attributed to Himself. Therefore these "spirit messages" do not come to us stamped with God's approval, for some of them have stated that hell does not exist or that at least it is not eternal, that Christ is not divine, and so forth. Statements such as these directly contradict God's revelation and therefore could not come from God as their source. Moreover, the frivolous, ludicrous means that are ordinarily used to communicate with the spirits desecrate the memory of the dead and are unworthy of being encouraged by God.

3. Satan. That Satan has, at least at times, a hand in these spiritistic seances may be concluded from (a) the evil doctrine which they teach, (b) the Church's condemnation of them, and (c) Holy Scripture's condemnation.

a) It is true that the "spirits" at these seances do encourage a God-fearing audience to pray, to trust in divine providence, to practice their religion. This is done at first so that the good will not be shocked by immoral advice into shunning future seances. After a few sessions, however, when interest and faith in spiritism have developed, the "spirits" try to stir up doubts about the sitters' religion. They say, for example: "Your religion teaches you that hell is eternal. Could an all-merciful God punish a man forever?" or "Do not novenas seem to be superstitious practices?" or "What magic power has the number nine?" Then, after the "spirits" have weakened the sitters' faith and thus prepared the ground, they sow the seed of their new religion. In this new religion hell is ruled out of existence, and the next life is pictured as a world full of amusements much like (though more appealing than) the ones we now enjoy. This new religion caters to one's emotionalism and sensuality, leads to easy morals, and appeals to one's curiosity. Not infrequently, for the Catholic, it leads to complete loss of faith.

b) The Church has explicitly condemned spiritism. The Holy Office, which is a Roman congregation whose special task consists in safeguarding the faith against error, has officially condemned spiritistic practices and attendance at spiritistic seances even though one does so out of mere curiosity and takes no part at all in the proceedings.

The prohibition of the Holy Office includes cases in which a Catholic wishes to attend a seance whose object is to communicate only with *good* spirits. This has also been expressly condemned by the Church. The reason for this latter condemnation seems to be the obvious danger to which a Catholic would expose himself: that of being drawn from attempted dealings with good spirits into actual dealings with the evil spirits. Moreover, it would be irreverent to presume that good spirits do the ludicrous or cater to vain curiosity. God does at times allow good spirits to communicate with us, as is evident from Scripture and the lives of the saints, but not in this unworthy manner. It should be noted that the Holy Office merely condemned spiritism without asserting whether or not spiritistic phenomena are produced through the agency of the evil spirits. The Second Council of Baltimore strongly denounced spiritism and branded it as an attempt to revive paganism. (See II Council of Baltimore, nos. 36-41.)

c) We read in Holy Scripture: "Neither let there be found among you any one . . . that consulteth . . . fortune tellers, or that seeketh the truth from the dead, for the Lord abhorreth all these things" (Deuteronomy 18:10-12).

For a Catholic to attend a spiritistic seance without grave necessity or without ecclesiastical approbation would be seriously sinful. For purposes of scientific research or for other valid reasons the bishop may allow, but only by individual permission, *passive attendance*—that is, assisting without in any way participating in the proceedings.

FAITH HEALING

The curing of ailments or diseases may be brought about in any of the following ways:

1. By natural means. Such means are the use of medicine, heat, X ray, surgery, or anything that depends upon the use of

natural resources or agencies external to the one to whom they are applied.

2. By suggestion. Because of the relationship between mind and body, hope and courage tend to maintain or to restore health, while fear and depression produce an injurious effect on the body. It is therefore evident that a strong suggestion received from one in whom we have confidence may be beneficial to health. This is particularly true if the ailment is merely imaginary or if timidity, brooding, or a vivid imagination makes it worse. It is for this reason that doctors and nurses make it a point to be cheerful and optimistic in dealing with patients. Physicians today are rather commonly convinced that numerous human ailments should be looked upon as psychosomatic (due partly to the *psyche* or mind and partly to the *soma* or body) and that they should be treated accordingly. Even if the mind had nothing to do with the onset of the ailment, as could occur in the case of a ruptured appendix, the mind can influence the rate of the patient's recovery.

3. By miracles. At Lourdes and other shrines there have been many cases of miraculous healing that were clearly effected by divine intervention.

4. By faith healing. The faith healer says that he possesses a special gift and that this gift, upon the occasion of praying, anointing, or the imposing of hands, is allowed by God to function. He claims no preternatural gift. It is merely the power of God that is working through him. He cites Holy Scripture in support of his contention. (See Mark 16:17-18.) The effectiveness of faith healers seems remarkable in cases of immoral habits, nervous ailments, and drunkenness. It would appear that the cures brought about by these healers are due merely to suggestion, and healing by suggestion is entirely licit. In certain cases religious considerations may prove the most effective form of suggestion.

Although faith healing or healing by suggestion is not sinful provided neither superstition, scandal, nor cooperation in fraud is involved in it, one must in serious illness have recourse to medical help, since to rely solely on a faith cure in such circumstances would be tempting God and practically demanding a miracle. Moreover, a Catholic may not go to faith healers who claim to have a divine gift, for this might easily lead to religious indifferentism. In most cases it would also involve scandal because it would give the impression that one accepted the religious teachings of those who practice faith healing and might be the occasion for leading uneducated or poorly instructed Catholics astray. If a cure by suggestion is sought, the patient should use autosuggestion or should entrust himself to someone who does not claim to possess a divine gift.

Vain observance

Vain observance is the superstitious attempt to produce a certain effect through the use of means which are known to be inadequate toward accomplishing such results. Examples are seeking health by absurd methods (wrapping a red string nine times around a tree in order to cure a fever); wearing amulets or charms to ward off danger; reciting prayers a certain number of times or in a certain place or with certain gestures and attributing the entire efficacy of the prayers to these conditions. Since one realizes that the effect cannot be obtained in this way either from God or from nature, the action is at least an implicit appeal to the devil for help. Hence to expect that the desired results will *infallibly* follow the mere performing of such actions is matter for grave sin. However, many who indulge in these practices because of their simplicity or their ignorance do not clearly understand the utter disproportion between the means employed and the effect hoped for. If they do not realize the malice of the act, they do not, of course, commit serious sin. Moreover, in many cases the one who engages in such practices places but imperfect confidence in their efficacy.

On the other hand, it is not wrong for Catholics to wear medals, crucifixes, and the like, for these are not worn for any supposed magical powers attributed to them, but in order to foster devotion or to gain indulgences. Nor is it wrong to recite a set number of prayers (for example, in the case of the rosary, a novena, and so forth), provided we do not base our hope of obtaining the help sought in the supposed magic power of the number. However, a trace of superstition may creep into these pious practices, and this should be carefully guarded against.

SUPERSTITIOUS PRACTICES

We find frequent evidence of superstitious practices among all people of the world, and, strange to say, many of those puerile superstitions are international. In many countries thirteen is regarded as an unlucky number, so that one may not begin a trip on the thirteenth, and especially not on Friday the thirteenth. Thirteen persons may not dine together at the same table—"Otherwise," they say, "one of them is marked for death within the year." To marry on Wednesday or in May, to have the wedding group happen across a funeral procession—all these are looked upon by some persons as "signs of bad luck."

What of the sinfulness of these silly beliefs and practices? Today few people put any real credence in these superstitions, but rather they experience in their regard a sort of vague fear and uneasiness, or an indefinable hope. Why, then, do so many observe these foolish practices? They do so, not because they believe in the good luck or bad luck attributed to them, but in order to have nothing with which to reproach themselves in case anything does happen. They recognize the practices as silly, but, being of a nervous disposition, they would fret if they deliberately defied them.

For Catholics to engage in these practices can be a grave sin, a venial sin, or no sin at all. It is a *grave sin* if, after he has been duly instructed, he allows his whole life to be dominated by these signs. Such conduct would show that he took them seriously. It is a *venial sin* if he shows some slight credence in them. This is generally the case with most of those who observe these practices today. It is *no sin* if the observance of these practices is due solely to one's simplicity or nervous temperament.

CHAIN PRAYER

Chain prayer is a superstitious practice which consists in the saying of certain prayers successively by many individuals who hope for the favors requested, not so much from God's goodness as from the magic effect of this unbroken series of prayers. A written or printed prayer is sent to the person who is to form one of the links in the chain. He is requested to say this prayer and to continue the chain by persuading others to take up the praying where he leaves off. These others in turn are to pass the prayer on to still others. It is evident how irrational it is to place the efficacy of my prayer in the bare fact of continuousness accomplished, for the most part, by others. Whence does such prayer derive the special power which is attributed to it? God surely has not promised to answer petitions because they are made under such conditions. Prayer will be fruitful only when it is said with the proper dispositions; that is, when it is said with humility, confidence, perseverance, and attention. For an individual to participate in a chain prayer ordinarily involves a slight sin. It is a sin because the one who thus participates ordinarily places some credence in the power of this practice. It is but a venial fault because he does not take the matter too seriously.

The sins against the virtue of religion which have been considered up to this point are sins of *excess,* which as explained on page 69 consist in worshiping God in the wrong way or in giving to creatures the honor due only to God. We have now to consider sins against the virtue of religion by *defect.* We sin by defect by irreverence toward God or toward sacred persons or things. Such sins include sacrilege, tempting God, and simony.

Sacrilege

Sacrilege is the violation of a sacred (1) person, (2) place, or (3) thing. *Sacred* means *publicly dedicated to God.* A priest is sacred through ordination, a nun through her vows, a chalice through its consecration by the bishop.

1. Sacrilege may be committed against *persons.* It is a sacrilege and entails excommunication to lay violent hands (that is, to injure seriously) or to inflict great indignities on a cleric or a religious of either sex. For example, to spit upon a priest or unjustly to carry him off to prison would be a sacrilege.

2. Sacrilege may be committed against *places.* It is a sacrilege to perform in a church, chapel, or blessed cemetery any act that is especially repugnant to the holiness of the place; for example, to kill someone or to commit adultery in such a spot.[9]

3. Sacrilege may be committed against *things.* To receive any of the seven sacraments unworthily (that is, without the required dispositions) is a grave sacrilege. Not every sort of lie told during a confession, however, would make that confession sacrilegious. It is only when I tell a lie to cover over what I am seriously obliged to disclose that the falsehood would make the confession sacrilegious. To use phrases of Holy Scripture in jokes in a way that shows some irreverence is a venially sinful sacrilege. To steal

---

[9] To steal a watch in a church, however sinful it may be, is not a sacrilege.

money belonging to the Church (for example, from the collection basket or vigil-light box) would be a sacrilege, grave or slight, according to the size of the sum stolen. This is a violation of a sacred thing—that is, church property. To steal a priest's personal property is not a sacrilege.

Tempting God

Tempting God is an act or omission in which we try to test God's attributes (for example, His love, power, wisdom). One can tempt God either (1) explicitly or (2) implicitly.

1. I *explicitly* tempt God when I demand something from God or when I do or omit to do something for the actual purpose of ascertaining the extent of God's wisdom, power, and so forth. Such conduct manifests a real doubt about God's perfections. The following are examples of such tempting of God:

EXAMPLE 1. "If He be God, let Him come down from the cross," said some of those present at the crucifixion. The Jews here challenged Christ's power to free Himself.

EXAMPLE 2. A well-known atheist, with watch in hand, cried out: "If there be a God, I will give Him three minutes in which to strike me dead." After three minutes had passed he said: "You see, there is no God."

Explicitly tempting God is always a grievous sin because it is a direct insult to God.

2. I *implicitly* tempt God when, not doubting about His attributes, I rashly require a manifestation of divine power, wisdom, and so forth, here and now. The following are examples of this:

EXAMPLE 1. I engage in a duel and demand that God vindicate my honor by victory.

EXAMPLE 2. In trial by ordeal the suspected culprit is made to walk barefoot on red-hot coals. If he passes this test unburned, he is deemed innocent. Here one is trying to force God to work a miracle in order to defend the guiltless. It is said that trial by ordeal is practiced even today among some savage tribes.

EXAMPLE 3. Gravely ill, I refuse all medical aid and expect God to cure me. Here two things are to be observed: (1) If I refuse all medical aid because of imprudence or stubbornness or because of a desire to die, and not with any belief that God will cure me, I am sinning against the Fifth Commandment (by not taking due care of my health), but not against the First. (2) If I use the ordinary means for regaining my health and at the same time seek a miraculous recovery, resigning myself to God's will in the matter, I am not in anyway guilty of tempting God.

Implicitly tempting God is a serious sin in grave matters; a venial sin in slight matters. The matter of the sin would be considered slight if, for example, rashly counting upon God's curing me when I am suffering from some mild illness, I were to neglect the ordinary means of recovering my health.

Simony

Simony is to exchange (buy or sell) what is spiritual for what is temporal. In simony one attempts to class a material thing with spiritual things, and treats the spiritual as though he or some other human being had full ownership of it. (See Acts 8:20-22.) To attempt to purchase by money the power to absolve from sins or to impart indulgences is an act of simony. Simony is classified as a grave sin.

ACTS THAT ARE NOT SIMONIACAL

In order to save those with overtender consciences from unfounded scruples and to correct misinformed criticism we may note certain actions that are *not* simony:

1. To buy a consecrated chalice or an indulgenced rosary if there is no increase in price because of the blessing. (Rosaries, crucifixes, and so forth, when sold, lose all their indulgences.)

2. To offer Masses or prayers as stakes in betting. Since this might savor at times of irreverence, however, it seems preferable not to indulge in this practice.

3. To exact a fee on the occasion of granting marriage dispensations. (This fee is required in order to defray the clerical expenses involved.)

4. To pay money to a pawnbroker in order to obtain possession of relics of saints. (I may do this only with the bishop's permission.) Here I do not exchange the money for something spiritual; I merely fulfill a condition (that is, the payment of so many dollars) which is necessary in order to rescue a sacred thing from profanation.

5. To receive stipends for Masses. This practice is not simoniacal for two reasons: (1) The money is given for the support of the priest and not in payment of the Mass. The Mass stipend is one source of revenue that provides the priest with a means of livelihood (to which, of course, he has a perfect right), so that

he can freely serve the faithful. (2) The money helps to defray the expenses of the materials used at Mass (wine, candles, light, vestments, purificator).

Cases to be analyzed

1 A man dreamed that his recently deceased brother appeared to him and said: "I am coming for you soon." Frightened, he went to the sacraments the next day. The following night he was murdered by bandits. His sister believes that his dream was from God.

2 A girl visiting a large amusement park happens upon a gypsy fortuneteller and immediately consults her. "This fortuneteller," she claims, "is just one of the forms of entertainment here, and so I can consult her without sinning."

3 "To work is to pray," says George, and so he never recites any prayers except during Sunday Mass. He feels that, since he is busily engaged at the office all week, this is prayer enough.

4 A Catholic student, noticing that a professional hypnotist is giving exhibitions of his skill at a certain vaudeville theater, decides to go to that playhouse. "Assisting at such performances," says he, "is not sinful."

5 A fervent Catholic dines at the home of a Baptist minister. The minister says the usual grace before and after the meal and the Catholic joins him in these prayers.

6 A non-Catholic minister, in order to prove to his audience that he is inspired by God to preach the gospel, allows himself to be bitten by a rattlesnake. "The power of the Spirit," he says, "will cure me." He relies on the scriptural text: "And these signs shall attend those who believe: in my name . . . they shall take up serpents; and . . . it shall not hurt them" (Mark 16:17-18).

7 A Catholic is careful to attach a St. Christopher medal to his automobile. Confident because of his strong faith in St. Christopher's protection, he drives very recklessly and takes many chances. His mother tells him that he is guilty of tempting God.

8 A young man has a statue of Buddha in his bedroom. One evening while in a mirthful mood he made several deep bows and signs of worship before this idol. He intended it in fun. Though at the time he was alone in the room, he is now worried about those "idolatrous acts."

9 A Catholic eats lunch every day in a small downtown restaurant. Though he knows that most of the others who come there are Catholics, he deliberately omits saying grace before and after meals.

10 At Mobile, Alabama, a boy was struck down and killed by a truck. After the accident his mother mentioned that two nights before he had had a dream in which he saw himself run over by a truck driven by a certain man. It so happens that this man actually was the driver of the truck. Considering all this, the boy's mother concluded that his dream was sent by God.

11 A devout Catholic woman hangs her rosary in the garden when she wishes it to stop raining. Her friend tells her this is vain observance.

12 Thomas received a letter from an acquaintance that read as follows: "Dear Tom, This novena to the Little Flower was sent to me and I am passing it on to you in hopes that you will not break this chain. The fourth day after you receive this letter some special favor will come to you. Make three copies of this letter before the fourth day and mail them to three friends and say three Hail Mary's for nine days. If you do not write the letters, you will regret what happens to you on the fourth day. Sincerely, ..." In order to obtain something he wanted very much, Tom fulfilled his acquaintance's request. His prayer was granted.

Topics for discussion[10]

1 Without considering for the moment the morality of trying to acquire such knowledge, would knowledge of the free future in general be for man's best interests?

2 All the phenomena that occur in spiritistic seances may be attributed to trickery. Explain.

3 Discuss the so-called "prophecy of St. Malachy" of A.D. 1142. Is it worthy of credence?

4 Discuss black magic.

5 What is witchcraft? Briefly give its history in this country. Is witchcraft purely imaginary?

Bibliography

Bastion, R. and J. Hasdon. "An Evaluation of Moral Rearmament." *American Ecclesiastical Review* 135:217-26, October 1956.

Bouyer, Louis. *Liturgical Piety*. Notre Dame: University of Notre Dame Press, 1955.

Coreth, Emerich. "Contemplative in Action." *Theology Digest* 3:37-45, Winter 1955.

Davis, Henry. *Moral and Pastoral Theology*, seventh edition, edited by L. W. Geddes, Vol. 2, pp. 1-41. 4 vols. New York: Sheed and Ward, 1958.

Duff, Edward. "Verdict on MRA." *Social Order* 6:274-90, June 1956.

Ellard, Gerald. *Christian Life and Worship*. Milwaukee: Bruce Publishing Company, 1950.

Fenton, Joseph C. *The Theology of Prayer*. Milwaukee: Bruce Publishing Company, 1939.

Jone, Heribert. *Moral Theology*, pp. 92-107. Westminster: Newman Press, 1957.

---

[10] Not all the assertions contained in the topics are true. The student is to judge the truth of any assertions made and to explain his decision.

Journal of the American Medical Association 168:186-89, September 13, 1958 (on hypnotism).

Jungmann, Josef A. *Public Worship,* translated by Clifford Howell. Collegeville: Liturgical Press, 1957.

Knox, Ronald. *Enthusiasm.* New York: Oxford University Press, 1950.

Noa, Thomas. *Pastoral Instruction on Faith with a Directive on Catholic Participation in Moral Re-armament.* Marquette, Michigan, 1958.

O'Shea, William J. *The Worship of the Church.* Westminster: Newman Press, 1957.

Pius XII. *Mediator Dei.* Washington: National Catholic Welfare Conference, 1948.

Poulain, Augustin F. *The Graces of Interior Prayer.* St. Louis: B. Herder Book Company, 1950.

Rahner, Karl. *Happiness through Prayer,* translated by J. Hennig and M. Carroll. Westminster: Newman Press, 1958.

Thurston, Herbert. *The Church and Spiritualism.* Milwaukee: Bruce Publishing Company, 1933.

CHAPTER V

The
second
commandment

"Thou shalt not take the name of the Lord thy God in vain."
Exodus 20:7

T HOUGH negative in form, the Second Commandment is positive in meaning, for it implicitly commands us to show reverence for the name of God. The Jews of old, we know, held the name of God *(Yahweh)* so much in awe that they generally refrained from pronouncing it and used in its place the word for Lord *(Adonai)*. Reverence for God's excellence and gratitude for His countless benefits bid us to treat His name in a respectful manner. Its misuse dishonors His holy person.

Every decent man speaks respectfully of his parents and wishes others to speak of them with respect. Our Father in heaven, who has given us gifts of all kinds and who could not for a moment fail to look upon us with love, is far more deserving of our respect than any parent could be, yet He is often treated with disrespect that borders on contempt.

The Second Commandment points out our duty of venerating the name of God as well as the names of those who are especially dear to Him—the saints. All irreverence to the holy name is explicitly forbidden by this commandment. God's name is dishonored by (1) irreverent use, (2) blasphemy and cursing, (3) unlawful oaths and perjury, and (4) the violation of vows.

THE IRREVERENT USE OF GOD'S NAME

"To take God's name in vain" means to use it without good reason or proper reverence. God's name may be taken in vain (1) to show surprise; for example, "Great God, what is it?"; (2) to show impatience; for example, "Good Lord, let me alone"; (3) to punctuate remarks; for example, "Christ, I'll show him." Often today "God" and "damn" are flippantly written as one word—"Goddam." The irreverence against God is present nevertheless. "Gosh" (God), "Gee" (Jesus), and other words that are corruptions of the holy name have today lost their original meaning, and their use is not sinful.

THE SINFULNESS OF USING GOD'S NAME IRREVERENTLY

1. To use God's name reverently in even our everyday occupations is praiseworthy. In Ireland, for example, this is often the case in exclamations that are also a prayer: "Glory be to God, he is home already."

2. Using God's name in vain is ordinarily a venial sin. It is a sin against the virtue of religion, which requires that, because of its relation to Him, God's name be used with due reverence.

3. Using the names of the saints in an irreverent manner is also a venial sin.

4. Any irreverent expression that is a sin is in itself equally sinful even if used at a time when no one is present to hear it, though in this case there is not the element of scandal that might otherwise be present.

5. Using vulgar language is not sinful. However, it is ill-befitting a lady or a gentleman and is offensive to decent people.

THE HABIT OF USING GOD'S NAME IN VAIN

There are individuals in whom the habit of using God's name has become so fixed that they scarcely realize what it is that they are saying. It is not easy to determine the imputability of individual acts in such cases. One who realizes that he ought to get over the habit and is taking means to correct it may slip occasionally and use God's name without advertence, or the imputability may be lessened because of emotion or some other factor, or he may go against his good resolution deliberately and be fully responsible. Others will realize that they ought to stop the bad habit but will not force themselves to take positive steps. Others will knowingly refuse to do anything about overcoming it. If they do not advert to what they are doing in a particular act, they are not guilty here and now but are guilty for failing to take measures to overcome the habit or for deliberate refusal to take such measures.

BLASPHEMY AND CURSING

Blasphemy is speaking against God in a contemptuous, scornful, or abusive manner. Included under blasphemy are offenses committed by thought, by word, or by deeds (for example, shaking one's fist at the heavens; deliberately and with contempt slashing holes in a picture of the crucifixion). Serious, contemptuous ridicule of the saints, of sacred objects, or of priests or nuns in their capacity as sacred persons would also be blasphemy because through these God is indirectly attacked. The following are examples of blasphemy: "God is unjustly loading me with hardships"; "God is unjustly allowing the bad to prosper."

Jokes or criticism about certain priests' defects as men, and not as representatives of God, would not constitute blasphemy and would be sinful or not according to the general laws of charity and justice that govern our speech with regard to anybody. We should remember, however, that to gossip about the faults of a priest as a man generally lessens reverence for him as a priest.

THE SINFULNESS OF BLASPHEMY

All fully deliberate blasphemy is a grievous sin. Not infrequently it happens that the blasphemy is uttered during a sudden, spontaneous burst of anger. When such is the case there is not present the complete advertence which is necessary to make the sin mortal. In order that one really blaspheme he must (1) use blasphemous words and (2) realize the blasphemous meaning of these words.

One who realizes the irreverence involved and uses blasphemous words, but only for the purpose of showing his anger or terrifying others, is nevertheless guilty of blasphemy, for he is bound to avoid causing the dishonoring insult to God which, from the very meaning of the words, such an act entails. If on the other hand he does this with the intention of dishonoring God, the malice of the blasphemy is greater.

To narrate an incident, repeating the blasphemy used, is allowable, provided there is a good reason for doing so. Blasphemy in plays, elocution pieces, and so forth, cannot be justified on the grounds of realism. One may, however, quote blasphemous passages in an article criticizing a play or in a book review.

DEFINITION OF CURSING

Cursing (or damning) is calling down evil on someone or something. Cursing should not be confused with swearing (that is, taking an oath), with blasphemy, with the irreverent use of God's name, or with the use of vulgar or obscene language.

There is great danger of rash judgment and self-deception in efforts that are made by pious and zealous souls to do good to others by praying that God may send some physical evil upon an individual who they think needs to be brought to a better state of mind or prevented from being a source of harm to his neighbor. Nevertheless it cannot be said that such prayers are always sinful if the intention is truly sincere.

THE SINFULNESS OF CURSING

Cursing may be licit or it may be sinful. God, we remember, cursed the serpent in the Garden of Eden. He also cursed Cain because of his murderous deed. The sinfulness of cursing varies with the nature of the curse.

1. To curse or damn the devil is not a sin.

2. To curse animals (for example, a vicious dog, an unruly horse) or objects (for example, tools, knife, golf club) that have caused us pain, annoyance, or inconvenience, though not sinful in itself, generally indicates a fit of anger or impatience which should have been controlled, and as such is venially sinful. If God's name is included in the curse (for example, "Goddamn that hammer") there will be added the sin (venial) of using God's name in vain.

3. To call down *moral evil* (that is, spiritual harm or ruin) on a person is always sinful. This occurs in such expressions as "May God curse (damn) your soul"; "Go to hell"; or "Go to the devil."

Although to pronounce such expressions deliberately and seriously could be gravely sinful, still today such speech ordinarily constitutes a venial sin against charity. If such expressions do not include the irreverent use of God's name and are made in a jocose and friendly manner, they are not sinful.

In ancient times the expression "You fool!" meant "You atheist!" and since such an accusation was considered by the Israelites as the worst of insults, this was a grave sin against charity. Today, however, this phrase has lost its original meaning. To use it now would ordinarily be either no sin at all or at most a slight sin against charity.

4. To call down *physical evil* (sickness, bodily injury, or loss of some kind) upon anyone is sinful unless the evil hoped for is desired as something that will be productive of good for the individual himself or for others. Physical evil might be desired as a good (1) as an effective means for converting a hardened sinner (for example, sickness very often awakens in a reprobate thoughts of eternity and causes him to repent) or (2) as an obstacle to hinder the evil work of some sinner (for example, a dope peddler might be prevented from corrupting young people because he is confined to bed).

5. Maliciously to wish someone *physical evil as evil* is a serious sin if the evil desired is grave, and a venial sin if the evil desired is slight. One wishes another *evil as evil* if one desires that some misfortune overtake him, not because of the salutary effects that might result, but because of the suffering, hardship, or inconvenience which he will thus experience.

THE HOLY NAME SOCIETY

This society, approved and encouraged by many popes, has for its principal purpose the fostering of love and reverence for the name of God. In achieving this it takes the positive means of making known the power[1] and glory[2] of the name of Jesus, and the negative means of endeavoring to put an end to blasphemy, profanity, perjury, and irreverent language in general. There are

---

[1] "If you ask the Father anything in my name, he will give it to you" (John 16:23).

[2] "Therefore God also has exalted him and has bestowed upon him the name that is above every name, so that at the name of Jesus every knee should bend of those in heaven, on earth and under the earth" (Philippians 2:9-10).

rich indulgences to be gained by membership in this confraternity. The good that the Holy Name Society has accomplished is well known to all.

ILLICIT OATHS AND PERJURY

An oath is invoking God to witness the truth of what one says. One takes an oath, for example, in an affidavit before a notary public. We may call on God as witness either by naming Him expressly or through an act that implies calling on God as witness (for example, by placing one's hand on the Bible, the cross, and so forth, in certain circumstances).

THE LICITNESS OF TAKING AN OATH

That an oath be licitly pronounced it must fulfill the three following conditions:

1. The statement sworn to must be true. One has the grave obligation of excluding from oaths all lies, even slight ones.

2. One must have a sufficient reason for swearing. To swear without a good reason would amount to using God's name in vain, and so would be venially sinful. Such would be the case were one to say: "I swear by God that I thoroughly enjoyed that glass of wine." A *sufficient reason* means a matter of some importance; for example, to rid oneself of the habit of drink, one takes a pledge under oath.

3. The making of the statement must not be sinful. The making of a statement may be sinful either because we are revealing a secret which we are not free to disclose or because we are expressing a determination which we are not free to entertain.

EXAMPLE 1. A witness in a damage suit reveals some hidden sin of the defendant, but this sinful act of the defendant has no bearing upon the case being tried and hence there is no reason for referring to it. The witness, being under oath, is asking God to confirm the truth of a statement that is sinfully made because it is detraction. If the sin revealed is serious, the offense is serious; if venial, the offense is venial.

EXAMPLE 2. Z swears that he will lie to A (Z's oath is venially sinful) or that he will murder B (Z's oath is mortally sinful).

OATHS NOT ALWAYS ILLICIT

Some Protestant sects maintain that all oaths are forbidden by the Bible, alleging in proof the following texts: "I say to you not to swear at all" (Matthew 5:34) and "Above all things, my brethren, do not swear, either by heaven or by the earth, or any other oath" (James 5:12). In answer we note the following points:

1. The followers of Christ are in general forbidden to swear, for oaths are unnecessary in a Christian society where everyone is honest and truthful. But in a world where lies and mistrust have arisen among men, an oath is at times necessary to establish the truth. Men who in many instances would not hesitate to tell a lie may have enough reverence for God not to commit perjury.

2. St. Paul repeatedly took an oath to confirm the truth of his words. See Romans 9:1-2; 2 Corinthians 1:23 and 11:31.

3. The Church has condemned as false the doctrine denying the lawfulness of oaths.

THE BINDING POWER OF AN OATH

One who takes an oath is bound thereby to speak the truth or to fulfill his promise if he has a real intention of taking an oath. Such an intention is presumed to be present if he uses a generally accepted formula. One who uses such a formula (even if he does not have the intention to bind himself) and testifies falsely is held by the state to have been guilty of perjury.

FEIGNED OATHS

An oath is feigned (or fictitious) if one uses the usual formula of an oath but has no intention of calling upon God as witness to the truth of the statement made. Such a hollow formula would not bind as an oath. However, one might sin grievously by taking a feigned oath, in the following ways:

1. When grave injury is done thereby to a third party.

EXAMPLE. A, relying on my feigned oath, enters into a contract with B, and as a result loses a large sum of money.

2. When grave injury is done to the common good.

EXAMPLE. A witness who takes a feigned oath preparatory to testifying in court violates the state's right to require that an oath taken in court be genuine.

3. If one confirms a promise by an oath but has no intention of fulfilling his promise, serious sin is committed. This would be grave abuse of God's name, for one would exteriorly call God to testify to the truth of what he knows to be false.

105

In itself taking a feigned oath is but venially sinful, for it is a lie, coupled with using God's name in vain. Only in the cases that have been mentioned above would the taking of a feigned oath be seriously wrong.

THE OBLIGATION OF PROMISES MADE UNDER OATH

A promise under oath imposes a grave or slight obligation to fulfill the promise according to the seriousness or slightness of the matter involved.

> EXAMPLE. A soldier, promising under oath to defend his country, is under grave obligation to do so; a very emphatic woman, sincerely promising under oath to accompany her friend to the theater, ordinarily would be under slight obligation to do so.

PROMISES MADE UNDER OATH TO PERFORM SINFUL ACTIONS

A promise under oath to do something sinful does not bind at all. Hence the following sworn promises would entail no obligation in conscience:

1. A Catholic swears that he will get married by a Protestant minister.

2. I swear that I will help a friend rob a certain bank.

3. The members of certain secret societies take an oath to maintain secrecy regarding everything that occurs in their meeting, and so forth, no matter what it may be and under all circumstances. State and church authorities have at times a right to such knowledge.

THE FORMULA OF AN OATH

"I swear to God," "God is my witness," "So help me God," and the like, are proper formulas of an oath. The oath taken by a witness in court is thus worded: "The evidence that you shall give to the court and jury, touching the matters in question, shall be the truth, the whole truth, and nothing but the truth, so help you God."

"Before God," "As God lives," "God knows I'm hungry," "I swear this is true," "May I die on the spot if this is false," and so forth, are ordinarily not real oaths, though they could be in certain circumstances; for example, when used in answer to a request for an oath. These phrases are usually employed merely to lend conviction to one's words. One should be on his guard against taking an oath about every declaration that his hearer seems inclined to doubt.

MAY A CATHOLIC SWEAR ON A PROTESTANT BIBLE?

Ordinarily a Catholic should not swear on a Protestant Bible, for such an act would give tacit approbation to that Bible and would not infrequently cause scandal. A Catholic, however, may licitly swear on any Bible that is presented to him for this purpose in a court of law, even though it is a non-Catholic one, because in these circumstances there is a sufficient reason for so acting. Here he clearly regards this Bible simply as a book containing the word of God without reference to what version it may be.

The Catholic Church does not forbid the use of Protestant Bibles because she believes that their contents have been falsified, although it is true that the canon (the list of sacred books that are included) is not the same for Catholic and for Protestant Bibles. As a matter of fact, some Catholic biblical scholars consider certain Protestant versions at least equal to the best Catholic versions in fidelity to the original text and in general excellence. The Church, however, has an obligation to protect the faith of her members. She will not permit them to use even Catholic versions unless these versions have been examined and approved. Her prohibition is not so much against Protestant versions as it is against any unapproved version; and there is no reason why the Church should undertake to scrutinize every Protestant version that appears, since her members have been provided with more than one good Catholic version.

OATHS OF ALLEGIANCE BY IMMIGRANTS

Immigrants who have sworn allegiance to their native country but now wish to become United States citizens may now swear allegiance to the United States, for the obligation of fidelity to a nation is understood to cease if with good reason one seeks a new land without harm to his former fatherland.

DEFINITION OF PERJURY

Perjury is swearing to a falsehood. Perjury is never permissible and is always a grave sin, even though one swear to the truth of only a slight lie. Even in this latter case the sin is serious, because great dishonor is shown to God by calling upon Him to witness the truth of what is known to be false. Perhaps the majority of those who testify nowadays consider the oath, not as having any religious force, but only as a solemn declaration that the truth will be told. Such witnesses are made more careful to avoid lies during the court proceedings through fear of the heavy penalties prescribed by the law for perjury.

VOWS, ADJURATION, AND EXORCISM

A vow is a free, deliberate promise made to God to do something that is good and that is more pleasing than its omission. The one vowing must realize that a special sin is committed by violating this promise. A vow binds under pain of sin (grave or slight) according to the intention of the one taking the vow. If one vows with regard to grave matter, one is presumed to intend to bind oneself under pain of serious sin. If, for example, a resident of Chicago vows to make a pilgrimage to Midland, Ontario, the matter of the vow would be considered grave, since the pilgrimage would be a long and costly one.

THE VALUE OF A VOW

Vows better our actions because:

1. They unite the soul to God by a new bond of religion, and so the acts included under the vow become acts of the virtue of religion. Hence they are more meritorious.

2. One surrenders to God the moral freedom of acting otherwise, like one who not only gives at times of the fruit of the tree, but gives up the tree itself.

3. Vows forestall weakness, since they do not leave matters to the indecision of the moment.

WHEN A VOW CEASES TO BIND

A vow ceases to bind in the following cases:

1. When it is canceled. Provided that the material of the vow be within their jurisdiction, a husband can annul his wife's vows and a father his minor children's private vows. A bishop or privileged confessor can release from most private vows.

2. When fulfillment becomes impossible. For example, I vowed to donate a marble altar and now I am reduced to poverty. If, however, I can still afford to give a wooden altar and this is

acceptable to the superior of the convent or to the pastor of the church to which I vowed I would donate a marble altar, I am obliged to donate a wooden altar, for I am obliged to fulfill that part of the obligation that has not become impossible. I cannot give a *marble* altar, but I can give an altar of some kind.

DEFINITION OF ADJURATION

Adjuration is using the name of God or of a saint or the mention of a holy thing to confirm a command or a request. For example, the high priest said at the trial of Jesus: "I adjure thee by the living God that thou tell us whether thou art the Christ, the Son of God" (Matthew 26:63). Many of the liturgical prayers of the Church end with the adjuration: "Let us pray. Graciously hear us, O God . . . through our Lord Jesus Christ, Thy Son, who liveth . . ."

THE LICITNESS OF ADJURATION

To be licitly employed, an adjuration must fulfill three conditions. It must be made (1) in the name of the true God, (2) in order to obtain a lawful object, and (3) concerning a thing of some importance.

EXORCISM

Exorcism is adjuration that has as its object the expelling of evil spirits. The formula used by the Church is found in the Roman Ritual: "I adjure thee, serpent of old . . . that thou go out of this servant of God (the name of the individual) . . ."

We know that God does at times allow the evil spirits to exert a certain influence on human beings, either by way of attacking their bodies from the exterior (obsession), or by inner control of the actions of the body (possession). The victim's liberty of soul always remains intact. Although the Roman Ritual mentions as probable (not certain) signs of obsession such things as speaking or understanding an unknown tongue or showing strength above one's natural capacity, it warns against concluding too hastily that a person is possessed by the devil. Many so-called cases of obsession are no doubt to be attributed to mere illusions, hysterics, or fraud. Holy Scripture, however, recounts many instances of diabolical possession. In these scriptural accounts the one attacked is sometimes described as being deprived of his sight or speech

(Matthew 12:22), at other times as being hurled to the ground (Mark 9:16-26), and again as endowed with preternatural strength (Mark 5:2-5).

It appears that diabolical possession is not altogether unheard of today, especially in pagan countries. An example of diabolical possession is found in *The Question of Miracles*,[3] by Reverend G. H. Joyce, S.J., pages 125-29.

Cases to be analyzed

1 A coach who has developed many champion football teams finds that the squad often needs the stimulus of strong language. Hence he curses and uses God's name in his pep talks. "God knows that I mean no irreverence," says he, "and so there is no sin."

2 A wealthy contractor promised under oath to give a thousand dollars to a very poor man. Now, when he is about to carry out that promise, he finds that the man has become wealthy by reason of an inherited fortune. He never would have made such a promise unless the man were poor, but still he feels bound to give him the thousand dollars.

3 "I vow I'll never listen to that program again," said a teen-age girl, turning off the radio in disgust. A week later, however, she is anxious to hear it just once more, but she is afraid of contracting serious guilt by violating her vow.

4 A gravedigger, much given to drink, takes a solemn pledge never to touch another drop. A week later he drinks a pint of whisky at a single sitting. Though he did not become intoxicated on that occasion, he accuses himself in confession of having committed the mortal sin of breaking his solemn pledge.

5 An emotional Catholic had great devotion to St. Francis, and so he prayed to that saint for three weeks for a very special favor. Impatient that his prayers were apparently unanswered, he took his picture of St. Francis and tossed it into the furnace, exclaiming in disgust: "You sure have great influence with God!"

6 A confirmed bachelor solemnly promises under oath to marry a girl within a month's time. He has, however, no real intention of keeping his word. The girl, believing the sincerity of his promise, orders her trousseau and makes other arrangements for the wedding.

7 In order to show his appreciation for a special favor from God a man makes a vow to visit a certain shrine. Later, however, he remarks: "All right. I'll go. I don't see what else I can do about it. I don't want to commit a mortal sin by violating my vow, but I never would have made that vow if I had known the expense and inconvenience involved in such a trip."

_____
[3] London: Manresa Press and B. Herder, 1914.

8 "May Satan destroy me on the spot if I'm not telling the truth," exclaims an impassioned speaker. His friend quietly warns him against using such an oath as that.

Topics for discussion[4]

1 How does honoring the Blessed Virgin and the saints honor God?
2 What is to be said of the use of slang?
3 Why should one join the Holy Name Society?
4 Explain some effective method that could be used for overcoming the habit of taking God's name in vain.

Bibliography

Cotel, Peter. *Catechism of the Vows for the Use of Religious,* twenty-eighth edition, revised by Emile Jombart and translated by William H. McCabe. New York: Benziger Brothers, 1924.

Davis, Henry. *Moral and Pastoral Theology,* seventh edition, edited by L. W. Geddes, Vol. 2, pp. 42-58. 4 vols. New York: Sheed and Ward, 1958.

Jone, Heribert. *Moral Theology,* pp. 107-20. Westminster: Newman Press, 1957.

---

[4] Not all the assertions contained in the topics are true. The student is to judge the truth of any assertions made and to explain his decision.

CHAPTER VI

The

"Remember that thou keep holy **third**
the sabbath day. . . . thou shalt do
no work on it."
Exodus 20:8-10 **commandment**

SOMETIMES at least during their lives all men are required by the natural law to worship God. In the Old Law God imposed on the Israelites the obligation of exercising public worship on the seventh day of each week. In the New Law the Catholic Church, in the fullness of power given her by Christ, changed the time of the obligation from Saturday (that is, the Sabbath) to Sunday. Just when this ecclesiastical law was enacted has not been determined by historians. It is known, however, that the change from the Sabbath had taken place within the first centuries. It is possible that Christ Himself made the change after His Resurrection, or it may be that the apostles made the change because it was on the first day of the week and not on the Sabbath that Christ rose from the dead. There is no certain proof from Scripture, however, indicating when and for what reasons the Sabbath obligation was changed by the Church to Sunday.

The church law of today that defines the obligations of Catholics as regards the matter of the Third Commandment reads as follows: "On holydays of obligation Holy Mass must be heard, and one must abstain from servile work and from judicial proceedings; also . . . from public markets, fairs, and other public buying and selling" (Canon 1248).

THE OBLIGATION OF HEARING MASS

Attendance at Mass is required under pain of mortal sin on all Sundays and holydays of obligation. In the universal Church there are ten holydays of obligation; in the United States, however, there are but six: January 1, Ascension Thursday, August 15, November 1, December 8, and December 25. Those in this country have been dispensed as regards the prescribed observance of the four other feasts: those of the Epiphany (January 6), St. Joseph (March 19), SS. Peter and Paul (June 29), and Corpus Christi. Nevertheless, if someone from the United States happened to be traveling or visiting in another country where these latter feasts are still days of obligation, he too would be bound to observe them as such during his stay in that place.

In Canada January 6 is a holyday of obligation but August 15 is not. With the exception of these two, the holydays of obligation are the same in the United States and in Canada. A Canadian who is in the United States on August 15 is obliged to hear Mass on that day, but if he is in our country on January 6, he shares during his stay here in our dispensation regarding that holyday.

WHO ARE BOUND TO HEAR MASS

All Catholics who enjoy habitual use of reason and who have completed the age of seven years are under the grave obligation of hearing Mass on Sundays and holydays of obligation. Hence we see that, if a youngster attains the use of reason at the age of 6 or fails to attain it at the age of 9, he is not bound by this church law. Adults who are so mentally deficient as not to have attained to the use of reason are of course exempt from this law.

HOW MASS MUST BE HEARD

Too much cannot be said about the reverence with which one should attend Mass, which is a repetition of the sacrifice of Calvary; but to fulfill the church obligation only four things are required under pain of sin: (1) bodily presence, (2) a whole Mass, (3) sufficient attention, and (4) the proper intention.

BODILY PRESENCE

To be bodily present at Mass means to be there physically, so as to be considered as belonging to the group that is assisting at the Holy Sacrifice. Anyone who is actually inside the church fulfills the condition of bodily presence. A lone worshiper in any part of an immense basilica is present at the Mass being said there. If one is in the sacristy with the door closed, he may satisfy his obligation provided he can follow what is going on at the altar. The ringing of the bell, for example, or the sound of the congregation rising or kneeling, or the singing of the choir makes it possible for him to know what part of the Mass has been reached. If one is outside the church, even then he is sufficiently present provided he can be reasonably considered part of the congregation. The following would be regarded as present at Mass:

1. One in a house quite near the church, if he can see the priest at the altar.

2. One of a crowd extending for some yards outside an overcrowded church.

PERSONS NOT CONSIDERED BODILY PRESENT

One would not be considered present at Mass if he were at a great distance, even though he could follow the actions of the priest perfectly by means of a telescope and could hear the priest's exceptionally resonant voice clearly. Hence Mass cannot be heard by radio. During the Spanish civil war it was said that Pius XI allowed the Catholics in Red Spanish territory to fulfill their Sunday Mass obligation by radio. That merely meant that he recognized existing conditions and granted them a dispensation from fulfilling the church law in the ordinary manner. Such exceptions cannot be used as a norm for interpreting church law.

WHAT IS A "WHOLE" MASS?

On Sundays and holydays of obligation one is obliged to assist at a whole Mass, and this embraces everything from the prayers at the foot of the altar at the beginning up to and excluding the Last Gospel. Though the Last Gospel is, strictly speaking, not part of the Mass, decent regard for divine worship would at least counsel one not to leave the church before the Last Gospel is finished. If a notable part of the Mass is omitted, one's obligation is not fulfilled.

It is not easy to estimate exactly what would constitute a grave omission in this matter. In forming a judgment regard must be had, not only for the duration, but also for the importance of the parts missed. The parts close to the Consecration rank, of course, highest in dignity. The following estimate is commonly looked upon as a safe guide. It would be a serious omission:

1. To miss everything up to and including the Offertory.
2. To miss everything up to and including the Gospel, together with all that follows the Communion of the priest.
3. To miss everything from the end of the Preface to the beginning of the Consecration.
4. To miss everything from the end of the Consecration to the beginning of the Pater Noster.
5. To go outside the church during the Consecration and then again during the Communion of the priest, although one is present for all the other parts of the Mass.

Less than the above would constitute slight matter; for example, to omit all before the Gospel or after the Communion.

COMPENSATING FOR PARTS MISSED

In case one misses a notable portion of the Mass, the missing of which would prevent him from fulfilling his obligation, he must make up for the omission by hearing in another Mass the portion which he missed. Under all circumstances one should be present at the Consecration and Communion *of the same Mass.* One cannot fulfill the precept by hearing simultaneously complementary parts of different Masses. For example, I would not fulfill my obligation if I arrived at the Consecration of the Mass being said at the main altar and left at the end of this Mass, even though a priest at a side altar was on my arrival beginning his Mass and had finished the Consecration when I left.

To make up slight omissions in hearing Mass is praiseworthy but not obligatory. For example, A deliberately and without excuse intends to miss a small part of the Mass and not to make it up. A is guilty of venial sin. B, on the other hand, misses a small part of the Mass through necessity. B commits no sin. At the end of the Mass neither A (who sinned when he made the evil intention of not hearing a *whole* Mass) nor B (though he could do so without any inconvenience) has the obligation of staying for a following Mass to make up the part missed. C deliberately misses all up to the Gospel of the Mass, intending to stay up to the Gospel of the next Mass. He is guilty of no sin, but he must under pain of venial sin remain in the next Mass for the part missed.

Deliberately to miss, without an excusing cause, a slight portion of the Mass (for example, everything from the beginning of the Mass to the Gospel) is a venial sin.

SUFFICIENT ATTENTION

To fulfill one's obligation it is necessary that one assist at Mass in such a way that he realizes, at least in a confused manner, what is going on at the altar and that he refrain from any action which of its nature is incompatible with this attention. Examples of actions incompatible with this attention are writing, reading a novel, earnest and continuous conversation, and deep sleep. Hence if I fall into a deep sleep (nodding occasionally is not the same as deep sleep) or read a newspaper during a part of the Mass that cannot be missed without serious sin, I have not satisfied my obligation and I am bound to make up the part missed.

If one yields fully to *willful distractions* the whole time, he is not obligated to hear another Mass. Though in this case it would be preferable to attend another Mass, it is not strictly necessary, since distractions, even though voluntary (and hence venially sinful), do not prevent one's fulfilling the strict requirements of this church law, which looks only to external decorum and proper behavior. The following acts do not exclude sufficient attention: (1) singing in the choir, (2) acting as an usher, (3) going to confession, or (4) making the Way of the Cross.

WHAT IS A PROPER INTENTION?

In order to satisfy this church precept one must have the intention of worshiping God by participating in the Mass. It is by no means necessary, however, to intend this *explicitly*. I have the proper intention as long as I go to church to participate in the Mass like other Catholics. Devout Catholics may take it for granted that they always have the proper intention, at least implicitly and hence sufficiently. The intention necessary is that of worshiping God, and does not include that of satisfying the obligation. Therefore if I attend Mass out of devotion on Ascension Thursday, forgetting what day it is, and then remember later in the morning that it is a holyday of obligation, I need not attend another Mass.

If one fulfills the requirements for attendance at Mass on Sundays and holydays, he is undoubtedly doing something very pleasing in the eyes of God. His attendance is an act of obedience to the authority exercised by the Church and involves an act of faith in the reality of the sacrifice of the Mass. However, there are many degrees of participation in the sacrifice of the Mass. One could attend Mass conscious of unrepented mortal sin. His attendance at Mass would still be a good action; God often gives such a person the grace to repent. Another could attend Mass while in the state of grace but offer himself up only partially with Christ. The perfect disposition for attendance at Mass is the complete offering of oneself to God with Christ. This complete offering involves the determination not to commit even venial sin (although we know that we will occasionally do so) and the acceptance of the will of God in all phases of our life. It is not easy to make such an offering sincerely, but a Catholic who wishes to imitate Christ more perfectly must at least strive to develop this disposition of perfect submission to the will of God.

ATTENDANCE IN ONE'S PARISH CHURCH

It is not necessary to attend Sunday Mass in one's parish church, though to do so is generally recommended. One may attend Sunday Mass in any church or public or semipublic oratory (for example, in chapels of hospitals, religious communities, colleges, prisons, and so forth) or under the open sky. Moreover, the Mass which one attends may be celebrated in any rite, such as the Byzantine, that is approved by the Church.

WHO ARE EXCUSED FROM MASS

If because of circumstances attendance at Mass would cause me moderately grave inconvenience, I am excused from the obligation of attending. One may tell oneself that any reason or any state of affairs that would cause him to put aside urgent business of some importance would justify one's omitting Mass. Hence the following classes of persons would be excused because of the moderately grave inconvenience that would result for them if they were to attempt to assist at Mass:

1. The sick, or persons who must remain at home to care for those who cannot be left alone such as the sick, young children, or the very aged.

2. Those who would be obliged to walk over an hour (one way) to church. Somewhat less would excuse from the obligation in inclement weather or if one were weak. If it would involve moderately grave inconvenience (for instance, because of the expense or great length of time involved) to take an automobile, streetcar, or train to Sunday Mass, one is not obliged to do so.

3. Servants who are forbidden by their employers to go. They should obtain if possible another position where they will be allowed to attend Sunday Mass.

4. Workmen, if by going to Mass they would deprive themselves of reasonably necessary sleep.

5. Those who cannot give up their work without relatively grave loss.

FACTS TO BE NOTED CONCERNING SUNDAY OBSERVANCE

The following comments concerning Sunday observance may serve to settle doubts that sometimes arise:

1. The fact that one has committed mortal sin does not excuse one from attending Mass on Sundays.

2. The fact that one is legitimately excused from the obligation of hearing Mass merely means that one will commit no sin by not attending Mass. It does not mean that in many cases it would not be preferable to attend the Holy Sacrifice in spite of all difficulties.

> EXAMPLE. A farmer would have to walk two hours to reach the nearest church. He is not obliged to go; but if he does so in spite of the grave inconvenience, his act is most praiseworthy.

3. There is no obligation to assist at Sunday Vespers, Benediction, or other services. However, attendance is recommended.

4. Even though one is excused from the church law in regard to attendance at Mass, he still has the obligation from the natural law to worship God and obey His commandments. If such a person finds that frequent absence from Mass results in failure to pray at all and in frequent serious violations of the commandments, he must either change his circumstances so that he will be

able to attend Mass or make use of some other means to remain close to God.

5. If for some good reason (and not just to escape the obligation of assisting at Mass) I wish to start out on a trip on Saturday evening, knowing that Sunday will find me far from any church, I may do so.

> EXAMPLE. A father leaves on Saturday for a week-end visit with his son who lives in a churchless section of the country. Because of his valid reason he is justified in acting as he did.

Because they lived in places far from any church, many Catholics lost their faith. Hence one should be very slow about choosing such a place for his residence. Those who are so situated should strive to hear Mass (even on a weekday) at least three or four times during the year even though this should cost them great effort. Some religious practices at home, though not obligatory, would undoubtedly help to keep their faith alive. Families could, for example, recite in common the rosary of the Blessed Virgin either daily or on Sundays.

WHO MAY BE DISPENSED

If one wishes to absent oneself from Mass for some reason that is not of itself grave enough to excuse from this obligation, he may ask for a dispensation from his pastor.

> EXAMPLE. A man who is seldom able to get away from his work would like to take a day's outing on a boat that leaves very early Sunday morning, for he feels that the change would do him much good. He has sufficient reason to ask for a dispensation.

SUNDAY REST

SERVILE WORK

Canon 1248, quoted earlier in the chapter (page 113), stipulates that we must abstain from servile work, judicial proceedings, and public buying and selling. The Church has never defined officially what is meant by servile work, and anyone familiar with theological writings knows that there is no common agreement among theologians as to its precise meaning. One of the papers given at the Twelfth Annual Convention of the Catholic Theological Society of America in 1957 was entitled "The Changing Concept of Servile Work." Catholics may be surprised to hear that a concept which seems so clear to them is the subject of debate among theologians. Catholic lay persons are for the most part familiar only with the concept of servile work which has prevailed since the sixteenth century and which is usually attributed to Cardinal Cajetan. According to this concept a work is judged to be servile solely by the nature of the thing done with no regard for the intention or the circumstances. Some books on moral theology still define servile work as work which is chiefly physical. However, in the last two decades many moral theologians have questioned this definition. They base their objections to it on the purpose of the law, its history, and the changed conditions of modern society.

The purpose of the law is to free men from their ordinary everyday work so that they will be free to worship God in a fitting manner. This purpose can be attained even if one does some manual labor for exercise or recreation. Other things which no one considers to be forbidden could interfere more with the worship of God than manual labor.

Laws in regard to Sunday rest go back to the fourth century; even before that time customs were in effect throughout the Church. The earliest laws forbade public activities which would interfere with the worship of God but did not explicitly forbid manual labor. In fact, some manual labor was to be preferred to useless idleness. In the Middle Ages servile work was the work done by serfs from which they were freed on Sundays and holydays in order to worship God. The prohibition of manual work was necessary in their case if the purpose of the law was to be attained. Gradually servile work and manual work were identified. It is argued that this identification came about through interpretation of the church law by theologians and that modern theologians can interpret the law in a new way because of changed circumstances.

In our society many people get little physical exercise from their everyday work. Even those who work in factories do most of their work by machines. However, they are under a considerable amount of nervous strain, especially those who spend all their time in a busy office. Such people find it a real relaxation to do light manual work. They need the exercise and recreation which it affords them. It is true that they could get exercise and recreation by engaging in sports such as golf or boating, but many of them prefer to get it by doing some manual work around the house or in the yard. In some places customs have grown up; Leo XIII recognized such a custom when he did not forbid French mine and factory workers from gardening on Sunday.

Taking all these factors into consideration, some moral theologians would hold that it is a legitimate interpretation of the law to allow some manual work done for exercise or recreation on the basis of custom, and that custom is indicated by the lack of scandal on the part of good Catholics. Father John R. Connery recommends this as a reasonable interpretation of the law.[1] There are enough moral theologians of repute who hold this opinion (or one which is equivalent to it) to make it probable and applicable in practice. Several have suggested a change or clarification of the church law by the Church herself. In this interpretation heavy manual work (plowing, ditch digging) would still be forbidden and would constitute a serious violation of the law if done over a period of several hours.

JUDICIAL PROCEEDINGS AND CIVIL OCCUPATIONS

Judicial proceedings consist of the ordinary everyday business of the courtroom, such as pleading cases, acting as witnesses, passing judgment. Judges and lawyers are not forbidden to do legal work privately (for example, preparing a brief in getting their case ready for trial or holding private consultations). By civil occupations are meant public buying, selling, or trading. Hence merchants are not allowed to engage in business on Sundays.

WHAT IS ALLOWED ON SUNDAY

The following activities are permitted on Sundays and holydays of obligation:

1. Housework. This consists of cooking, sweeping, washing dishes, making beds, and so forth.

2. Liberal works. Among these are drawing, painting pictures, embroidering, crocheting, amateur photography, typewriting, studying, and other similar activities.

3. Games, such as football, baseball, golf.

4. Forms of recreation such as hunting, fishing, hiking.

---

[1] See John R. Connery, "Current Theology: Notes on Moral Theology." *Theological Studies* 19:552-53, December 1958.

5. To "putter around" the garden, trimming plants, watering the grass, or removing weeds.

EXCUSING CAUSES

One would be excused from the church law regarding servile work for the following reasons:

1. Serious inconvenience. If I would experience serious inconvenience because of the fact that I refrain from doing certain work on a Sunday or a holyday of obligation, I would be excused on that day from the obligation which is imposed by this ecclesiastical prohibition.

> EXAMPLE. Since he has little spare time during the week, a salesman dismantles and repairs his automobile on Sunday, so that it may be in good condition for his business trips.

2. Works of charity toward those in need. We may tend the sick, bury the dead, make clothes for one badly in need of them, and so forth.

3. Necessity. This may be (a) public necessity or utility (for example, the work of policemen, firemen, railroad employees, and so forth) or (b) private necessity (for example, the work of druggists, restaurant personnel, gasoline-station attendants, newspaper boys, chauffeurs, tailors finishing clothes that must be ready for wear on Monday).

Although necessity may require some people to engage in civil occupations on Sundays because others in the same business are open, Catholics ought to take all possible means to stop such abuses. Civil occupations interfere directly with the purpose of the Sunday rest. If one business opens—for example, drugstores (which actually sell many items proper to hardware store) or automobile dealers—others will use this as an excuse for opening. Gradually more and more people would have to work on Sunday, a form of "enslavement" which the law tries to prevent.

Realtors often remain open on Sundays to take prospective customers to examine lots or houses that are for sale. In a certain city realtors whose consciences told them that they ought not to engage in buying or selling on Sundays felt that they could not afford to close if they wished to remain in business. A Catholic realtor proposed to his fellow realtors, many of them non-Catholics, that they should all agree that they would do no selling on Sundays. The suggestion was accepted, and thus an abuse was corrected. This is an example of what can be done by persons who sincerely believe in the sanctity of the Sabbath and who refuse to accept the principle, held by so many today, that the law of God should never be permitted to interfere with the making of money.

DISPENSATIONS PERMITTING SERVILE WORK

For a good reason one may seek from one's pastor a dispensation from the law prohibiting servile work, just as in the case of the Mass obligation.

Cases to be analyzed

1 A farmer lives five miles from his church, but in spite of the fact that he has an automobile he believes he is excused from going to Mass on Sunday because of the great distance.

2 A steam fitter confesses that he missed Mass through his own grievous fault on Holy Thursday.

3 Since a certain druggist is able to attend no other church on a particular Sunday, he assists at Mass at a Greek Orthodox church.

4 A man 23 years old who has the mentality of a boy of 9 is kept home Sundays by his mother. She says that he is excused from the Sunday obligation because of his mental deficiency.

5 A boy who is serving Sunday Mass absents himself after the "Orate frates" to get the sanctus bell that is in the house of the priest about a block away. He returns just before the Consecration. He hears no other Mass that day.

6 A man arrived at the last Mass on Sunday just after the Consecration. He would have been on time, but he was delayed in thawing out his automobile. He does not believe he sinned gravely.

7 A middle-aged woman has no hat that she could wear to Sunday Mass. Besides, she cannot spare any money for the collection. Hence she remains at home.

8 A doctor has a fairly bad cold and, although he could attend Mass with little risk to himself, he is afraid of communicating his cold to others. Hence he feels that he is excused from the Sunday obligation.

9 A good Catholic makes it a point to hire for his small factory only non-Catholics. With these he can without scruple keep his plant working all day on Sunday.

10 A college girl finds that she must frequently miss Mass during the summer because she has to accompany her parents (lukewarm Catholics) on Sunday outings. They generally start at 7 A.M. and she would find it difficult to refuse to go along.

11 A stenographer brought from the office a batch of business letters and typed these out on Sunday. This work took her over three hours.

12 A teen-age boy generally arrives at Sunday Mass during the First Gospel. He himself is always ready on time, but he has to wait for his sister to bring her to church in the family automobile.

13 A girl spent most of Sunday afternoon and evening decorating her house for the birthday party of her young sister. The party was to take place the next day.

14 A young man usually spends his Sunday afternoons overhauling his Ford. He looks upon this occupation as recreation and enjoys it more than seeing a movie. Hence he feels that it is allowed.

Topics for discussion[2]

1 What is to be said about the conduct of one who always tries to avoid high Masses on Sunday?

2 There is no obligation to attend Sunday Vespers.

3 How may one best occupy oneself during Mass (for example, by saying the beads, using a prayer book, meditating)?

4 The church law regarding Sunday observance promotes the social good of Christians.

5 Describe to an ignorant Catholic what action of the celebrant indicates the beginning of the Offertory of the Mass; the end of the Communion.

Bibliography

Bussard, Paul. The Meaning of the Mass. Washington: The Catholic University of America Press, 1942.

Connery, John R. "Current Theology: Notes on Moral Theology." Theological Studies 19:552-53, December 1958.

Conway, J. D. "What Is Servile Work? Catholic Mind 56:514-19, November-December 1958.

Davis, Henry. Moral and Pastoral Theology, seventh edition, edited by L. W. Geddes, Vol. 2, pp. 59-68. 4 vols. New York: Sheed and Ward, 1958.

Howell, Clifford. Of Sacraments and Sacrifice. Collegeville: Liturgical Press, 1952.

Jone, Heribert. Moral Theology, pp. 121-26. Westminster: Newman Press, 1957.

Kelly, Gerald. "Current Theology: Notes on Moral Theology." Theological Studies 9:105-08, March 1948.

Pettirsch, Frank X. "A Theology of Sunday Rest." Theology Digest 6:114-20, Spring 1958.

Quigley, Joseph. "The Changing Concept of Servile Work." In Proceedings of the Twelfth Annual Convention of the Catholic Theological Society of America, pp. 145-53. New York: Catholic Theological Society of America, 1958.

---

[2] Not all the assertions contained in the topics are true. The student is to judge the truth of any assertions made and to explain his decision.

CHAPTER VII

The
fourth
commandment

"Honor thy father and thy mother."
Exodus 20:12

O BLIGATIONS arising from our relationships with God are covered by the first three commandments. The rest of the commandments concern the obligations of man in regard to his neighbor. The acts which they command, however, are ultimately directed to God both because they are done in obedience to God and because our reason for loving and respecting our neighbor is that he is created by God and participates in the highest of God's perfections in his life, intelligence, and freedom. These commandments presuppose a fundamental attitude of reverence and love for our neighbor. Unless one has that fundamental attitude, they simply become a series of burdensome obligations imposed on us by God.

The necessary attitude can be developed chiefly by a true knowledge and appreciation of Christ. Christ taught love of the neighbor as the second requirement for gaining eternal life. He showed us its meaning by the way in which He treated His associates. His love and reverence for them was not based on their moral worthiness but on the fact that they were His Father's children. Even at the moment of His betrayal He showed His love for Judas by giving him a last chance to repent. He was gentle and considerate of Peter after the latter's denial. He chose Zacchaeus, a publican despised by his neighbors, for special friendship. In every case He reverenced the individual and spared him embarrassment; more than that, He loved each of them individually and continually strove to bring them to eternal life with His Father. Unless we realize that the commandments which regard our neighbor are simply a concrete expression of the love and reverence which we should have for him as a child of God, we will never experience the joy of joining with Christ in His work for the salvation of man. Without it our practice of the commandments can never be perfect and we are in danger of disobeying them when temptations assail us.

The Fourth Commandment directly looks to those duties of children toward their parents that arise from the natural law; indirectly it concerns the obligations of parents toward their children. In this commandment are also implied the duties of all inferiors toward their superiors and of superiors in relation to their inferiors. The special virtue that has to do with the love due to blood relatives is called piety. Filial piety is the virtue that regulates the conduct of children toward their parents. Holy Scripture extols the virtue of piety in the following words: "And he that honoreth his mother is as one that layeth up a treasure. He that honoreth his father shall have joy in his own children, and in the day of his prayer he shall be heard. . . . He that feareth the Lord, honoreth his parents, and will serve them as his masters that brought him into the world. . . . Remember that thou hadst not been born but through them: and make a return to them as they have done for thee. . . . Honor thy father, in work and word and all patience. . . . Son, support the old age of thy father, and grieve him not in his life" (Ecclesiasticus 3:5-14; 7:30).

DUTIES OF CHILDREN

The duty which children have of honoring their parents requires in general that children do three things. It demands:

1. That children love their parents because of the natural bond arising from the fact that parents are coauthors with God

of their being and because of the many benefits that they have received from them.

2. That children reverence their parents because of the dignity and authority given them by nature.

3. That children obey their parents because, since parents have the duty of caring for and educating their children physically, intellectually, morally, and in matters of religion, they have the right to exact the obedience necessary for this.

Actions that violate charity or justice are, when directed toward one's parents, more serious than when they are directed toward strangers.

THE OBLIGATION OF LOVE

Children have the obligation of showing their parents both internal and external affection, and this duty endures all their life long. Children must sincerely love their parents in their hearts, and they would sin gravely by really hating them or by wishing them serious evil. A burst of anger or impatience at times prompts children to say that they hate their parents, but as a rule they do this without reflecting and do not really mean what they say. Children also are obliged to relieve their parents' needs, to show them signs of affection, and to protect them from physical or spiritual harm. Hence children may sin against this duty of filial love in the following ways:

1. By refusing to help parents in need of housing, food, clothing, medical care, or other necessities when it is possible for them to help.

2. By unjustly causing sorrow or anger to their parents by their actions.

3. By speaking to them sharply and in a hostile manner.

4. By failing without good reason to visit or write to them when they are sick or in some way afflicted.

5. By neglecting to see to it that they have an opportunity of receiving the last sacraments.

THE OBLIGATION OF REVERENCE

Children are bound to respect their parents by venerating them interiorly and by manifesting in their language and conduct proof of this deference and respect. This duty of filial reverence arises from the very fact that this man or this woman is one's father or one's mother and does not result from the existence of the good qualities that parents ordinarily have. Hence even though one's parents have become objects of public disgrace or are leading sinful lives, they still retain their right to reverence from their children. In spite of everything they are still the parents, and their children must acknowledge this lifelong right even after they have reached their majority. Children would sin against filial reverence in the following ways:

1. By unjustly striking their parents.

2. By unjustly threatening them (for example, by word or clenched fist).

3. By showing contempt and by ridicule, or insults, either in word or deed.

4. By being ashamed of them because of their poverty or lack of culture and by refusing to recognize them in public.

THE OBLIGATION OF OBEDIENCE

Children should regard their parents as commissioned by God to take charge of them and consequently as deserving to be obeyed in all things that pertain to their behavior, education, and training. Obviously, they may not do the bidding of their parents if what is commanded is surely sinful. The laws of the Church concerning fast and abstinence, attendance at Mass on Sundays and holydays, and the avoidance of servile work on Sundays and holydays are not intended to be binding if their observance would cause serious inconvenience. When there is question of these precepts children can obey their parents with a clear conscience. Parents are far better prepared than children to decide whether under the circumstances a sufficient reason for not observing the precept exists. A child gifted with a good mind and a fund of common sense, particularly if he is attending a Catholic school, might at times be convinced that his parent is wrong. If the parent reacts unfavorably to a quiet question or suggestion, the child may still obey because of the serious inconvenience of putting himself in open opposition to his parent. On the other hand, a parent could not command a child to receive Holy Communion an hour after eating, nor would a young person be justified in contracting marriage before someone other than a priest because his parents wished him to do so. In cases of doubt a priest should be consulted.

EXAMPLES. A 14-year-old girl is told by her mother to eat the meat served at home on Friday. A boy of 15 years is ordered by his father to help him plow fields on Sunday. Children in such cases may usually take it for granted that the parents, in giving such orders, have some sufficient reason that would excuse from the ecclesiastical prohibition.

Obedience is due to parents as long as their children live under their authority. The obligation ceases when children have reached their majority (according to civil law the age of majority is usually 21), or when they marry or enter religious life. If, however, a person who has reached his majority continues to live at home with his parents, he must obey them in all that pertains to domestic discipline.

EXAMPLE. A man 22 years old, unmarried and living at home with his parents, is told by his father that he must be home every night by twelve o'clock. He must obey.

HOW SINFUL IS DISOBEDIENCE?

Parents may command their children under pain of sin or not, just as they see fit. In things of great importance they may impose a grave obligation or a slight one, and the sinfulness of the child's disobedience will accordingly be grave or slight. In most cases commands regarding even serious matters are, perhaps, binding only under pain of venial sin. Such would probably be the case if John, known to be a somewhat reckless driver, is forbidden by his mother to drive over forty miles an hour. If a parent, however, very earnestly and in an impressive manner gives an order about a matter of grave importance, it is presumed that he wishes to bind under pain of mortal sin; for example, if a girl's father, foreseeing great danger to his daughter's virtue, solemnly forbids her to keep company with a divorced man. Very often, however, in telling their children to do something, it may well be that parents are simply expressing their wishes in the matter or are using persuasion, and that they have no intention of imposing an obligation under pain of sin, as when a mother says to her 17-year-old daughter: "Mary, don't eat any more of that candy. You will spoil your appetite for dinner."

It is not necessary that parents should *explicitly* demand obedience or *explicitly* intend to bind under pain of sin. God has given them a right to obedience, and the extent of the child's obligation depends upon *how much the parent wishes to be*

129

obeyed. Children, understanding this, often ask: "Mother, do I *have* to do that?"

THE CHOICE OF A STATE OF LIFE

Children are not obliged to obey their parents with regard to the choice of a state of life. Nevertheless they should, out of deference and for safe guidance, consult them about a matter of such importance. If, however, they have a grave reason for not informing their parents, they may, without divulging their intention, marry or enter the religious life. Even in this latter case, however, young persons should be very slow to trust their own judgment about the prudence of concealing their plans from their parents, and should be directed by the counsel of their confessor or of some other prudent adviser.

OBEDIENCE TO OTHER RELATIVES

Besides parents, other relatives should be shown love and reverence. If they hold the place of one's parents, as can happen by adoption, by court order, or by delegation of authority by the parents themselves, they must be obeyed. Younger members of the family are not obliged in conscience to do the bidding of an older brother or sister unless the parents have given these latter authority over them.

DUTIES OF PARENTS

Parents have the obligation of showing parental piety toward their offspring, loving them all equally and with due moderation. They should beware of excessive indulgence, manifested in giving in to their every whim and in failing to correct their faults. Parents would offend against their obligation if they showed marked favoritism toward one or another of their children and slighted the rest.

SUPPLYING CHILDREN'S TEMPORAL NEEDS

Parents are obliged to provide their children with suitable food, clothing, and other necessities. They must carefully watch over their children's lives and health and safeguard them against what would be injurious. This duty continues until children can provide adequately for themselves. What parents can do will depend upon their incomes; hence Canon 1113 says that they must provide for their children "to the best of their ability."

SUPPLYING CHILDREN'S SPIRITUAL NEEDS

Parents are under the serious obligation of looking to the spiritual instruction of their children. They must have their children baptized soon after birth and must see to it that they receive in due time the sacraments of penance, Holy Eucharist, and confirmation. Parents are obliged to take care that their offspring live up to Catholic practice and to protect them against destructive influences such as evil companions, harmful movies, immoral and risqué magazines or novels, and other things that may interfere with the development of a wholesome Christian character.

THE EDUCATION OF CHILDREN

Children should be given an education that is suitable to their condition in life. In most cases today, at least in our cities, a high-school education seems desirable. The children should be sent to a Catholic school, for according to church law (Canon 1374) Catholic children are forbidden to frequent non-Catholic schools, and this prohibition includes grade schools, high schools, colleges, and universities. Canon 1374, however, does not apply to colleges, universities, and technical schools in the same way that it applies to grade schools and high schools. For an explanation of the difference in application see T. Lincoln Bouscaren and Adam C. Ellis, *Canon Law: A Text and Commentary* (third edition), pages 744-45.[1]

Attending schools where there is no teaching of Catholic doctrine is generally injurious to both faith and morals. First of all, the student is not receiving the Catholic instruction that he should be getting at school: the systematic teaching of the dogmas of the Church and the orderly explanation of Christian morality. Only in rare cases are these provided for in the home. As a consequence the completion of his training in a non-Catholic institution will find in him a deplorable lack of theological knowledge and character training. Second, since religious truths and genuinely moral principles are sometimes passed over in complete silence in such schools, the student will readily conclude that knowledge of such

---

[1] Milwaukee: Bruce Publishing Company, 1957.

things is of little importance. This will pave the way for negligence in the practice of his Christian duties and may ultimately lead to atheism. A student in a non-Catholic school is apt to be corrupted by the example and teaching of some professors (for example, by the false views and imprudent discussions in courses on marriage) and by the evil influence of some of his textbooks and of reading that is prescribed. In non-Catholic universities and colleges many instructors require the reading of works that have a gravely harmful effect on the ordinary Catholic of college age. Experience has shown that such noxious reading has meant the undermining of morality and the loss of faith for many a Catholic who, up to that time, had been fervent in his religious practices. In some non-Catholic schools, though the doctrine taught is not especially inimical to the Catholic faith, danger to morals will arise from companionship with those who have no strict code of morality. If Catholic parents realized the disastrous influences at work in non-Catholic schools, they would never think of sending their children into the midst of such dangers.

The natural law forbids risking harm to one's faith or morals unnecessarily. Parents would sin grievously if they sent their children to any school or college where there was evidently proximate danger to faith or morals. This remains true even though parents have the most weighty reasons for so acting. To send their children to schools where these dangers are not proximate may be permitted by their bishop for good reasons (for example, in order to obtain technical instruction that is not to be had in any Catholic school in that vicinity), provided precautions are taken to make up for the lack of positive religious training by means of instruction at home or elsewhere. In all such cases the bishop must be consulted, for he is the proper judge as to whether one's reasons are sufficient (Canon 1374). This permission of the bishop is generally requested through one's pastor.

What has been said about attendance of Catholics at non-Catholic schools in no way implies a condemnation of the many excellent men and women who teach in such schools. Most of them have sincere religious convictions and try to help their students develop wholesome characters. Among them are many excellent graduates of our Catholic colleges who consider it a real vocation to teach and help form the characters of our young people. But neither teachers nor the authors of textbooks intended

132

for use in public schools are free to speak positively and in any detail about the nature of God, man's supernatural end, and the principles of conduct taught by God's revelation. Many non-Catholic schools are to be praised for their sincere efforts to do whatever is possible for their students in the existing situation. Large numbers of our leading statesmen and educators are concerned about the lack of religious training in our schools and would like to do something to remedy the defect, but so far no satisfactory solution has been found.

NEWMAN CLUBS

The bishops of the United States realize that some Catholics have legitimate reasons for attendance at non-Catholic schools and that others will attend such schools without legitimate reasons. They consider it their obligation to provide for the spiritual welfare of these students and have appointed chaplains or formed Newman clubs for their welfare. Their actions in no way imply general approval for attendance at such schools and should not be used as an argument for sending one's children there.

DUTIES OF HUSBANDS AND WIVES

Since the husband is the head of the family (1 Corinthians 11:3), his wife and children are subject to him in everything that pertains to family life and discipline (Ephesians 5:24). A wife would sin if she neglected her husband's legitimate commands, showed contempt for them, or assumed his authority without sufficient reason. The husband must support his wife and children and treat his wife, not as a servant, but as his loving helpmate. Husband and wife are under the obligation of living together, of cooperating in the marital act when the other seriously requests it and there is no just cause for refusing, and of showing each other mutual love.

DUTIES OF EMPLOYERS AND EMPLOYEES

The relations between employer and employee should be ruled by justice and should be equally beneficial to both. Each has certain rights, and consequently each has certain duties that are correlative to the other's rights. Leo XIII in *Rerum novarum* and Pius XI in *Quadragesimo anno* have given explanations of these rights and duties that are considered classics.

DUTIES OF EMPLOYERS

With regard to his employee the employer has the following fundamental duties:

1. To treat him as a fellow human being and not as a mere slave or machine.

2. To give him sufficient time for fulfilling his religious obligations (for example, for attending Sunday Mass).

3. To eliminate from his surroundings, insofar as possible, evil influences such as easy access to lewd women, narcotics, and gambling devices, and under no conditions to give support or encouragement to such evil influences.

4. To refrain from overtaxing the worker's strength. He must be especially careful in the case of young men or girls.

5. To pay a living wage.

DUTIES OF EMPLOYEES

With regard to his employer the worker has the following fundamental duties:

1. To be faithful to the duties agreed upon. Waste of working time, damage to property by neglect or willful act, and inexcusably inefficient service entail injustice.

2. To obey reasonable orders that pertain to his work.

3. To show his employer proper respect and to refrain from contempt and ridicule of him.

PROTECTION OF RIGHTS

Employers and employees have the right to protect themselves against injustice. For a long time the employee was frequently at the mercy of the employer, who usually could discharge him at will and defend himself by engaging competent lawyers and advisers. The situation has been greatly modified by the growth of large labor unions. Since it is almost impossible to determine the rights and duties of employers and employees with complete accuracy, they may both take means to get certain advantages or concessions which seem to them legitimate. There are bound to be disagreement and conflict in our present complicated economy. Both sides are obliged to use morally unobjectionable means in working for legitimate goals. Bribery and the exercise of undue influence on public officials and lawmakers can never be justified. Physical harm cannot be used to bring recalcitrants into line. Strikes which do more harm than good cannot be called. There will always be a certain amount of injustice in such conflicts; and while injustice cannot be condoned, neither should it be used as an argument for the destruction either of our capitalistic system or of labor unions.

The application of general moral principles to specific problems is made in courses on economics, sociology, and business. Students in these fields should become familiar with the social encyclicals and with current Catholic thought and opinion as found in learned Catholic publications such as *Social Order*.

DUTIES OF CITIZENS

Every citizen is obliged to love his country and to pay honor, obedience, and loyalty to the duly constituted civil rulers. Since every nation has the right to defend itself against unjust aggression, it may justly use the means necessary to resist its enemies. At times citizens are conscripted to serve their country for this purpose, and in such a contingency they have the duty of defending their country's rights, even at the cost of their lives.

DUTIES TOWARD ECCLESIASTICAL SUPERIORS

Every Catholic owes obedience, not only to the general laws of the Church, but also to the decrees and regulations of his ecclesiastical superiors. These are the living teaching body established for his daily guidance in things spiritual.

THE SOVEREIGN PONTIFF

The pope of Rome is the successor of St. Peter and the vicar of Christ on earth. He is the supreme shepherd of the faithful, and his chief concern is the spiritual welfare of his charges. Since the pope enjoys the primacy of universal jurisdiction in the Church, he has the power to command and direct each and every member, clergy and laymen alike. It is his duty to preserve the purity of Catholic doctrine, and so in order to clarify doubts which endanger faith or morals he makes at times infallible pronouncements; that is, he speaks *ex cathedra* to the universal Church on matters concerning what must be believed (for example, the assumption) or what constitutes right or wrong conduct. Every Catholic must accept these teachings of the Church as infallibly true.

At other times the pope makes pronouncements which do not infallibly define dogma or morality, but have for their purpose the imparting of salutary advice and wise guidance to all the faithful. These utterances of the pope must be received with great respect by every Christian. In them he is speaking as the chief shepherd of his flock, guarding his sheep from wolves and leading them to suitable pastures. It should be remembered that he who is speaking is a man of wide experience and that he is aided by the expert counsel of some of the world's best students of the subjects discussed. Hence one who disregards these papal warnings and counsels would ordinarily be guilty of temerity.

In addition to his power of teaching the pope also exercises the power of ruling over the whole Church. He makes laws and performs judicial functions. Many of these functions (for example, deciding on the validity of a marriage) are delegated to sacred congregations. The decisions of the latter are binding upon the individual or upon the whole Church, depending on the matter in question. This ruling power of the pope should not be confused with his power to teach.

THE BISHOP

The bishop is by divine right a successor of the apostles, endowed with the same rights and duties as they had in the ordinary ministry of the gospel. He is the spiritual director, the authentic teacher, and the official judge of his flock. He is the ruler in spiritual matters in his diocese. Hence he has the power to make local laws and regulations. He has the duty of protecting those committed to his care, and we observe how solicitous he is about preserving untarnished the faith and morals of his charges. He sees to it that the sacraments are properly administered; he provides as best he can for the religious instruction of all his subjects. He directs and guides both clergy and laity. It is clear that all those under his jurisdiction must obey his laws and decrees. Moreover, they must love and reverence him, show proper deference for his counsel, and be grateful for the many blessings and benefits that he procures for them. "Obey your superiors and be subject to them, for they keep watch as having to render an account of your souls; so that they may do this with joy, and not with grief" (Hebrews 13:17).

THE PASTOR

The bishop, we have seen, has the spiritual care of his whole diocese. Since he cannot personally administer to the needs of all his subjects, he delegates part of his authority to various representatives. To these delegates, called pastors, he gives jurisdiction over a section of his territory that is designated as a parish. The pastor, then, has authority over his parishioners, and his subjects owe him, not only love and reverence, but also obedience in those things that pertain to his office. The Catholic should bear in mind the numberless benefits that come to him through his pastor. It is the pastor who supervises the faith and morals of his parish, who protects it against various sources of temptation, who says Mass for his people, who builds church and school, who sees to it that the young are instructed, who cares for the poor and friendless, who visits the sick, who hears the confessions of his flock, who gives them the Bread of Life, and who would willingly risk even death itself in order to administer Viaticum.

Parishioners, then, are clearly obliged not to interfere with their pastor in the performance of his duties. They should, moreover, feel deep gratitude for his Christlike solicitude for their eternal salvation, and they should generously proffer the help he needs in caring for those who have been committed to his guardianship. They can cooperate with him in a practical way by joining some of the parish organizations. They should pray for him and for the success of his work.

Cases to be analyzed

1 A Catholic mother sends her boy for his college education to a large state university. "After all," she explains, "the evils one hears about such places are quite exaggerated, and my boy has had four years of Jesuit high-school training. He should be able to take care of himself now. The change will broaden him and give him desirable standing."

2 A boy, 17 years old, leaves home to make his own way in the world. His father, who had always squandered the little money the boy earned, strenuously objects to the boy's departure. The boy is now worried about having disobeyed his father.

3   A girl's parents threaten to leave the Church if she becomes a religious. Nevertheless she enters the novitiate. From that day neither of her parents ever sets foot in a church.

4   The daughter of bitterly anti-Catholic parents is convinced that the Catholic Church is the true church, and so she ardently wishes to join it. However, to do so would mean going directly counter to her parents' wishes and perhaps would result in her being ejected from home. Hence she delays her reception of baptism.

5   A policeman warns a friend that her 17-year-old daughter has been seen several times at a cheap dance hall where there is much immorality. "You needn't worry about her," says the mother; "she is an exceptionally good girl and such places would not harm her. I have such confidence in her that I let her go where she wishes."

6   A college student cheats repeatedly in order to pass his examinations. His professor has warned him against using unfair methods to succeed. The student is worried about the sinfulness of his acts.

7   A senior in high school, ordered by her mother to return from the dance before 1 A.M., comes home at 2:30 A.M. "My mother," she explains, "is very old-fashioned. Maybe she won't speak to me tomorrow, but she'll get over it."

8   A high-school sophomore often provokes her mother to anger because of the way she answers back. At times, too, she blushes at the mistakes in English that her mother makes in the presence of visitors.

9   A college student often violates the school regulation against smoking in the building. Moreover, he avoids attending the Friday Mass for students, though all are obliged to be present. Still he believes that none of this is sinful.

10 A sophomore in college takes a liking to a good Catholic. He often comes to see her but is received coldly by her parents. Without any apparent reason her father forbids her to go out with the young man. May she continue to go out with him?

11 A woman has to take care of her aging father. Often he insists on doing things that might cause him serious injury; for example, he crosses a busy thoroughfare without waiting for someone to help him; he goes outdoors in cold weather without an overcoat. On such occasions she must speak very sharply to him in order to persuade him to obey her orders. She worries at times because she feels that she may have been guilty of irreverence.

Topics for discussion[2]

1   Discuss the Catholic attitude on education.
2   Religion should be an integral part of our public-school education. How could this be accomplished? What are its practical difficulties?

---

[2] Not all the assertions contained in the topics are true. The student is to judge the truth of any assertions made and to explain his decision.

3 Has a citizen the duty of voting?
4 Using fictitious names, describe some actual cases where Catholic students in non-Catholic colleges have given up the practice of their religion and trace the causes of their falling away.
5 A student may be considered to have done his full duty at school if he succeeds in all his examinations.
6 How in a practical way can a college student show his gratitude to his parents by his conduct at home?
7 Comment on the action of a college boarding student who writes home only when in need of more funds.
8 What of the practice of parents who treat their children as "chums"?

Bibliography

Davis, Henry. *Moral and Pastoral Theology,* seventh edition, edited by L. W. Geddes, Vol. 2, pp. 69-140. 4 vols. New York: Sheed and Ward, 1958.

Hull, Ernest R. *Formation of Character.* St. Louis: B. Herder Book Company, 1910.

Jone, Heribert. *Moral Theology,* pp. 126-33. Westminster: Newman Press, 1957.

Moody, J. N. "Church and State." In *Catholic Encyclopedia,* Supplement II, Vol. 18.

Pius XI. *Christian Education of Youth (Rappresentanti in terra).* In Joseph Husslein, editor, *Social Wellsprings,* Vol. 2, pp. 89-121. 2 vols. Milwaukee: Bruce Publishing Company, 1940, 1942.

Pius XII. *Humani generis.* New York: Paulist Press, 1950.

Voight, John J. "Moral and Spiritual Values in Public Education." In *Proceedings of the Eleventh Annual Convention of the Catholic Theological Society of America,* pp. 92-116. New York: Catholic Theological Society of America, 1956.

CHAPTER VIII

The
fifth
commandment

"Thou shalt not kill."
Exodus 20:13

W HEN God, our Creator, placed us in the world, it is evident that He intended that we conserve the life which He imparted to us. It is clear, then, that we have the duty of protecting our body against any forces that would interfere with God's gift of life and health. It is clear, too, that we have the right to preserve our life, and so we also have the right not to be unjustly deprived by others of this gift of God. It is this right that the Fifth Commandment safeguards.

The Fifth Commandment is the first of several prohibitions against unjust injury to one's own or to another's bodily integrity, against violations of rights acquired by marriage, and against violations of one's rights to his earthly possessions. The first of these is a command intended to protect our neighbor's life. Primarily the Fifth Commandment forbids all unjust killing of fellow men. Secondarily it forbids illicit mutilation and wounding, laying violent hands on others, and quarreling, which prepare the way for unjust killing. Killing and mutilation of self are also prohibited by this commandment, because such acts are directly against God's right over us. Finally, the commandment forbids anger, hatred, and jealousy, by which we are moved to do harm or wish harm to others.

SUICIDE

It is never lawful directly to kill oneself on one's own authority. The reason is that destroying life is exercising ownership over life itself. But exercising ownership over life itself is lawful to Him alone who exclusively owns life. Now, God alone exclusively owns life; He is the supreme and exclusive owner of all things that exist. Therefore exercising ownership over life itself is lawful to God alone, and destroying our life is lawful to God alone. One who destroys his life is violating God's right by doing what only God may lawfully do.

TAKING ONE'S LIFE ON GOD'S AUTHORITY

We have stated that it is never lawful directly to kill oneself *on one's own authority.* Clearly it is lawful to kill oneself or another on God's authority, for then the exclusive owner of life gives leave to exercise an act of ownership over life. Hence we can understand how it was that the holy patriarch Abraham, in obedience to God's command, so unhesitatingly prepared to slay his son as a sacrificial offering. (See Genesis, Chapter 22.) In the case of some of the martyrs who, when condemned to be burned, are said to have rushed into the flames of their own accord, it is commonly believed that they did so in response to an inspiration received from God. History, however, appears to present few fully authenticated instances of this kind. God may have sent death to many who longed for it, but He has done nothing to create the impression that impulses toward self-destruction frequently come from Him.

Probably it is allowable for a criminal, justly condemned to death, to be his own executioner when the state so appoints him.

INDIRECT KILLING OF ONESELF

"Directly to kill" means to intend death either as the end of my act or as the means for obtaining the end in view. Death would be intended as the *end* of the act if one who longed for death as synonymous with total oblivion were to blow his brains out. Death would then be the purpose of the act, not the means to an end. Death would be intended as a *means* to an end if one trapped on the top floor of a burning building were to shoot himself in order to avoid the intense suffering of being consumed by fire. Death here is intended directly as the means of avoiding the torture of the flames.

If, on the contrary, a soldier attempts to approach and set fire to an enemy powder magazine, he does not necessarily directly intend his own death. Though he foresees that he cannot escape alive, still he merely permits his own destruction. He would prefer to return alive if possible. His objective is inflicting grave injury on the enemy, and to accomplish this he permits (but does not desire) his own destruction. Another example of the indirect killing of self would be the action of soldiers in World War II who strapped dynamite around their waists and flung themselves at enemy tanks.

MUTILATION

Mutilation is an action (an excision or the equivalent) by which an organic function or the use of a member of the body is partially or wholly destroyed; for example, to amputate one's hand, to pluck out an eye. The following do not constitute mutilations within our meaning of the term: stripping off skin (for example, for grafting), a blood transfusion, face lifting. The use of these measures, however, is not licit without a justifying reason.

It has always been recognized by theologians that a man has the right to sacrifice members of his body for the well-being of the whole body. The most obvious cases are those in which death would follow unless an amputation or operation were performed. Lesser reasons than danger of death also justify mutilation. If a serious pathological condition can be removed by an operation, there is a sufficient reason for the operation even though without it there would be no danger of death, provided the evil to be removed is in proportion to the seriousness of the operation and the success of the operation is reasonably certain.

It should be pointed out that the organ removed or suppressed in an operation or other mutilation need not itself be diseased. In certain cases of cancer, for instance, a healthy organ stimulates the growth of the cancer and may be removed or suppressed in order to stop the growth of the cancer.

In some extreme cases it happens that a person amputates one of his own members. There have been examples in shipwrecks and fires where a person amputated a leg or an arm in order to escape from the wreckage in which he was pinned. Obviously this is simply a somewhat gruesome application of the principle enunciated above.

STERILIZATION

Sterilization means depriving the body of the power of either begetting or of bearing children. It consists in rendering the faculties of generation unfruitful. This effect may be accomplished by the surgeon's knife, by X ray, or by intravenous injections. In general, the operation that is involved, especially in the male, is slight, but the loss of the power of procreation is grave. Sterilization may be direct or indirect. Sterilization is direct if it is done in order to take away the power of procreation; it is indirect if done to remedy a pathological condition. We will consider direct sterilization first and then take up a few special cases of indirect sterilization, also called therapeutic sterilization.

DIRECT STERILIZATION

Punitive sterilization is an operation performed on criminals as a punishment for their crimes. This type of punishment is advised by some for certain types, such as the habitual sex offender. Eugenic sterilization has for its object preventing the propagation of subnormal offspring (that is, the mentally defective or the diseased). Eugenists contend that certain physical or mental defects and certain evil tendencies such as alcoholism are either directly transmitted by parents to the child or at least are acquired by the child through its early environment. The defect causing the greatest concern is feeblemindedness.

THE MORALITY OF PUNITIVE STERILIZATION

The licitness of this operation is disputed by moralists. Strong arguments are alleged both for and against the licitness of punitive sterilization. Those who defend the operation argue that the state has the right to decapitate for grave crime and that it must have the right to inflict on a grave offender a lesser punishment—mutilation. Sterilization is a real punishment, for it deprives the criminal of a physical good—his corporal integrity and the precious power of begetting or bearing children. Those who condemn the operation as illicit argue that sterilization is not a real punishment, since little if any suffering is involved. Besides, sterilization offers the culprit an opportunity for wanton indulgence with no possibility of undesired consequences that may follow upon pregnancy and the need to care for children. A penalty may be inflicted only if it is deemed psychologically efficacious to prevent subjects from violating the law. Sterilization is not efficacious in this. Today criminologists agree that sterilization is not an effective penalty.

The conclusion here proposed is as follows. Theoretically, the state may sterilize criminals if sterilization is a genuine punishment. In practice, however, sterilization seems clearly to encourage rather than to deter the sex offender in his crime. Hence punitive sterilization for sex crimes is not licit. Consequently surgeons may not perform such an operation when it is inflicted as a punishment.

THE MORALITY OF EUGENIC STERILIZATION

Eugenists endeavor to justify the practice of eugenic sterilization by the following reasons:

1. Defectives are a source of disease, misery, and crime, and so the state is justified in using sterilization to prevent these undesirable members of society from coming into the world. Only healthy citizens make for the good of the state.

2. Defectives are a great burden to taxpayers, who must provide institutions for their care. Sterilization would eliminate the necessity of such taxes.

To eugenists who thus defend the righteousness of their cause we admit that their objectives are very praiseworthy, but we ask: "What of the means you advocate for accomplishing these objectives?" Promoting a healthy citizenry and lessening the taxpayers' burden—these are good *ends*, but the *means* through which eugenists would achieve them are evil. Eugenic sterilization, for the following reasons, is immoral.

The state does not have supreme power over its citizens, but only such power as is conformable with the accomplishment of its end. The state has the right to punish adequately and even to execute duly condemned criminals. This power is necessary for accomplishing the purpose of its existence; that is, for maintaining peace and right order in the community. But the state has no right to kill or to mutilate an innocent man. To give the state such a right would be to empower it to use one human being as it willed for the benefit of others—a thing contrary to natural justice. The individual as such is antecedent to the state by priority of nature, and so certain rights of the individual are prior to those of the state. Life and bodily integrity are given man before he enters society and he does not lose the right to them because he becomes a member of society. Every citizen, then, has from the natural law an inalienable right to his life and bodily integrity. The law may interfere with this sacred right only when a man has, through some serious crime, subjected himself to the higher right of the state to punish evildoers. Now, a man has not become guilty of any crime because he is mentally defective or physically diseased. Hence the state may not punish him because of his misfortune. The state may not mutilate an innocent citizen.

We quote that scholarly pontiff, Pope Pius XI, on the subject of eugenic sterilization:

> Public magistrates have no direct power over the bodies of their subjects; therefore, where no crime has taken place and there is no cause present for grave punishment, they can never directly harm, or tamper with the integrity of the body, either for the reasons of eugenics or for any other reason.[1]

STERILIZATION AND FEEBLEMINDEDNESS

Sterilization, as we have seen, is never allowable for eugenic purposes. To employ it to try to rid the human race of the mentally deficient (that is, morons, imbeciles, and idiots) is to use an evil means to accomplish a praiseworthy end. But even if sterilization were allowed, would it actually prove successful in purifying the race to any great extent? We shall here record some of the findings of authorities in this matter. These data show us the expected results of sterilization, interpreted in a very favorable light. Some very highly esteemed authorities would deny that

---

[1] Pius XI, *Christian Marriage in Our Day (Casti connubii)*, in Joseph Husslein, editor, *Social Wellsprings*, Vol. 2, pp. 148-49. 2 vols. Milwaukee: Bruce Publishing Company, 1940, 1942.

even the physically good effects here mentioned, comparatively insignificant though they are, would *certainly* follow.

1. About 50 per cent of the cases of feeblemindedness arise from nonhereditary causes. This 50 per cent would in nowise be affected by sterilization.

2. The remaining 50 per cent of the cases may be attributed to hereditary causes. Feebleminded offspring come from two sources: from feebleminded parents and from normal parents who are carriers of feeblemindedness. If all the feebleminded parents were prevented by means of sterilization from procreating children, the procreation of feeblemindedness by the second group would not be affected.

3. Of the cases due to hereditary causes only a small fraction come from feebleminded parents. Sterilization of this fraction would not appreciably reduce feeblemindedness in the generations to come. According to the carefully considered calculations of sound authorities, if the entire feebleminded group were sterilized, it would take at least 2,000 years of constant sterilization to reduce feeblemindedness from a proportion of 1 per 1,000 to 1 per 10,000.

INDIRECT OR THERAPEUTIC STERILIZATION

Because of the presence of cancer or for some other reason one of the generative organs may need to be removed or to be rendered inactive as a means of preserving a patient's life or of saving him from acute pain or from grave inconvenience. This type of sterilization is called therapeutic because its purpose is the restoration of health. It is called indirect because the thing that is directly intended is not the sterilization itself but the removal of a threat to life or health which may licitly be removed for a sufficient reason.

Therapeutic sterilization is licit when a competent and conscientious physician declares that it is necessary. Two things, however, should be pointed out. Because patients or the members of their families may bring pressure to bear upon a physician in order to induce him to perform a sterilizing operation, the physician must be careful to avoid performing the operation because of the wishes of others and without sufficient regard for what is medically necessary. The "grave inconvenience" that sterilization is intended to remove should not merely be the inconvenience of bearing another child. Second, a sterilizing procedure must not be used if some less drastic remedy is available.

TEMPORARY STERILIZATION

In recent years certain drugs have been developed which render a woman temporarily infertile. The use of such drugs would be judged according to principles already enunciated. If the drugs are used in order to produce infertility and avoid pregnancy, their use constitutes a direct temporary sterilization. If they are used to remedy some pathological condition they might be licit: if the condition is serious and there is a proportion between the good to be accomplished (remedy of the pathological condition) and the evil which is foreseen but not intended (infertility), their use would be licit; if these conditions are not fulfilled, their use would be illicit.

THE DUTY OF CARING FOR THE BODY

Everyone is obliged to use the ordinary means for preserving his life. When God gave us a living body He indicated that He wished us to keep that body alive; otherwise, why would He have given us the gift of life? To fail to use the ordinary means for preserving life is thus going counter to God's wishes and is virtually equivalent to committing suicide.

We must use *ordinary means* to preserve our life. There is as a rule no obligation to use *extraordinary means* to keep alive, for God surely does not exact from us what is beyond the ordinary power of men in general. If we had to employ very difficult and extraordinary means to preserve our lives, we would be held to a rule of conduct which would exceed the normal strength of men in general. Hence one would not be obliged to use the extraordinary means mentioned in the following cases:

EXAMPLE 1. The life of a very old man could be preserved for a few months by continual blood transfusions, intravenous feeding, and oxygen. He has very little money and the cost would be borne by a son who has a growing family. The son's children would be deprived of the type of education he thinks they should have if he spent the money to preserve his father's life. There is no obligation in this case to use these extraordinary means.

EXAMPLE 2. A woman could be cured by submitting to a very painful operation which involves no danger to life. If no anesthetic could be

147

given, she need not undergo this operation, for it would be an extraordinary means. Today, however, anesthetics prevent all such pain, and so ordinarily she would be bound to have the operation.

EXAMPLE 3. A man with a serious heart condition could perhaps prolong his life for many years by having a particular operation. The operation, however, is quite dangerous and he might die on the operating table. Hence he is not obliged to submit to an operation that would put his life in such immediate danger.

At times one may be bound in charity to one's dependents or to one's fellow citizens to employ extraordinary means to preserve one's life. In order that such an obligation be present, two conditions must be fulfilled:

1. One is necessary to one's family or to one's fellow men.
2. The success of the extraordinary means is very probable.

EXAMPLE. The father of a large family is told by doctors that, unless he moves to Denver or to some similar place, he will die within six months. Such a change of residence would entail great hardship for him; but if he dies, his family will be unprovided for. Charity in such a case might easily oblige him to move to a better climate.

The decision as to when a means is ordinary and when extraordinary is often a very difficult one. Usually several factors are involved and a decision as to the obligation of using or not using the means in question depends on the weighing of all the factors. The age of the person, the seriousness of the operation or treatment, the probability of success, the pain involved, the obligations of the person to others, and many other factors must be considered. It should not be surprising, therefore, if there is some disagreement among theologians in the application of the general principles to particular cases. Some take a rather strict position and uphold the obligation to use a means unless it is clearly extraordinary; others are more liberal and would classify as extraordinary means which would be considered ordinary by the first group. There is some diversity in different Catholic hospitals in this same regard. Following the principle of liberty which affirms that an obligation is not to be imposed unless it is certain, we can say that the faithful are free to follow the advice of a competent moral theologian in a particular case, even though they might be advised differently by some other competent theologian.

Whether there is question of a patient who is sincerely devoted to his family or of members of the family who must care for the patient, it is a consolation to know that all possible means for preserving life were used; but there are other human factors which might make the acceptance of death a better thing than the preservation of life.

SHORTENING ONE'S LIFE

We must carefully distinguish between the action (1) of one who does something expressly in order to shorten his life and (2) of one who regrets that the length of his life will be lessened because of some action that he performs.

1. Directly to intend the shortening of life is sinful. For example, though other good jobs are available, a man who is tired of living goes to work in a quicksilver mine in order to shorten his life. The degree of sinfulness depends on the extent of the injury intended. If one directly intends to shorten one's life notably, the fault is grave. To administer a fatal blow to oneself or another, though death is imminent from sickness or from some other cause, is always gravely wrong.

2. Not to intend directly but merely to permit the shortening of one's life may be sinful or sinless. The decision depends upon whether the conditions necessary for the principle of the twofold effect are verified or not. For a proportionate reason one may allow his health to be exposed to serious injury. Hence though their work endangers or will probably shorten their life, the following will be justified in performing their required duties:

   a) workers in paint factories, glassworks, steel mills, certain types of foundries, or in sulphur mines;

   b) steeple jacks;

   c) priests, physicians, and nurses administering to those who have contagious diseases.

If one does not have a proportionate reason and the act either involves proximate danger of death or notably shortens one's life, the sin is grave.

> EXAMPLE. A gourmand is warned by competent physicians that, unless he stops eating meat, he will die within a few months. Abstinence from meat will prolong his life for several years. He keeps on eating large quantities of meat. The sin of injuring his health is in this case grave.

THE OBLIGATION OF SOBRIETY

Sobriety is a virtue that moderates one's appetite concerning the pleasures of strong drink. Sobriety makes for man's perfection, since it leads him to exercise due moderation. The pleasures of intoxicating liquors are often very alluring, and as a consequence the practice of moderation is not always easy. It is well known how often drinking too freely of alcoholic beverages has led to temptations and sins. "Wine drunken with excess raiseth quarrels, and wrath, and many ruins. . . . Wine hath destroyed very many" (Ecclesiasticus 31:38, 30).

The virtue of sobriety, then, should be carefully cultivated. This virtue is especially important for young persons because it serves to aid them in keeping passions in check and in developing self-control. Women in particular should strive to acquire this virtue, for experience shows the grave dangers to which a woman addicted to drink exposes herself. Alcoholic beverages induce a happy, carefree attitude. Immoderate drinking causes inhibitions and self-restraint to disappear and one's sense of modesty and self-respect to be forgotten.

EFFECTS OF OVERINDULGENCE

Excessive drinking of alcoholic beverages is attended by quite a number of undesirable effects, of which the following are the most serious:

1. It ordinarily leads to earlier death, since it may cause acute and fatal alcoholism, tends to render one more susceptible to disease, and often influences one rashly to expose oneself to grave physical dangers.

2. It opens the way to some mental diseases.

3. It lessens physical endurance.

4. It is known to weaken to a serious extent one's judgment, will, and sense of responsibility.

5. It often results in neglect of one's dependents, waste of needed funds, unemployment, broken homes, and disgrace for oneself and one's family.

Those who tend to underestimate the effects of excessive drinking should investigate modern psychological and sociological studies. It is true that excessive drinking is often a symptom of some other psychological disturbance, but the excessive drinking adds new problems and has many harmful effects on the individual, his family, and society in general. The fact that there are 4,000,000 alcoholics in the United States today should make us realize the gravity of the problem and should discourage us from creating conditions in which people, and especially young people, are under pressure to drink.

THE MORALITY OF DRINKING

To partake with moderation of alcoholic liquors in itself involves no sin. It is only excessive drinking that is sinful. The degree of sinfulness depends upon how this excess is known to affect this particular drinker. We may evaluate the gravity of the fault as follows:

1. It is *grave matter* if it is foreseen that this drink will cause me to lose the use of my senses or will put me in such a state that I am no longer able to distinguish between right and wrong.

> EXAMPLE. A salesman knows that this glass of whisky will render him unconscious. Nevertheless, to celebrate a big sale he made that afternoon he drains the glass.

It would also be a grave matter to get an innocent person intoxicated by deceit such as concealing the alcoholic content of a drink or "loading" a drink. For instance, a group of college students might get an innocent freshman girl drunk as a joke. Their action would be a grave sin against charity unless they did not realize its seriousness.

2. It is *venial matter* if one has reason for believing that this amount of drinking, though it is actually excessive, will neither deprive him of the use of his senses nor of the power to distinguish right from wrong.

> EXAMPLE. A boy takes a drink of wine, though he knows that it will cause him some dizziness. He is sure, however, that he will remain conscious and be aware of the morality of what he is doing.

3. Driving while somewhat under the influence of drink may involve some sinfulness. Drivers should realize that strong drink, besides slowing up one's normal reactions in an emergency, tends to make one careless or even reckless. Those who become exceedingly cautious when they know that they have drunk too much constitute only a small minority. Perhaps one has sinned only slightly in taking the liquor; but in some cases, by driving when one has not normal control of one's powers, one can be guilty of grave sin in seriously jeopardizing one's own life and the lives of others.

4. It is decidedly praiseworthy, and may under certain circumstances be an obligation of charity, to abstain from drinking

in the presence of one who we have reason for thinking would go to excess as a result of our example.

EXAMPLE. A businessman does not in the least tend to go to excess in drinking alcoholic beverages. One of his friends, however, has a decided weakness in this matter. The former often abstains from strong drink when out with his friend. His action is especially praiseworthy, since he will thus make it easier for his friend to avoid the occasion of sin and set him a good example.

5. Moderate drinking is good and can make social life more pleasant. Our Lord and His apostles certainly drank wine at times. Many good Catholic families have the custom of drinking wine with their meals. On the other hand, the Church encourages those who abstain from strong drink for a supernatural motive. The latter should not condemn those who use liquor moderately.

CARELESS DRIVING

The obligation not to endanger one's own life or the lives of others without a sufficient reason applies to all activities but is especially applicable to driving. Many serious accidents happen because people fail to take even the normal precautions. Their neglect may be due to excessive drinking or to some emotional factor. Younger people may tend to drive fast and take chances "just for the fun of it" or because they subconsciously wish to show resentment toward society. Older people do so because of frustration or anger or simply because they lack patience. Others begin to drive or continue driving even though they do not have the ability to drive safely. It would be a humiliation for them to admit their incapacity or very inconvenient for them to have to depend on someone else. Careless driving is almost always a manifestation of the lack of one or more fundamental virtues.

Parents have an obligation to see that their children are properly instructed before allowing them to drive. It would be most praiseworthy for them also to encourage organized campaigns for the improvement of driving habits.

Driving is an opportunity for the practice of many virtues. In addition to those absolutely essential for careful driving (prudence, patience, humility, meekness), it offers many chances for the practice of charity and resignation. Allowing someone to cross the street or slowing up so that another motorist can get on the main street may bring honks and even abuse from the man behind you, but it is a real act of charity and often offers an opportunity for accepting unjust abuse. Our forefathers developed many virtues by overcoming the hardships of their environment; modern traffic offers us a similar opportunity.

The bishops of Australia thought the problem of careless driving so important that they devoted to it their Annual Social Justice Statement for 1958. Their statement was reprinted in the *Catholic Mind*, Volume 56, pages 554-66, November-December 1958. It contains an analysis of the moral principles involved in driving and points out evils in much driving today: it is contrary to justice because it needlessly endangers the lives and property of others (we may add that the fact that insurance covers damages does not change the injustice); it is contrary to charity and temperance (especially when drinking is involved); it is a manifestation of arrogance, selfishness, and discourtesy. The statement also points out that others besides the driver have responsibility: passengers and pedestrians must not act in such a way as to occasion an accident. The statement ends with the "Driver's Prayer":

> Lord, lead me today in safety through the paths of this busy world. Help me to keep my mind and my eyes on the road while my heart rests in Thee. Let me see in each of those who walk or ride an image of Thee, dear Lord. Keep me in your gracious care so that all my journeying may lead at last to Thee. Amen.

A prayer for safe driving may seem strange to us. But the use of such a prayer will not only bring God's blessings; it will also have the salutary effect of making us realize that safe driving is a moral responsibility and that more than mere violation of a penal law is involved in careless driving.

CAPITAL PUNISHMENT

The state may take the life of duly condemned criminals if this maximum penalty is deemed necessary for the common peace and for the security of life and property. The reason is that the purpose of the existence of the state is to maintain social order and to protect the rights of its citizens. In order to procure this end the state may use the means necessary. God, the author of human society, could not wish public authority to exist and, at the same time, not confer on it the right to employ such measures as are necessary for its conservation and proper functioning. Without severe penalties the rights of citizens would be in constant jeopardy, and as a consequence the state may impose such penalties in order to protect its citizens. The inspired law of the Israelites confirms this right of public authority. "He that striketh and killeth a man, dying let him die" (Leviticus 24:17).

Police officers may, in case of urgent necessity, be given leave by public authorities to shoot on sight a dangerous public enemy who is certainly guilty of a crime punishable with death. However, this is an extreme case and should be looked upon as a last resort. Police officers may shoot a fleeing bandit in order to prevent his escape. They may also shoot when making a legitimate arrest, whether the act of shooting is necessary for effecting the arrest or as a means of protecting their own lives. Their purpose should be to subdue the one whom it is their duty to arrest, not to kill him. If circumstances are such that a shot in the arm or leg would be sufficient, they should not aim at a more vital part of the body. But since they can frequently expect a direct attack when they are performing their duty, they are not required to endanger their lives by being overcautious in regard to the part of the body at which they aim.

DEFENSE AGAINST UNJUST ATTACK

We have at times the right to use force, even a deathblow, against an unjust aggressor. Our right to life involves the right to use the means necessary to protect our life, provided such means do not violate the rights of others. In the case of unjust aggression the use of force and even of a deathblow may be the only means of saving our life. The rights of others are not thereby violated, for the assailant's right to live is suspended during his unjust attack. Moreover, he can easily protect his life by merely ceasing from the attack.

WHEN FORCE MAY LICITLY BE USED

We have, then, at times the right to use force against an unjust aggressor. Such a right is present if the following conditions are verified:

1. Recourse to civil authority must be impossible. The common good demands that as a rule the state alone use physical compulsion, for if any private citizen could at will employ force in

defending his rights, the peace and order of the community would be disturbed.

2. The attack must be actual or immediately imminent (for example, the assailant is reaching for his revolver or has his knife raised to strike me or is ready to kill me on sight). It is wrong to kill[2] before the attack, for there is grave danger that one may use force against many purely imaginary attacks. To allow the use of force against attacks that are merely possible would inevitably lead to grave abuses. It is not permissible to kill after the attack is over, for then defense is too late and the act of killing would constitute revenge.

3. The attack must be unjust. A robber, justly fired upon by police officers, may not kill them to protect his own life.

4. The force employed must be proportionate to the loss threatened and must not exceed what is necessary. Killing is not allowed if wounding would suffice for proper defense; wounding is not permitted if disarming the adversary or summoning help would be enough.

WHEN KILLING AN UNJUST AGGRESSOR IS LICIT

In order to justify killing an unjust aggressor the loss threatened must be one's life, a grave mutilation, or an object of great value. The sum threatened could be either of great value in itself or of grave moment to the owner because of his poverty and need. If the stolen property can be recovered later by recourse to civil authority or in some other way, killing would not be permitted. Chastity, as a precious possession, may also be defended by these extreme measures against the attack of an unjust aggressor. Even if the unjust assailant is intoxicated or insane, I may use proportionate force against him, for my right to defend myself is the same. It is not based on the sin of the attacker, and so, even though the assailant attacks inculpably, I may justly defend myself against him.

Ordinarily one would not be *obliged* to use this right to defend oneself, for one is bound merely to use ordinary means to

---

[2] When in this discussion we speak of killing we understand the use of means of self-defense that will probably or even certainly result in death. The one who is being attacked cannot aim at some nicely chosen part of the body where a wound will merely render the attacker temporarily impotent. He must effectively subdue the attacker, and this may mean that he must strike at some vital part. His purpose, however, must be to subdue, not to kill.

preserve one's life and the use of violence is considered an extraordinary means. If, however, one is needed by one's family or by one's fellow citizens, one would have an obligation in charity to protect oneself.

What I may do for my own self-defense I may also do in safeguarding the rights of others. At times one must go to another's defense. As we have seen (page 45), we are obliged *by charity* to go to the assistance of one in danger of death, even at the cost of grave inconvenience to ourselves. Hence we may use whatever force is necessary to save an innocent man from one who is attempting to murder him. At other times one must *in justice* protect another who is being unjustly attacked. For example, a policeman is required because of his office to defend a citizen against one who is attacking him.

MURDER

The unjust killing of an innocent person is murder. Directly to intend killing an innocent person is allowed neither to a private citizen nor to the state, and this not even in order to secure the common good. This is evident both from reason and from the divine law, for:

1. God has supreme and exclusive ownership over human lives, and so He is the only one who has the right to allow men to kill other men. He imparts to civil authority the right to kill criminals only when this is necessary for achieving the end of the state.

2. God Himself framed the following as one of the laws for the judges of the Chosen People: "The innocent and just person thou shalt not put to death" (Exodus 23:7).

MERCY KILLING

Mercy killing is administering (ordinarily at the victim's own request) an easy, painless death to one who is suffering from an incurable and perhaps agonizing ailment. Mercy killing is also called euthanasia (that is, "happy death"). The reason given in favor of mercy killing is that, with the advance of civilization, greater sensitiveness to the sufferings of others has been developed and that the law which condemns euthanasia as murder, framed in an age when indifference to human suffering was normal, is now out of date. Public sympathy tends to defend euthanasia, and some juries have refused to convict the mercy killer.

THE MORALITY OF MERCY KILLING

However, no matter what sentimentalists contend, euthanasia is always a grave crime and should be called by its proper name; that is, mercy murder. It is wrong for the following reasons:

1. God alone has the ownership of human life. In euthanasia the killer assumes the right of ownership over life, and so the crime committed is either murder or suicide. This is the fundamental reason that euthanasia is immoral.

2. Euthanasia takes no account of man's supernatural life, disregarding the value of pain and suffering in storing up merit and in shortening one's purgatory. Advocates of euthanasia ignore Christ's words, "If anyone wishes to come after me, let him . . . take up his cross daily" (Luke 9:23).

3. The practice of euthanasia would greatly lessen confidence in doctors, for the patient who was gravely ill might readily fear that his physician would judge his case incurable and so administer poison to end his suffering.

4. We may mention here a decision of the Holy Office. The Sacred Congregation of the Holy Office of Rome was asked: "Is it legal upon the mandate of authority directly to kill those who, although not having committed any crimes deserving of death, are yet, because of psychic or physical defects, unable to be useful to the nation, but rather are considered a burden to its vigor and strength?" The congregation's answer to the question was: "No, because it is contrary to the natural and positive divine law" (December 1940).

FETICIDE

It is never allowed directly to kill an infant in the womb, even though the life of the mother is in imminent danger. The reason is that any direct killing of an innocent person is murder, and a living fetus is an innocent person. Hence, no matter how noble may be the purpose of the operating surgeon, this means of saving the mother may never be used. The natural law, then, forbids craniotomy, decapitation, embryotomy, and evisceration of a living fetus or of a fetus that is *probably* alive.

ABORTION

Abortion consists in expelling an immature living fetus from the mother's womb. The fetus must, first of all, be living; if it is certainly dead, its removal is not only permissible but ordinarily necessary. Second, the fetus must be immature, by which is meant that it cannot live outside the womb, or that it is not viable. In ordinary circumstances a fetus is considered to be viable at the end of the twenty-eighth week of gestation or at the end of the twenty-sixth week if the child is to be born in a hospital where it can be placed in an incubator.

It is not abortion to hasten the birth of a viable fetus, but it is never licit for any reason whatsoever directly or indirectly to procure or intend an abortion. Such an action is murder, for it means removing the fetus from the only place where it can now live. Hence it is gravely wrong to procure an abortion, even though one is prompted by a praiseworthy motive.

> EXAMPLE. A doctor performs an abortion on a girl who has been criminally assaulted, so that by means of this operation he may save her good name, or on a mother whom giving birth to a baby would undoubtedly kill.[3] The end intended is good but the means chosen (that is, abortion) to accomplish this end is evil.

It is lawful, however, to extract from the mother a womb that is dangerously diseased (for example, cancerous), even though because of this operation the enclosed nonviable fetus will certainly die. This is not the same as direct abortion, though the effect for the fetus is the same. Here we have an application of the principle of the twofold effect:

1. The action (the removal of the womb) is good—it consists in excising an infected part of the body.

2. The good effect (the saving of the mother's life) is not procured by means of the evil effect (the death of the fetus).

3. There is sufficient reason for permitting the unsought evil effect to follow.

---

[3] There is very strong medical opinion to the effect that it can never be said that an expectant mother will "undoubtedly die" unless an abortion is performed.

4. The evil effect is not intended in itself, but is merely permitted as a necessary consequence of the good effect.

The womb belongs to the mother just as completely after the pregnancy as before. If the fetus were not present, she would clearly be justified in having removed a part of her body that was threatening her life. The presence of the fetus does not deprive her of this right.

DUELING

A duel is the meeting of two parties by private agreement to fight with weapons in themselves deadly. The natural law forbids exposing to grave danger, without just cause, one's own life or bodily integrity or that of another. Hence dueling partakes of the malice of both suicide and homicide. Dueling is not a case of justifiable self-defense, for the following reasons:

1. There is no attack occurring at the time, for the injury has already been inflicted.

2. The injured party may obtain satisfaction through legal or other channels.

3. Recourse to deadly weapons is obviously powerless to vindicate one's honor. In a duel the insult because of which one combatant challenged the other is not retracted.

4. Dueling is not an apt means of proving one's innocence, for the wicked may be more skillful than the good in the use of the weapon selected.

The Catholic Church brands dueling as a grievous crime and punishes very severely both the duelist and those who assist in such combats. This condemnation and punishment of the Church include student duels, in which the participants have only the face exposed to attack. Such duels were engaged in at some German universities.

PRIZE FIGHTING

The morality of modern prize fighting has been seriously questioned by a number of theologians. Medical studies have indicated that brain injury results inevitably from repeated blows to the head. The aim of the modern prize fighter is to win by a knockout, and a knockout is almost always achieved by head blows. Some theologians, therefore, argue that modern prize fighting is forbidden because the means (a knockout) to attain the end (victory) are evil: in order to win, a fighter must will to cause damage to the brain of his opponent. Ignorance may excuse from subjective guilt, but objectively there is serious matter. This damage could be justified only on the grounds of a proportionate good, since one may cause physical evil in certain cases for a proportionate good. In the case of prize fighting there is no proportionate good; money, fame, and entertainment do not justify the serious physical harm done to the neighbor. Prize fighting is also attacked from the viewpoint of the subjective attitudes of the participants and the spectators and of the effects which it has on them. It is contended that prize fighting encourages brutality in both the participants and the spectators.

In answer to these objections it is maintained that there is sufficient reason to allow physical harm in prize fighting, that it does not involve any more danger than many other sports, and that spectators are more interested in skill than in brutal slugging. Even granting that these arguments have some validity, they would not answer the principal objection: in other sports injuries are accidental—that is, they are not directly intended; in prize fighting the injuries are directly intended.

WAR

War is a conflict of force between independent nations, states, or tribes. The evils of war have always been great, but the disaster and destruction wrought by modern warfare are beyond words to describe. Still war is not intrinsically wrong. Given certain conditions, it could be justified even today, for the act of waging war is in itself indifferent and the evils resulting are merely permitted for a proportionately good reason. The conditions necessary for a just war are:

1. There must be actual or imminent violation of the nation's rights (for example, its independence or vital supplies are unjustly attacked).

2. All other means to obtain justice (for example, diplomatic protests and trade embargoes) have failed. If it is clearly foreseen that such measures would meet with no success, there is no obligation to try them, for one need not do what is useless.

3. Abstaining from conflict will entail greater evils for the cause of the nation than engaging in the war.

If war would bring greater harm than good to the wronged state, it is not justified. Under such conditions the state's welfare is better safeguarded by tolerating wrongs until they can be peacefully repaired.

EVIL METHODS OF WARFARE

The natural law and the divine law are still in force even during time of actual war. Hence the following are to be condemned as sinful:

1. Killing hostages, captives, or those trying to surrender.
2. Direct slaughter of noncombatants (chaplains, hospital attendants, civilians not engaged in promoting the war).
3. Broadcasting lies, slander, and any material that is unreasonably provocative.
4. Directly destroying buildings without any effect on the outcome of the war (for example, bombing a home for the aged of the Little Sisters of the Poor).

However, it is lawful:

1. To bomb military objectives in cities even though many civilians will indirectly be killed.
2. To sink a hospital ship that is carrying munitions or other supplies to the enemy.

THE USE OF ATOMIC AND HYDROGEN WEAPONS

There is probably no moral problem today which causes greater uneasiness for ethicians and theologians than that of the use of certain extremely destructive weapons of modern warfare. The responsibility in making a decision on their licitness is staggering. We stated above that if war, even though successful, would bring about greater harm than good, it would be illicit. The question arises as to whether a modern war in which atomic, and especially hydrogen, bombs were used would not be ruled out because the harm done would outweigh any conceivable good to be gained by the war. A few theologians take this position. All agree that it would be immoral to start such a war even for serious and just reasons. The real problem concerns defensive war.

Again, there is agreement that even in a defensive war weapons whose destructive power is uncontrollable could not be used.

This would certainly apply to the C-bomb; that is, a hydrogen bomb enclosed in cobalt. It would also apply to the use of hydrogen and atomic weapons to such an extent that a large percentage of the civilian population would be annihilated. On the other hand, it is agreed by most theologians that atomic or hydrogen weapons could be used against strictly military objectives such as a fleet of warships. There is disagreement on the use of such weapons for the bombing of industrial centers. The number of noncombatants who would be killed is so great that some theologians hold there is never a sufficient reason for such bombing. Others hold that, if there is no direct intention of killing noncombatants (their death is foreseen but not directly intended), a country in a justifiable war of self-defense could use atomic weapons on important industrial centers.

It is not the purpose of this book to settle problems so involved and complicated that even the most eminent theologians hesitate to present a solution as absolutely certain. Those who wish to pursue the question further may do so by reading the articles referred to at the end of the chapter. Further discussion may make the position of the Church clearer. For the present we can say that not all use of atomic weapons is forbidden but that their use is limited to strictly military targets and, according to some, to the destruction of a few very important industrial centers. In all that has been said it is presupposed, of course, that the nation which has been unjustly attacked has available no other means of self-defense that promise to prove effective.

CITIZENS' DUTIES IN TIME OF WAR

The duties of citizens during time of war may be summarized as follows:

1. During a just war a citizen must aid his country to gain victory, but he may not voluntarily provide help if his nation's cause is evidently unjust.

2. Those who are conscripted or who were already in military service when war was declared may, if they doubt about the justice of the war, assume that their nation is right. They may make this assumption because they do not have complete knowledge of the facts on which the declaration of war was based.

3. Volunteers must investigate in order to ascertain whether or not their country's cause is just. A volunteer freely chooses to

do battle, and so he himself must make sure that he is on the right side.

4. The conscientious objector must follow his sincere convictions in this matter. Hence if he cannot persuade himself of the licitness of war, he must abstain from active participation in it.

ANGER, ENVY, AND HATRED

Anger is a desire to take revenge upon another, to inflict harm on him as a punishment. Anger is either holy or unholy, its character depending upon the extent to which it conforms to the laws of justice and charity.

SINLESS ANGER

Sinless anger is a desire for vengeance, usually accompanied by a duly moderated display of displeasure, which is prompted by zeal for justice, honor to God, or some other good end.

EXAMPLE 1. The anger of Moses mentioned in the Book of Exodus, Chapter 32, verses 15, 19, was justified. "And Moses returned from the mount, carrying the two tables of the testimony in his hand, written on both sides. . . . And when he came nigh to the camp he saw the calf, and the dances: and being very angry, he threw the tables out of his hand and broke them at the foot of the mount."

EXAMPLE 2. A father has frequently warned his son about the sinfulness of lying and has often chastised him. He may be justly angered by the boy's refusal to mend his ways.

SINFUL ANGER

Sinful anger is an immoderate desire for vengeance. Desire for vengeance is immoderate:

1. If I wish the undeserving to be punished.

2. If I wish the guilty to be punished excessively.

3. If I wish the punishment to be meted out in a manner that is unlawful.

4. If I wish the punishment in order to vent my spite.

DEGREES OF GRAVITY IN ANGER

The sin of anger is not always equally grave. We may distinguish as follows:

1. It is *grave matter* if one sincerely desire (a) grave punishment for one who does not deserve such severe chastisement; or

(b) for the guilty, gravely excessive punishment or punishment to be inflicted in a gravely illicit way; or (c) punishment desired because of genuine hatred of another.

2. It is *slight matter* (a) if one desires but slight revenge or (b) if one merely allows oneself to become unduly worked up by angry thoughts. This type of anger, however, may easily lead to grave sins of blasphemy, cursing, and the like, into which one foresees that he will fall when he is thus aroused.

REMEDIES AGAINST THE HABIT OF ANGER

The sin of anger is one into which we may easily and repeatedly fall. A distinction should be made between those who have a convenient temper—that is, one they lose when it is to their advantage—and those who have a natural tendency to anger. The latter may have great difficulty in overcoming the habit of anger, even when they have a real desire to do so. The following remedies will help to overcome the habit, especially if used over a long period of time:

1. Meditation on the beauty of the virtues of meekness and patience as exemplified in Christ and the saints.

2. Recognizing our own faults and the punishment which we justly deserve from God for the many things in which we offend Him daily.

3. Thinking over the evil results of anger (for example, blasphemy, cursing, quarreling).

4. Promptness in resisting the first risings of anger.

5. Cultivating the habit of remaining silent for a few moments when provoked.

6. Constant prayer for help to overcome this habit.

7. The practice of asking forgiveness of those whom we have offended through anger; or, if the asking of forgiveness does not seem prudent, the indicating of our repentance by the way we treat them later.

THE NATURE OF ENVY

Envy is sadness that one experiences over another's good because one considers it as an evil to oneself—as a lessening of one's own excellence.

EXAMPLE. An athlete is sad because one of his teammates gets most of the publicity in the school paper.

Since fraternal charity urges us to rejoice over the good of our neighbor, envy is directly opposed to this virtue. Envy has its origin in pride. It usually has as its object a person who at one time was, or at least whom one considered to be, on about one's own level. Envy should not be confounded with the sadness that we may feel when we see some virtue or talent in our neighbor and regret that we do not possess such talent or virtue. This is not envy, since we are not sad because of our neighbor's good fortune but rather because of our own limitations.

The desire to imitate things we admire in others is called emulation. If the things we wish to imitate are good, emulation is praiseworthy. Education aims to encourage young people to emulate the virtues and achievements of the best men and women. The attaining of perfection in our spiritual life is identical with the imitation of Christ, the highest form of emulation.

It is very important to develop the habit of rejoicing over the good things which our neighbor has. Such rejoicing is an indication of real charity, it promotes peace in the family and in the community, it makes one's own life happier, and it helps one practice many other virtues. One who rejoices over his neighbor's success is not likely to live beyond his own means or pretend to be something which he isn't; he will be cooperative and gracious in his dealings with others; he will not be sensitive and imagine offense when none is intended. In short, he will be a magnanimous man, one who rises above the meanness and pettiness which pervade so much of the human race.

THE SINFULNESS OF ENVY

If the good of our neighbor that causes us envious sadness is of great value or importance, there is present the matter necessary for mortal sin. The greater the good that is the object of the envy, the greater the sin. Backbiting and detraction quite readily arise from the broodings of an envious person. Such a one tries by these sinful means to lessen the other's good name. Hatred, too, may be engendered by the sin of envy.

TYPES OF HATRED

Hatred is a voluntary act by which we regard a person or thing with bitter aversion. It is divided into (1) personal hatred and (2) hatred of a quality.

1. *Personal hatred* is hatred in which we wish another evil, not as a source of possible good, but precisely as evil.

EXAMPLE. An office worker who feels that he has been unjustly treated by his boss hopes that the boss will be fired and will not be able to find another job.

2. *Hatred of a quality* is hatred in which we regard another with dislike merely because of a certain quality or habit of his that irks us. It is hatred "of the sin but not of the sinner."

THE SINFULNESS OF PERSONAL HATRED

The sin of personal hatred may be either serious or slight.

1. If the evil that one wishes another out of personal hatred is grave, this is matter sufficient for mortal sin. The evil which the office worker in the example just given wishes his boss is certainly a grave one.

2. If the evil that one wishes another out of personal hatred is slight, there is question of venial sin only.

EXAMPLE. A girl who has been offended by her roommate hopes that the roommate will not get a good grade on a test. The roommate is a good student and would be only slightly upset by failing to get a good grade on one test.

THE SINFULNESS OF HATRED OF A QUALITY

This hatred may be good or evil according to the object of the hatred.

1. If the hatred is directed only toward some evil quality existing in another and does not touch the person himself, then the hatred is not sinful.

EXAMPLE. A businessman hates the injustice which he sees in some of his associates.

2. If the hatred is directed at some virtue in another, this hatred is sinful.

EXAMPLE. A criminal hates a judge because of his sense of justice.

Cases to be analyzed

1 St. Apollonia is said to have leaped into the flames and thus ended her life. She has been canonized by the Church. Thus suicide seems licit at times.

2 A priest enters a burning building to baptize a baby, though he knows for certain that he himself cannot escape alive.

3 One of the president's bodyguards leaped in front of his excellency in order to receive the bullet of an assassin. The president was saved but the bodyguard died.

4 The operator of a cutting machine in a large factory is badly in need of money. Knowing that his employer must pay him five hundred dollars compensation for the accidental loss of an index finger while at work, he deliberately places his finger in the path of the razor-edged blade and presses the control button. He then collects the five hundred dollars.

5 A beautiful girl in enemy-occupied territory fears assaults from hostile soldiers. In order to destroy her beauty and thus lessen the danger of violence against her person, she deliberately takes up a sharp knife and greatly disfigures her face.

6 A father refuses to allow the amputation of his young daughter's leg. Surgeons have told him that the daughter, afflicted with cancer of the thigh bone, will die within ten months unless her leg is amputated. On the other hand, an operation would give her one chance in ten of living—healthy, but crippled.

7 A man who is on trial for a criminal offense knows that one of his accusers is going to lie in order to have him convicted. The defendant considers it justifiable self-defense to hire some thugs to beat him up and threaten to do it again if he testifies falsely.

8 At about eleven o'clock one evening a teen-age boy decided that he would like something to eat. With this in mind he walked down to a hamburger stand which was closed for the night. He tried to awaken the proprietor by loud pounding on the door. The proprietor, thinking that it was a burglar attempting to gain entrance, took his rifle and fired from the window. The shot pierced the boy's heart.

9 A doctor, assisting at a birth, discovers that the baby is hopelessly crippled and so, out of regard for the mother, he allows the child to catch cold and die.

10 "And the young man . . . said: I came by chance upon Mount Gelboe, and Saul leaned upon his spear: and the . . . horsemen drew nigh unto him . . . and seeing me, he called me . . . and he said to me: Stand over me and kill me: for anguish is come upon me and as yet my whole life is in me. So standing over him, I killed him: for I knew that he could not live after the fall" (2 Kings 1:6-10).

11 A girl quarreled with her friend and now refuses to speak to her. She is worried about the degree of sinfulness involved in this outcome of the quarrel.

12 The State of .... has legally approved of euthanasia. A physician feels justified in practicing mercy killing in that state, since the law supports his action.

13 A woman tried by means of certain medicines to procure an abortion, but was not successful. She felt that she was guilty of no sin, since she actually brought the child safely into the world.

14 In retaliation for direct attacks on its own noncombatants a nation destroys several municipal hospitals of the enemy.

15 A soldier, acting on the orders of his lieutenant, deliberately shot three captured and disarmed enemy soldiers. The lieutenant explained that these deaths would save badly needed food for his men.

16 To prevent the recapture of a certain important site the commanding officer places prisoners of war in the front-line trenches as a shield against the enemy.

17 A jeweler was awakened one night by the burglar alarm attached to his shop. He tried to call the police but could not get the telephone operator to answer. Then, taking his rifle, he hurried to the shop, flung the door wide open, and jumped inside. He saw a shadow move and he fired one shot. Another shadow dodged. He fired again. No words had been spoken. The jeweler then called the police, who found in the shop the bodies of two young schoolboys and in their pockets three wrist-watch straps, valued at fifty cents apiece. The police exonerated the jeweler.

18 A man fond of mountain climbing has been warned about the danger involved in attempting to reach the top of Mount Clear, but nevertheless he tries to climb it. During the attempt he falls and is killed. Some consider his action the same as suicide.

19 At a surgeon's convention a famous doctor extracted the healthy appendix of a young boy. He wished to illustrate to his fellow surgeons a new technique.

20 Two men, caught in a mine explosion, find themselves in a narrow space with little air. If one of them were out of the way, the other could survive until he was rescued. If both continue to breathe the air, help cannot possibly reach them before they die of suffocation. Remembering the scriptural text "Greater love than this no one has, that one lay down his life for his friends" (John 15:13), one man cuts his own throat and thus saves his friend.

21 A religious fanatic had gravely sinned several times through the use of his eyes. Then, one day, meditating on that text of Scripture which says: "If thy right eye is an occasion of sin to thee, pluck it out and cast it from thee" (Matthew 5:29), he bathed his eyes in acid in order to destroy his sight.

22 A man was hired to guard the entrance of an apartment building while it was being fumigated. While engaged in this task he fell asleep, and two young boys, 10 years of age, entered the building and were killed by the poisonous fumigating gas. The guard is sorry about their death, but he does not feel in any way guilty of wrongdoing, for he knew nothing of the boys' entrance into the building.

Topics for discussion[4]

1 Dueling is not a satisfactory way of settling a personal affront.

2 Analyze the morality of risking life and limb in college initiations.

---

[4] Not all the assertions contained in the topics are true. The student is to judge the truth of any assertions made and to explain his decision.

3 Is it lawful for the commanding officer of occupied territory to order the execution of a certain number of noncombatant citizens of a district in reprisal for sniping that has occurred there?
4 Vivisection is forbidden by the Fifth Commandment.
5 Those who commit suicide generally do so while mentally unbalanced.
6 The doctrine of justifiable self-defense is opposed to Christ's teaching: "But I say to you not to resist the evildoer; . . . if someone strike thee on the right cheek, turn to him the other also" (Matthew 5:39).
7 What is to be said of the morality of prize fighting?
8 It is advisable for college students to practice total abstinence from alcoholic liquors.
9 Mercy murder, if legalized, would open the door to many murders committed under the pretext of showing mercy to the suffering.
10 Explain the attitude of the Catholic Church toward eugenics.

Bibliography

Australian Hierarchy. "Massacre on the Roads." *Catholic Mind* 56:554-66, November-December 1958.

Bernard, George C. *The Morality of Prizefighting*. Washington: The Catholic University of America Press, 1952.

Connery, John R. "Current Theology: Notes on Moral Theology." *Theological Studies* 19:549-52, December 1958 (on antifertility drugs); 19:543-45, December 1958 (on suicide).

———— "Morality of Nuclear Armament." *Theology Digest* 5:9-12, Winter 1957.

Davis, Henry. *Moral and Pastoral Theology*, seventh edition, edited by L. W. Geddes, Vol. 2, pp. 141-99. 4 vols. New York: Sheed and Ward, 1958.

De Letter, P. "The Pope on Medical Questions." *Clergy Monthly* 20:380-86, November 1956.

Fisher, Joseph P. "Some Thoughts on Pleasure and the Ascetical Life." *Review for Religious* 12:225-30, September 15, 1953.

Ford, John C. "Alcoholism." In *Catholic Encyclopedia*, Supplement II, Vol. 18.

———— *Depth Psychology, Morality and Alcoholism*. Weston: Weston College Press, 1951.

———— "Depth Psychology, Morality, and Alcoholism." *Theology Digest* Experimental Issue:46-52, December 1951.

———— "The Hydrogen Bombing of Cities." *Theology Digest* 5:6-9, Winter 1957.

———— *Man Takes a Drink*. New York: P. J. Kenedy and Sons, 1955.

———— "The Refusal of Blood Transfusions by Jehovah's Witnesses." *Linacre Quarterly* 22:3-10, 41-50, February, May 1955.

Gibbons, William J. and Thomas K. Burch. "Physiological Control of Fertility: Process and Morality." *American Ecclesiastical Review* 138:246-77, April 1958.

Healy, Edwin F. *Medical Ethics*. Chicago: Loyola University Press, 1956.

Jone, Heribert. *Moral Theology*, pp. 133-45. Westminster: Newman Press, 1957.

Kelly, Gerald. *Medico-Moral Problems*. St. Louis: Catholic Hospital Association, 1958.

———— "The Morality of Mutilation. Towards a Revision of the Treatise." *Theological Studies* 17:322-44, September 1956.

———— "Pope Pius XII and the Principle of Totality." *Theological Studies* 16:373-96, September 1955.

Laforet, Eugene. "Boxing, Medicine, and Morals." *Catholic Mind* 57:21-32, January-February 1959. Reprinted from *Linacre Quarterly*, May 1958.

Murray, John Courtney. "Remarks on the Moral Problem of War." *Theological Studies* 20:40-61, March 1959.

Pepler, Conrad. "War in Tradition and Today." *Blackfriars* 35:62-67, February 1954.

Pius XII. "Sport and Gymnastics in Their Relation to the Religious and Moral Conscience." *Catholic Documents* 12:1-8, July 1953.

Sieber, Sylvester A. "Racism." In *Catholic Encyclopedia*, Supplement II, Vol. 18.

Straus, Robert and Selden D. Bacon. *Drinking in College*. New Haven: Yale University Press, 1953.

Zamayon, Pelayo. "Morality of War Today and in the Future." *Theology Digest* 5:2-5, Winter 1957.

Zolli, Eugenio and Sophia Cavalletti. "Anti-Semitism." In *Catholic Encyclopedia*, Supplement II, Vol. 18.

CHAPTER IX

"Thou shalt not commit adultery." The sixth
Exodus 20:14

"Neither shalt thou desire his and ninth
[thy neighbor's] wife."
Exodus 20:17 commandments

P ROBLEMS which arise in connection with the Sixth and Ninth
Commandments cannot well be treated without first saying a few
words about different attitudes toward sex. The Reverend E. C.
Messenger, in his excellent work *Two in One Flesh*,[1] discusses the
attitude found in many Catholics and encouraged to some extent
by the terminology and teaching of certain moral theologians.
Although his book was written in 1949, many false attitudes still
persist; students are urged to read at least the first part in order
to develop or foster a healthy attitude. A shorter treatment which
covers some of the same matter can be found in the issue of
Social Order for May 1957.[2]

To develop a proper attitude one must begin with correct
ideas about the purpose of sex. Here there is little difficulty, for
few would deny that the continuation of the human race is a good

---

[1] Westminster: Newman Press, Vol. 1, pp. 1-19.
[2] John L. Thomas, "The Place of Sex." *Social Order* 7:195-201, May 1957.

thing or that God willed the continuation of the human race by sexual actions. It follows from this that sexual actions are good in themselves because they are the natural and ordinary means for the continuation of the human race. Even those outside the Church who advocate artificial insemination would limit its use to cases in which generation is impossible by the ordinary sexual union of husband and wife.

Since sexual actions are something good in themselves, the real problem of sex concerns the circumstances and manner in which one can rationally express his physical love for another person by sexual union. The Church, basing her teaching both on the Old Testament and the words of our Lord, maintains that such an expression of physical love can be made rationally only between married people. They alone are capable of bringing children into the world in a fitting manner because only in marriage can children be reared and educated in a way proper to them as free and intelligent creatures.

The purpose of sexual union is a noble one and the union itself, if done rationally, participates in the nobility of the purpose. St. Thomas does not hesitate to say that it can be an act of religion (*Summa theologica*, III Suppl., q. 41, art. 4). What is said of the acts can obviously be said of the organs by which these acts are accomplished. They are something good in themselves, created by God for the generation of intelligent beings to give Him honor and glory. At the same time they enable a man and a woman to express their mutual love for one another in the most intimate way.

Unfortunately, current attitudes toward sex in our society often seem to be either puritanical and Jansenistic or an extreme reaction against puritanism and Jansenism. Even those who flaunt sex for the purpose of making money seem to have a subconscious conviction that sex is somehow evil. For this reason they fail to see the difference between the noble and purifying use of sex and the ignoble and debasing. Sex in marriage is no different from sex outside marriage, but for some the second may be more interesting because there is the thrill of doing something forbidden.

Catholics have by no means escaped the puritanical attitude toward sex. Because complete control of the sex urge is imposed on them before marriage, some have transferred their condemnation of the illicit use of sex to sex itself. Unfortunately, this tendency has been encouraged in some of the clergy and the laity by Jansenistic expressions. The organs of sex have been labeled "indecent parts" and those closely connected with sexual organs the "less decent parts." Thoughts about sex have been called "impure" even when the person engaging in them has a perfect right to do so; for instance, a doctor studying the anatomy of the human body. Sex for many has become a problem: before marriage it causes concern and worry because of the continual fight for control; after marriage it frequently is a burden for the woman, who often wants children but still thinks that there is something evil about begetting them, and an embarrassment for the man, who feels that he is too carnal or animal; sometimes, of course, the roles are reversed.

These attitudes are not based on the teaching of the Church but are due to influences from outside and to certain members of the Church who have been influenced by Manichaean and Jansenistic thought. Many moral theologians and sociologists have been combating them for years but have not completely succeeded in replacing them with a more positive attitude.

Catholics should keep in mind the following principles as guides in their thinking about sex:

1. The organs of sex are good because they were created by God and are intended for a noble purpose: the preservation of the human race.

2. The sexual act in marriage is good and beautiful both because of its ordination to the generation of children and because it is an expression of true mutual love.

3. Sex is essentially unselfish because it is ordered to others: its ultimate ordination is to the offspring; its proximate to the marriage partner.

4. When sex is used for selfish purposes it is disordered. The deordination may occur because the ultimate purpose is frustrated by contraception or because the sexual act is had in circumstances where offspring would be brought into the world without proper provision for their upbringing and education (fornication and adultery). Or the deordination may be due to the fact that sexual union is sought merely to satisfy the selfish desire of one of the partners—as, for example, when the other partner is sick.

5. There must be justification based on sound reasons for any actions that bring about sexual stimulation either directly (for ex-

173

ample, touches) or indirectly (for example, looking at pictures). Of course, direct sexual stimulation can be had only between those who are married. Others may often have good reasons for permitting indirect sexual stimulation.

6. Directly venereal actions—that is, actions whose direct and exclusive purpose is to stimulate or further venereal passion—are always forbidden to the unmarried. They are opposed to the virtue of chastity. Indirectly venereal actions—that is, actions which serve some other purpose than venereal stimulation but which may result in it—are good, venially sinful, or seriously sinful according to the intention of the one performing the actions and the circumstances in which they are performed. The moral quality of such actions is determined by the principles applicable to the double effect. Modesty is the virtue by which we exercise control over such actions.

The statement that there is no parvitude (smallness) of matter in regard to the Sixth Commandment applies only to directly venereal actions.

7. The application of principles to a particular individual must take into consideration his temperament, habits, past experience, and physical make-up; therefore prudence is required to decide what is licit or forbidden to an individual in each particular case. One should never conclude that the advice given to him is applicable to others nor that the advice given to others is applicable to oneself.

Unless one keeps these principles in mind, he is in danger of being caught in the general abandonment of restraint common to many of our contemporaries or of obeying the teaching of the Church without understanding that it alone gives true meaning to sex. One who obeys without understanding is almost certain to suffer from frustration or even a certain amount of resentment.

With these principles in mind we can proceed to a treatment of the Sixth and Ninth Commandments. The Sixth Commandment expressly forbids adultery; the Ninth forbids the desire to commit adultery. Other parts of the Old Testament and the New Testament give us further revelation as to the proper use of the sex faculty.[3] From these and her constant tradition the Church derives her teaching on chastity.

---

[3] See Messenger, *Two in One Flesh,* Vol. 1, pp. 20-36.

Both the Sixth Commandment and the Ninth Commandment treat of the same subject matter (that is, whatever is opposed to the orderly propagation of the race according to the dictates of nature). Hence we shall deal with them together. Since thought and desire precede action, we shall follow the logical order by discussing first the Ninth Commandment and then the Sixth.

These observations are intended to deal only with the life of the unmarried. When a Catholic is about to be married, he should see to it that he receives detailed instructions about conjugal chastity and marriage rights and duties, either through reading or by private conference with his pastor.

VENEREAL PLEASURE

Chastity is a virtue that disposes one to abstain from all illicit venereal pleasure. Venereal pleasure is commonly defined as that pleasure which is experienced in the organs of generation from a stirring sensation or motion. It is described as the pleasure felt when the sex organs become noticeably aroused. This bodily reaction is for the most part produced by sexual stimuli; that is, by thoughts, touches, sights, words, or imaginations.

VENEREAL PLEASURE NOT IN ITSELF SINFUL

Experiencing this venereal pleasure is not in itself sinful for the unmarried, even though it is present for hours at a time. The mere physical presence of such pleasure in the body is not sinful, for it arises from an instinct implanted by God in human nature for the propagation of the race. It is sinful, however, for the unmarried to yield to that pleasure (that is, to want it in the body, to enjoy and consent to it). Deliberately to accept and enjoy venereal pleasure outside marriage is grievously sinful. Whether that pleasure has been intentionally procured or has risen spontaneously, yielding to it is in both cases gravely sinful. Deliberately to accept and take pleasure even in the first beginnings of this bodily sensation is mortally sinful, no matter whether this occupy a brief time or not. Later in the chapter we will give some principles for determining whether or not one has deliberately engaged in thoughts contrary to chastity or taken pleasure in impure desires. God's intention is clearly that this pleasure may be licitly indulged in between man and wife and that it should attract them to the marital act so that they may be induced to propagate the race and to accept the many burdens that arise from begetting and rearing children. This is the primary reason for venereal pleasure. Hence it is against God's designs to use it outside married life.

VENEREAL PLEASURE AN INDUCEMENT TO SIN

Although experiencing venereal pleasure in itself is no sin at all, it is a strong inducement to sin. The very presence of carnal pleasure in the body entices one strongly to yield to it, and so it may easily constitute a proximate danger of sinning when protracted. Hence we are obliged to avoid experiencing venereal pleasure insofar as it is possible for us to do so. It will come at times unbidden and we cannot escape it. Then, even though we feel the pleasure, as long as we do not desire to feel it we do not sin. It is possible to have the pleasurable sensation and not at the same time consent to it. Let us take an example to explain the difference between feeling the pleasure and wanting the pleasure there. John offers Tom some delicious-looking chocolates, and Tom avidly puts one in his mouth. While he is chewing it with much relish, John discovers that the candy is poisoned and tells Tom this. Tom immediately spits out the poisoned candy. However, since it has partially dissolved, getting rid of it takes some minutes. All during the time that Tom is trying to expel from his mouth every vestige of the poisoned candy, he experiences the pleasant taste of the chocolate. Nevertheless, it is clear that he does not want it there, for he is taking every available means to end it. He feels the pleasure but does not want to feel it.

THE RELATION OF THOUGHT TO ACTION

God requires purity, not only in our outward dealings with self and others, but also in regard to the inner life of our souls. Thoughts and desires can be regarded as the beginning of action and naturally tend to be externalized. Free external actions always start in thought and desire, and so, by properly controlling thought and desire, the external conduct is safeguarded. In fact, chaste conduct cannot be realized unless one's thoughts are kept chaste as far as possible. Moreover, Christ explicitly mentions the sinfulness of impure desire: "But I say to you that anyone who so much as looks with lust at a woman has already committed adultery with her in his heart" (Matthew 5:28). Christ also branded the Pharisees as despicable in the eyes of God because, though externally they were fair to the eye, internally they were as filthy as corrupting corpses.

THOUGHTS

Thinking about the sex organs or sexual actions is not wrong in itself, but it is forbidden if engaged in without a sufficient reason. A group of psychologists who discuss sexual aberrations in order to get further knowledge of them and make suggestions to help combat them are doing something good. It does happen, however, that even those who are thinking about sexual actions for a good reason will experience venereal pleasure. Presupposing that they do not intend it and do not consent to or encourage it, no sin is committed. This is an evil effect (if one willed it directly, it would be a sin) which follows from a good action and which may be permitted for a sufficient reason.

If without a sufficient reason one deliberately engages in thoughts which tend to arouse venereal pleasure, there is always some sin involved. The degree of sin must be judged by the circumstances. Let us take the case of a person who reads an article or book out of curiosity and who begins to experience a mild sexual reaction. He does not read the book for that purpose, however, and is certain that he will not give consent to any venereal pleasure which might arise. Such a person has some reason for reading the book in question, but his reason is insufficient and does not excuse him completely from sin. However, his sin would ordinarily be venial. The same would be true of one who is somewhat slothful in putting away thoughts that are likely to cause venereal pleasure.

A person who engages in thoughts which ordinarily cause venereal pleasure and has no reason for so doing is guilty of serious sin if his action is fully deliberate. Such a person is placing himself in a proximate occasion of sin with no justifying reason. If a particular individual knows that such thoughts will not cause venereal pleasure, they would not be a proximate occasion of sin for him; such individuals, however, are very rare.

If a person engages in thoughts which arouse venereal pleasure for the express purpose of arousing the pleasure, he obviously commits a serious sin.

Very often thoughts will arise spontaneously in the mind and will persist for some time. If the person involved attempts to turn his mind to something else, there is no sin even if the thoughts return again and again. In concrete cases, however, there is often confusion as to whether or not a person "consented" to such thoughts. In deciding whether the thoughts were sinful (and the same would be true of words, desires, or actions) one should keep clearly in mind that three things must be present before mortal sin is committed: grave matter, full advertence, and full consent. The element of sufficient reflection is often lacking, especially with regard to sins of thought.

Immediately after I have been besieged by thoughts or desires I may ascertain whether or not I have sinned by asking myself the following questions:

Question 1: Did I want to have those thoughts or desires? Did I wish them to continue?

a) If the answer is no, there is no cause for anxiety, even though they haunted me for hours.

b) If the answer is yes, then before deciding that I have sinned, I must ask myself Question 2.

Question 2: Did I want these thoughts or desires to remain after I realized their sinfulness?

a) If the answer is no—that I drove them away as soon as I realized that evil thoughts or desires were in my mind—then I have not sinned.

b) If the answer is yes—that I fully consented to the thoughts or desires—I have sinned gravely.

c) If the answer is both yes and no—that I hesitated and was slow in trying to expel them—then I sinned venially.

d) If the answer is that I do not know, I have certainly not sinned seriously and I may have committed no sin at all.

DESIRES

Deliberately to consent to an impure desire is always a grave sin. The malice of the sin varies with the object of the evil wish— whether one desires to sin impurely with oneself or with a single person or with a married person. This object of the evil desire (for example, an unmarried man or woman) should be mentioned in confession. Impure desires of their nature include thoughts, and so when one accuses oneself in confession of impure desires, one need not mention the corresponding thoughts that accompanied them. On the other hand, it may happen that one entertains thoughts that arouse venereal pleasure without desiring to commit any impure action. Hence it would not be sufficient as regards the integrity of confession to accuse oneself of thoughts contrary to chastity if one yielded to impure desires also.

> EXAMPLE 1. A woman thus confesses an impure desire: "I was guilty of one thought contrary to chastity and of one impure desire." She should not mention the thought involved in the desire.
>
> EXAMPLE 2. A boy is guilty of five impure desires deliberately entertained. He confesses: "I gave in to five thoughts contrary to chastity." That is not enough. Evil desires are greater sins than thoughts.

FORBIDDEN SOURCES OF DANGER

The Sixth Commandment forbids expressly only the crime of adultery (that is, sexual intercourse with the married partner of another). Implicitly it prohibits all impure actions—that is, all external sins against the virtue of chastity—because all these, insofar as they are opposed to the orderly propagation of the human race, share with adultery the reason for the prohibition. This commandment forbids some actions because they are sources of spiritual danger and others because of themselves they work directly against the good of the human race. We will here treat the forbidden sources of danger.

Looks

The sight of the human body, either one's own or that of another, is in itself not sinful. Why, then, is it in general forbidden for one to look at an unclothed adult[4] of the opposite sex? The reason is that this would ordinarily arouse venereal pleasure in the one looking at such a sight, and hence would involve strong incitement to the grave sin of yielding to that pleasure. Such looks (that is, looking at the nude of the opposite sex or at actions which tend to cause venereal pleasure) are forbidden, not be-

---

[4] We use the word "adult" because the sight of a nude infant of the opposite sex would ordinarily arouse one's passions only slightly or not at all, and so would not entail grave danger of sinning. However, such looks can be venially sinful. In case an individual is certain that the sight of a nude infant would constitute for him no danger at all (not even slight danger), then for him such looks would not be even venially sinful.

cause the mere seeing of such things is wrong—for it is not—but because such things create for the normal person a proximate occasion of serious sin. All such sights, then, that would naturally arouse the passions are forbidden because of the danger of sinning with which they are associated.

These sights are, in general, forbidden but they are not prohibited in all circumstances. Since they are not wrong in themselves, they can at times be good, at other times bad. Looking at an unclothed adult of the opposite sex is permissible when there is a sufficient reason to justify risking the danger involved (for example, a physician examining or operating on a patient) and no venereal pleasure is intended or consented to. Looking at an unclothed person of the opposite sex to arouse one's passions would always be grievously wrong. If one were to look merely out of curiosity and very briefly, there would be present some danger of sinning, though not a great one, and so such a glance would ordinarily constitute matter for venial sin.

THE NUDE IN ART

What of looking at pictures or statues of the nude of the opposite sex? If such representations are clear, attractive, and life-like, they would constitute about the same danger of sinning as living persons. Hence we may apply to the nude in movies, magazines, and advertisements the same principles that have been laid down in the preceding paragraph. One would ordinarily be justified in viewing paintings and statues of the nude in art museums for the sincere and useful purpose of cultivating one's sense of the artistic or to develop one's talents as an artist, provided these paintings and statues are not of a lascivious nature.

The all-but-nude dancers and actresses of some theaters, night clubs, and floor shows are in general sources of grave temptation to the normal man. Although some scanty clothing is worn by the performers, still their beauty and natural attractiveness, their provocative movements, the fact that they are the center of all eyes, and the softening influence of the music create an atmosphere that tends greatly to arouse venereal pleasure. Hence men are obliged under pain of mortal sin to refrain from looking at performances in which actresses do not wear at least the minimum essentials of trunks and brassieres. In this same category must also be placed veil or fan dancers and strip-tease performers.

Priests are often asked about the binding force of the classifications of films by the Legion of Decency. These classifications do not have legislative force but are meant to be a guide for prudent choice. The obligation to avoid shows which are an occasion of sin comes from the natural law. When a picture is classified as C the meaning is that in the judgment of prudent interviewers the picture constitutes a proximate occasion of sin for many people, especially those who are young and impressionable. There might be circumstances in which a mature person would have sufficient reason for attendance at such a show, but this would rarely be the case. Even one who knows that such a show would not be a proximate occasion of sin for him would ordinarily be giving scandal by attending it. There is also the danger that one who thinks such shows are not occasions of sin for him is rationalizing. Pictures classified as B are objectionable in part for adults. In the present system of classification many pictures which were formerly classified as B are now classified as A III, so the present B classification includes only the more objectionable pictures of the former B classification. Attendance at such pictures could be a proximate occasion of sin for some people. The danger from frequent attendance at such movies is much greater than that from occasional attendance. From such frequent attendance one can easily pick up attitudes harmful to faith or morals; for example, that divorce with remarriage is the best solution to some marriage problems.

The concern which the Church shows about some motion pictures does not imply any condemnation of motion pictures as such. On the contrary, popes and bishops have stressed the possibilities for good inherent in this form of art and have exhorted Catholics to make use of it for the common good.

Touches

Touching the human body (or any part of it) is in itself not sinful at all. Such touches may be good if they are performed with the right intention and serve a useful purpose (for example, bathing, surgical operations). Such touches are bad (1) if they are intended to arouse the passions or (2) if they have to do with the sexually exciting parts of the body and are engaged in without sufficient reason. There are certain touches that ordinarily bring with them venereal pleasure and so involve danger of yielding to that forbidden pleasure. In this class must be placed kissing and petting.

KISSING

Kissing is a mark of affection which may or may not be licit. Because there are so many ways in which this act is performed and because individuals are so different in their reactions to it, it is difficult to draw up a rule that would clearly indicate what is sinful and what is sinless.

Kissing can be such that it does not usually arouse any venereal pleasure at all. This is true of kisses exchanged between a boy and his mother or sister. In such acts real affection is felt, but there is normally no exciting of the passions. A kiss of this type is of course not sinful at all, even though it be exchanged between a young man and woman. This kind of a kiss we shall call the nonpassionate kiss because it is of such a nature as not to arouse the passions of the normal person.

There is, however, another kind of kissing that may be termed passionate kissing. Kisses of this type, because intense or passionate, ordinarily cause venereal pleasure. Hence such kissing is forbidden under pain of serious sin. Even kisses that at first are not passionate ordinarily become so if the act is prolonged for some time; hence prolonged kissing is classified as passionate.

Although the nonpassionate kiss is not in itself sinful, it may easily prepare the way for passionate kissing, especially when indulged in by young persons of opposite sexes.

KISSING "FOR THE THRILL"

Sometimes boys kiss girls "just for the thrill," as they say. Are such kisses sinful? We must distinguish according to the meaning of that term. Kissing just for the thrill may mean:

1. Kissing in order to arouse venereal pleasure. In this case the intention of the boy is obviously gravely sinful, and so such kissing is illicit.

2. Kissing in order to experience the general "good feeling" produced by the excitement (nonvenereal) over the act. Here there is no reaction in the organs of generation. There is merely an increase of pulse and respiration that causes a feeling of exhilaration. In this case the act itself is not sinful. Such kisses, how-

ever, could in certain circumstances easily prove a source of danger because they prepare the way for arousing the passions.

3. Kissing out of a spirit of mischievousness (for example, forcing a kiss on a girl who resists) or just because of the novelty of the act. Here there is hardly question of a sin against the Sixth Commandment, but the act may involve a sin, more or less serious, against the virtue of charity.

PETTING

Petting, as we shall use the term, means a hugging, embracing, or caressing of the body that is of such a kind as ordinarily to produce venereal pleasure in the one being fondled. It does not include holding hands with a girl, stroking her hair, patting her shoulder, and the like. These latter actions do not arouse venereal pleasure in the normal persons, at least ordinarily speaking. If they happen to do so in this or that individual and are indulged in for the purpose of arousing the passions, they are in that particular instance grievously sinful. Or if these ordinarily harmless actions do in certain cases arouse the passions, one would of course sin gravely by consenting to this pleasure.

Petting as defined above is always mortally sinful because it tends of its very nature to stir up venereal pleasure. Even though it stops short of producing complete sexual satisfaction, it is naturally a proximate preparation for the complete act. One who indulges in petting is enkindling in himself and in the other party a burning desire for an act allowed only to the married. Even though a certain individual discovers that thus touching another indecently does not arouse in him any venereal pleasure, still he may not perform such actions, for his petting would, it must be presumed, awaken passion in the other party and thus he would be inducing another to commit grave sin.

DUTIES OF THE ENGAGED

Those who are engaged to be married are allowed no exemption from the law of God that prohibits to the unmarried any indulgence in venereal pleasure. They are not yet married, and so may not make use of the rights that marriage alone gives. However, the engaged should foster their mutual love for each other and they have a right to show each other certain marks of this love. Hence they may make use of the nonpassionate kiss and embrace. They must realize, nevertheless, that continual hugging and kissing, even of the nonpassionate type, may readily bring on serious temptations and that it should therefore be avoided. Because of the fact that the parties involved are in love with each other, are of an age when passions are very strong, are in circumstances where these passions are quickly aroused, and are strongly drawn to make their embraces as ardent as possible, to indulge in continual hugging and kissing of the nonpassionate type may readily lead to grave sin. This is especially true at times when they are free from observation by others (for example, when they are alone in an automobile parked at a deserted spot).

Engaged couples who act thus are acting imprudently and putting themselves in an occasion of sin without sufficient reason. Though on this or that occasion they may stay within the bounds of what is licit, eventually they will be certain to fall. "He that loveth danger shall perish in it" (Ecclesiasticus 3:27). Everyday experience of human nature proves this to be the normal consequence of such conduct. Moreover, such continual kissing and embracing is not at all necessary as a means of expressing their love. Their tone of voice, their general attitude, their facial reactions to the deep love they feel, the little attentions and courtesies they show each other—these will provide an evident indication of their genuine affection. Genuine love seeks the good and not the injury of the one loved. It is not true love to make the person of the beloved an instrument for arousing unlawful passion. This is merely a display of selfishness that ignores the best interests of the other. A man should remember that it is not merely the body but the whole person of the one loved, and especially her soul, that should be the object of this affection. If he concentrates on considering the beauty of her virtues (for example, her purity, meekness, humility, generosity, and so forth), this will help to spiritualize his love for her and raise him above the dangers of attachment to mere physical attractiveness.

Steady dating

Those who seek each other's company with a view to becoming engaged are expected to show a normal amount of affection. They have, then, good reason for making use of the ordinary marks of love. However, the same dangers are present for them as for engaged couples, and so they would weigh well the warnings given above against frequent kissing and embracing.

The current custom of steady dating by boys and girls of high-school age and by college men and women who will not be able to marry for several years has been widely discussed by moralists and sociologists. Arguing from the general principles on occasions of sin, some moral theologians hold that this practice is always either seriously or venially sinful if there is no prospect of marriage in the near future or no thought of marriage at all. If the couple, so these moralists hold, find that steady dating has frequently led to serious sin, the practice itself would constitute a proximate occasion of sin and would have to be avoided under pain of serious sin; if it has never led to serious sin, it would be venially sinful because they would be putting themselves in a remote occasion of sin without sufficient reason. Others disagree with this opinion and think that such cases should be handled on an individual basis. Couples who can sincerely say that "going steady" has not been an occasion of sin for them should not be told that they are committing venial sin. Those for whom it is a proximate occasion of sin must avoid it under pain of serious sin. Experienced counselors do not think that the latter is usually the case with conscientious young Catholics.

The moral theologians who hold this less strict opinion do not necessarily approve of the practice of "going steady"; many of them think the earlier custom of free dating until the time when a couple are seriously looking forward to marriage had many advantages and would like to see it revived. In the meantime, however, they do not wish to condemn the present practice as sinful in all cases. Young people are under pressure to live according to the customs of the society; and although practices which are sinful cannot be permitted, we should avoid giving them false consciences and adding to the difficulties which they already have in leading good Catholic lives.

Conversation

First of all, a distinction must be drawn between vulgar language and impure or obscene language. Vulgar language consists in the use of coarse expressions that are unseemly in polite society; for example, the use of "damn," "hell," or words that refer to the functions of the toilet. Impure or obscene language, on the other hand, has to do with talk that refers to sex life. It tends to arouse in the hearer venereal pleasure. Vulgar talk is in general not sinful, though it is unbecoming in a Catholic and may at times shock or scandalize. Talking about things which refer to sex life is in itself not sinful. It may be perfectly licit if engaged in for a sufficient reason and without danger of sin to oneself or others. The danger of sin arises from the fact that such conversation may readily arouse one's passions and that as a consequence there is present the temptation to consent to venereal pleasure.

A medical student has sufficient reason for talking about sexual topics; and if he takes precautions against consenting to forbidden pleasure and avoids scandalizing others, he may carry on such discussions without sin.

The following principles apply to conversation on sexual matters by those who lack a sufficient reason for such conversation:

1. If such conversation is really obscene and is protracted, it is generally matter of mortal sin, especially when engaged in between those of opposite sexes. Such talk arouses more than passing venereal pleasure and constitutes proximate danger of consenting to that pleasure.

2. If only one or two obscene words are spoken between those of the same sex, the matter is venially sinful.

3. If the conversation is merely a little suggestive or only slightly objectionable, the sinfulness is venial. However, in the case of those who are not mature even this type of talk could easily lead to serious sin.

4. To listen to impure talk out of mere curiosity or to smile at an impure joke because afraid not to do so is venially sinful. If a person cannot avoid overhearing impure talk (for example, the talk of fellow workers in office or factory), he commits no sin provided he neither desires it nor consents to it nor encourages it in any way.

It must be remembered that any sort of talk, if engaged in *for the purpose of arousing venereal pleasure* either in oneself or in another, is gravely sinful. In this case the intention of the speaker is evil.

What has been said of the sinfulness of obscene language is based on the known reactions of the normal person. Some individuals, however, who have become thoroughly accustomed to such talk would experience only slight temptation even from very obscene conversation. Hence, scandal apart, these could engage in such conversation without serious sin.

Dancing

In itself dancing is perfectly lawful. At times, however, it may become a source of evil either because of the way in which it is done or because of the fact that it is an occasion of sin for this particular individual. The general rule, then, for gauging the licitness of dancing in any given case may be stated thus: If dancing is not a proximate occasion of sin for the dancer, then it is licit for him or her.

In some places there is a special prohibition of the bishop or pastor against dances held at certain times or under certain conditions. Such a prohibition must be obeyed. Ordinarily in these instances dancing is banned because of various evils attendant upon gatherings of this kind in that locality.

Nudism

Nudism is a cult which has as its chief doctrine the belief that both sexes should live together in the state of complete nakedness. Such a way of living, nudists contend, makes for greater health of body and mind. It prevents sex obsession and morbid curiosity by satisfying once and for all one's natural inquisitiveness regarding the mystery of sex.

Perhaps complete nakedness would at first bring quiet to many who are abnormally attacked by sex images, but it surely would not extinguish or lessen the ardor of their sex instinct. It would, on the contrary, rather urge on that instinct to satisfaction, for certain looks always tend to awaken a desire to indulge in forbidden pleasure. Once a person has complete knowledge of the anatomy of the opposite sex, his scientific curiosity is satisfied; but even after that, the sight of an object agreeable to his passions does not fail to attract and to arouse him. Nourished by such sights, the carnal instinct grows stronger and leads to frequent and promiscuous sins of impurity. This is a fact that has been confirmed by repeated experience.

Nudism, then, ordinarily occasions severe temptations in the cultists. Though it may be that in their gatherings no external sins of lust are in evidence, still, evil desires are fostered by such surroundings and these afterwards easily lead to external deeds of impurity. Very many persons who have not accepted the Catholic viewpoint concerning purity defend the principle that only external actions against the virtue can constitute wrongdoing. They overlook the sinfulness of impure thoughts and desires that are freely indulged. Hence we may understand how some do not realize the grave evil of nudism.

ACTIONS OF THEMSELVES EVIL

ADULTERY, FORNICATION, AND SELF-ABUSE

Deliberately to enjoy and yield to venereal pleasure outside marriage is a grave sin. Hence for the unmarried any action whose purpose is the procuring of venereal pleasure is grievously sinful. Thus adultery, fornication, and self-abuse must be classed as mortal sins. Adultery, as applied to the unmarried, is sexual intercourse with the married partner of another. Fornication consists in sexual intercourse, mutually agreed to, that is performed between an unmarried man and an unmarried woman. Self-abuse is the act of trying to arouse in oneself venereal pleasure by self-stimulation. In adultery and fornication there is the added guilt of cooperation in another's sin. Moreover, adultery has an additional malice, since it entails violation of the conjugal rights of the spouse of the one who has sinned, and this violation of another's conjugal rights will always be there, even if the innocent spouse openly favors the sin.

PRUDISHNESS

Catholics are urged to cultivate the virtue of modesty but to avoid prudishness in the matter of the Sixth Commandment. Prudishness is an habitual attitude of extreme propriety and overdelicacy. A prudish person detects wrong where no wrong exists. A young person, for example, is ashamed to ask where the toilet is located. A mother insists on her daughter's speaking of "stomach" when "belly" or "abdomen" is obviously meant. Christ did not hesitate to call things by their right names.

Modesty, on the other hand, is not prudery. It is the golden mean between prudishness and pruriency. The latter is morbid curiosity about sex and sex life. Modesty is a virtue that regulates one's conduct in things that are apt to induce forbidden pleasure or a desire for it. Chief among these things are one's dress, one's language, and one's general deportment. By prompting one to avoid acts that would be for self or for others an incitement to passion, modesty removes sources of danger, closes the approaches to impurity, and safeguards chastity. A person who ignores the urging of modesty must be accused at least of making it extremely difficult for himself to preserve his purity and of embroiling himself in a constant battle that he could have avoided.

Although all Catholics should have a high regard for modesty in dress, they should not try to reduce modesty to mathematical formulas. It is true that girls usually do not realize how much more sensitive boys and men are to sexual stimulation and that they may need guidance in determining what is modest and what is not; but this guidance should come from mothers or other prudent women rather than from a set of mathematical formulas as to how much of the body must be covered. Stress should be put on the type of clothes worn and on modesty in gestures, bearing, and general deportment. One girl can be modest in a swimming suit, another immodest when clothed from toe to neck.

THE CASE FOR CHASTITY

Chastity is a virtue that greatly ennobles, for by it man exercises control over the body by the spiritual faculties of the mind and the will. Chastity preserves man's innate dignity by keeping him from the selfish and degrading indulgence in pleasures forbidden him by the natural law. Chastity is not unnatural; it does not impede man's proper development; it does not prevent the rational expression of sexual love. Man is intended by nature to be guided by reason and to be ruled, not by the cravings of the body, but by the dictates of the soul. Chastity does not wither up man's personality, but rather increases his moral stature and helps toward the development of his higher faculties. The more impure a man becomes, the nearer he approaches the evil spirits and the more enslaved he finds himself to blind passion. On the contrary, the more chaste he is, the closer he draws to God and the greater is his liberty in exercising the higher powers of his spiritual nature. Chastity retains for man his freedom from the entangling tendrils of a lower appetite and disposes him to follow the guidance of his conscience.

THE BEAUTY AND MERIT OF CHASTITY

Chastity is a strong and beautiful virtue. It is strong because to possess it requires fortitude, strength of character, and genuine virility. To spurn temptations to other types of sin (for example, stealing, lying, disobedience) is not difficult for the ordinary Christian, but to refuse the pleasant, insistent, and seductive attraction to impurity demands real moral courage. By yielding one chooses the easy way, the cowardly way. By resisting one becomes more manly. "For thou hast done manfully and thy heart has been strengthened because thou hast loved chastity" (Judith 15:11). In the chaste person shines forth the virtue of constancy; for chastity implies, not merely a single victory, but a long series of conquests over passion.

Chastity is a beautiful virtue as well, for it preserves untarnished the splendor and beauty of the superior part of man, that of his soul. The wholesome attractiveness of the pure stands out in striking contrast to the appeal of those who have given themselves up to impurity. One may see the radiant luster of this virtue in the spotless Lamb of God, in the immaculate Mary, in the pure St. John, and in other saints. "O how beautiful is the chaste generation with glory" (Wisdom 4:1).

Why is chastity so emphatically praised? It is because this virtue preserves man from sins that are especially shameful and keeps his vision clear to see the value of heavenly things. Impurity, on the contrary, blinds man's mind and fills him with disgust for the things of God. Just as chastity may in a sense be called the foundation of sanctity, so impurity may be branded as one of the most common causes of man's spiritual ruin.

"The life of man upon earth is a warfare" (Job 7:1), and the struggle to preserve chastity is one of life's greatest battles. Victory is won only by sternly disciplining the body. The fight must be directed against a very alluring pleasure. To subdue this appetite one must practice many virtues; for example, modesty, sobriety, humility, and mortification. "For the flesh lusts against the spirit, and the spirit against the flesh; . . . And they who belong to Christ have crucified their flesh with its passions and desires" (Galatians 5:17-24).

The person who, with regard to the matter of the Sixth Commandment especially, intends to go as far as he can just short of sin is very imprudent. Such a one shows little appreciation for the priceless value and the enhancing beauty of the virtue that is jeopardized by this way of acting. "No price is worthy of a continent soul" (Ecclesiasticus 26:20). Moreover, he seems to possess little knowledge of the weakness of human nature. Experience proves that one who rashly endangers the virtue of chastity will not long continue without serious sin. "He that toucheth pitch, shall be defiled with it" (Ecclesiasticus 13:1).

HELPS TO CHASTITY

The following means are usually of great aid in cultivating the virtue of chastity:

1. Training the will to rigorous control over one's thoughts. An unbridled imagination gives rise to many temptations, and the imagination can and must be brought under the control of the will. A properly disciplined will can be very effective in excluding dangerous thoughts.

2. Self-denial regularly practiced. It is difficult to practice perfect chastity without self-denial in other physical pleasures, especially in food, drinking, smoking, and sleep. The performing of disagreeable tasks and willing submission to hardships help greatly in developing the self-control necessary for a more perfect practice of chastity.

3. Developing keen interest in some study, work, or hobby that will take up all one's spare time. It is well known that "an idle mind is the devil's workshop," and so we must be sure to keep ourselves occupied. Moreover, a person who has many interests is far less likely than others to develop those attitudes of self-pity and selfishness which weaken the will and make us less able to resist temptation.

4. Regular and frequent reception of the sacraments of penance and Holy Communion. One should, if possible, always confess to the same confessor.

5. Devotion to the Blessed Virgin Mary and St. Joseph.

6. Meditation on the beauty of chastity and on the degrading effects of impurity.

7. Guarding the eyes, the ears, and the hands.

8. Avoiding as far as possible the circumstances which have in the past led one into sin or which reason tells one will surely prove a source of temptation.

9. Remembering that to acquire the virtue of chastity is quite possible. Not to become discouraged by the number or persistency of the temptations. Recalling the promises of God—"God is faithful and will not permit you to be tempted beyond your strength, but with the temptation will also give you a way out that you may be able to bear it" (1 Corinthians 10:13)—the long list of saints who shone by their purity, and the vast multitude of Catholic men, women, and children in every part of the world today who are leading beautifully pure lives—priests, nuns, brothers, lay men and women, boys and girls in school and out of school.

10. Bearing in mind the words of St. Paul: "Or do you not know that your members are the temple of the Holy Spirit, . . . and that you are not your own? For you have been bought at a great price" (1 Corinthians 6:19-20).

11. To make it a rule during the time when one is tempted in thought:

a) To use quick distractions. The application of this means will differ with individuals. In general, the more interesting the thing I turn my mind to, the more effective it will be in driving out unwanted thoughts. For some, it may be sports; for others, a story which they have heard. Each should develop his own method of getting his mind on some interesting topic.

b) To think of God's omnipresence, of the crucified Christ, of death, of hell.

c) To call to God for aid by short prayer; for example, "My Jesus, have mercy."

d) To recall that every temptation resisted is merit gained and every sin committed (though later forgiven) increases one's purgatory. Remember that by giving in to temptations against purity one does not lessen them except for the moment. By yielding to them we make them grow ever more insatiable.

e) To avoid being afraid or terrified at the idea of impure thoughts besieging you. Say to yourself: "If they come, I'll simply resist them and thus increase my reward in heaven." Cultivate a calm and serene attitude.

Decide beforehand, when calm and untroubled by temptation, the exact means which you will employ during the temptations that are to come—the exact aspiration, the exact joke; whether you will think of hell or of death or of Christ crucified. If you wait until the temptation is on you before trying to choose your weapon, you will waver in your choice and your delay may prove costly.

Cases to be analyzed

1 A young man is frequently tempted by thoughts against chastity. Though he never consents to these temptations, he is disgusted with himself, for he concludes that he would not have such thoughts if he were really a good Catholic.

2 Another young man deliberately has immoral relations with a girl to help him decide whether or not he wishes to get married. Besides, he feels that he should so act at least once for the sake of the experience.

3 A girl allows her boy friend full liberty with regard to petting. "Priests are too strict about this," she says; "and besides, nearly all the Catholic girls I know allow it."

4 A Catholic often goes to a restaurant where there is a lewd floor show. "The meals there," he says, "are better and cheaper than at the more conservative eating houses."

5 A student goes to a condemned movie. He excuses his action on the score that there are only two very bad spots and the acting is excellent.

6 A girl at a dance with a chance acquaintance drinks several highballs.

7 A secretary just out of high school at times goes to the theater, to dinners, and to athletic events with married men. She enjoys their company and sees no harm in helping them spend a pleasant evening. The wives of these men know nothing of this.

8 A boy of very delicate conscience finds that he is tempted by many of the illustrations in the daily newspaper and especially in the Sunday rotogravure section. Though his parents and teachers wish him to keep up on the news of the day, still he feels obliged in conscience to give up reading these newspapers.

9 A young businessman knows that he is sure to hear immoral stories if he delays long in the locker room after his round of golf. Though these stories generally cause him very grave temptations, he makes it a practice to listen to them, especially if the narrator happens to be a business prospect of his.

10 "I want to be natural," avows a college girl. "I just cannot understand how anybody can call practicing modesty really a normal way of acting. It seems to me that it generally makes a person very stiff and stilted."

11 "Chastity after all is a feminine virtue," declares the town he-man. "Why should a real he-man pay much attention to acquiring purity? Always trying to be perfectly chaste can't do anything else but make a man effeminate. A fellow has to have more freedom in such things than a woman."

12 "I never take liberties with any girl who objects to them," says a handsome young man; "consequently I don't see anything very wrong about the way I act."

13 A budding intellectual knows that a certain popular movie is obscene in parts. "I favor such movies," says he, "because they portray life just as it is."

Topics for discussion[5]

1 Sexual abstinence is not injurious to one's health.

2 Instruction in matters of sex should be imparted to the young only when such instruction is necessary.

3 Depicting the nude in statue or oil is perfectly licit provided the artist produces a thing of beauty.

4 There is no harm in suggestive stories if they are really funny.

5 Is the sex instinct in itself evil? Explain.

6 The only cure for the prevalent modern immorality is a return to the practice of religion.

7 The virtue of chastity brings true liberty to those who practice it.

Bibliography

Arnold, Franz X. "The Theology of Sense and Sex." *Theology Digest* 2:107-10, Spring 1954.

Connery, John R. "Steady Dating Among Adolescents." *Theological Studies* 19:73-80, March 1958.

Connors, Charles. "Teen-Agers 'Going Steady': Whose Problem?" *Homiletic and Pastoral Review* 58:249-54, December 1957.

Davis, Henry. *Moral and Pastoral Theology*, seventh edition, edited by L. W. Geddes, Vol. 2, pp. 200-36. 4 vols. New York: Sheed and Ward, 1958.

Ford, John C. and Gerald Kelly. *Contemporary Moral Theology*, Vol. 1, pp. 157-66. Westminster: Newman Press, 1958.

Gardiner, Harold C. "Moral Principles for Discerning the Obscene." In *Proceedings of the Ninth Annual Convention of the Catholic Theological Society of America*, pp. 126-39. New York: Catholic Theological Society of America, 1954.

Haring, Bernhard. "Love and Celibacy." *Theology Digest* 7:11-14, Winter 1959.

Jone, Heribert. *Moral Theology*, pp. 145-61. Westminster: Newman Press, 1957.

Kelly, Gerald and John C. Ford. "The Legion of Decency." *Theological Studies* 18:387-433, September 1957.

Kelly, Gerald; B. R. Fulkerson; and C. F. Whitford. *Modern Youth and Chastity*. St. Louis: Queen's Work, 1940.

---

[5] Not all the assertions contained in the topics are true. The student is to judge the truth of any assertions made and to explain his decision.

Lochet, Louis. "The Ends of Marriage." *Theology Digest* 1:21-26, Winter 1953.

Lynch, John J. "Current Theology: Notes on Moral Theology." *Theological Studies* 19:172-76, June 1958 (on the Legion of Decency); 19:183-87, June 1958 (on modesty in dress); 19:170-72, June 1958 (on steady dating).

Messenger, Ernest C. *Two in One Flesh.* 3 vols. Westminster: Newman Press, 1949.

Mooney, Philip T. "Dating in Charity." *Catholic Mind* 57:212-17, May-June 1959.

Pius XI. *Christian Marriage in Our Day (Casti connubii).* In Joseph Husslein, editor, *Social Wellsprings,* Vol. 2, pp. 125-73. 2 vols. Milwaukee: Bruce Publishing Company, 1940, 1942.

Ple, A. "The Virtue of Chastity." *Theology Digest* 5:13-17, Winter 1957.

Sorokin, Pitrim. *The American Sex Revolution.* Boston: Porter E. Sargent, 1957.

Thomas, John L. "Clothes, Culture, and Modesty." *Social Order* 4:386-94, November 1954.

———— "The Place of Sex." *Social Order* 7:195-201, May 1957.

CHAPTER X

"Thou shalt not steal." The seventh
Exodus 20:15

"Neither shalt thou desire . . . and tenth
any thing that is his."
Exodus 20:17
commandments

T HE Seventh Commandment is directed to the protection of
the rights that man possesses in reference to the ownership of
property. It expressly forbids all external violation of commutative
justice such as stealing and the unjust damaging of others' property. The Tenth Commandment forbids unjust desires. It empha-
sizes the fact that the morality of man's actions depends on his
will and intention.

Although we have already treated the virtue of justice briefly
in Chapter 3, it may be helpful to develop it at greater length in
connection with the Seventh Commandment. As we said in the
same chapter, the virtue of charity is the greatest of the virtues.
Charity vitalizes all the virtues and gives them supernatural value.
Charity, however, cannot be a substitute for justice. The latter is
a most important virtue in regard to our neighbor. Moral theologians spend a great deal of time over questions of justice and
are somewhat concerned about the lack of a sense of justice in
many persons today, even in those who are well educated and in

those who have been brought up in a Christian atmosphere. Many men and women who lead good Catholic lives in other respects seem to engage in business practices which are clearly unjust. They excuse their practices on the score that it is impossible to stay in business without them. While no one should judge the subjective guilt of others, we can without lack of charity affirm that there is something awry in their thinking. It is probably not far from the truth to say that the everyday martyrdom of the modern American Catholic consists in a strict adherence to justice. Christ did not promise that following Him would be easy. The acceptance of the privations and humiliations which result from the strict practice of justice is one of the best ways of bearing witness to Christ in our society. A man who lives in a smaller home and drives a less expensive car because he refuses to be unjust may feel that he is looked down on by his more successful neighbors as a simpleton, but he has the consolation of knowing that he is leading a life of integrity and that he is acting in a way most pleasing to Christ. The same could be said for a woman who refuses to join in conversations which unjustly destroy the good name of her neighbor.

On the other hand, there are some Catholics who err by thinking that they have obligations in justice when none actually exist. Because problems of justice are so complicated, it is often difficult to determine the rights involved in a particular case. If after a serious effort to arrive at the truth the right of another remains doubtful, a person can act for his own best interests; the ceding of his claim might be a virtuous act, but he is under no obligation to give to another what may belong to himself. Those who tend to be very strict in judging the actions of others should be careful not to condemn those who follow opinions which are solidly probable and hence tenable. For instance, if it is *doubtful* that a person was capable at the time of making his will, it would not be unjust for relatives to attempt to break the will by legal procedure. This is an opinion which may be followed despite the fact that some moralists might require *certainty* of incompetency in the one who signed the will. Nor should the fact that a man is financially successful be considered as indication that he has been dishonest. Certain people have a knack for business which others do not enjoy; the legitimate use of this natural talent is good and should not be the occasion for jealousy on the part of those who do not have it. We ourselves can be unjust because we rashly judge our neighbor to be unjust.

It would not be out of place to recall also what was said in Chapter 3 about the virtue of fortitude. It applies, not only to fear arising from physical danger, but also to fear arising from human respect. Most of us do not have occasion to exercise fortitude in the face of physical danger very often in our lives, but we are constantly under pressure from the society in which we live, from the "world," if you will, to give up our ideals and to act as others do in order to avoid embarrassment. Fortitude is necessary for the practice of any virtue, but it is particularly necessary for one who wishes to be just. St. Thomas said that there can be no *perfect* virtue unless we have *all* the virtues. A Christian who tries to live in the modern world without developing fortitude will find himself unable to practice the other virtues, especially those in opposition to the dominant social trends of the times.

God, a generous provider, has through nature put at the disposal of the human race more than enough of this world's goods to meet the needs of all mankind. Since man has the duty to preserve his own life and health and to provide for the necessities of his dependents, each one has the right to acquire in a legitimate manner, and to own, at least as much of nature's resources as is necessary for his own conservation and that of his family. The existence of this right is established in general ethics. Moreover, once he has justly acquired certain property, he is justified in demanding that others respect this right of ownership. The Seventh Commandment is an implicit command to observe the rights of others according to the virtue of justice.

THEFT

The nature of theft

Theft is the secret taking of another's goods against his reasonable wish. The following would be included under theft:

1. "Borrowing" an article without the owner's consent and with the intention of giving it back. This is equivalent to stealing the article temporarily.

2. Taking goods as a loan with the owner's consent and then refusing to restore them.

3. Running up a charge account that one foresees one will never be able to pay.

4. Living so extravagantly when burdened with debts that the payment of these debts is rendered impossible.

BORROWING WITH PRESUMED CONSENT

To borrow an article with the owner's presumed consent is entirely permissible. To borrow with the owner's presumed consent means that I take it for granted that the owner, if he were asked, would freely give me permission to use the object in question. One may presume such consent only when the owner cannot conveniently be consulted and when one can honestly judge that he would not object to one's borrowing it without his explicit consent; one must afterward inform the owner about the action that was taken.

EXAMPLE 1. A boy in need of a dollar for dinner takes it from his father's desk without asking permission. His father is out of town and his mother will not be home till late in the evening. The father always gives him that amount for dinner, and consequently his consent may be reasonably presumed in this particular case.

EXAMPLE 2. A suburbanite borrows his neighbor's lawn mower without asking. His neighbor always lends the lawn mower when requested to do so. This action would not be contrary to justice but it might be contrary to charity, especially if the neighbor's consent could have been easily obtained. The neighbor might want to use the lawn mower himself and might consequently be inconvenienced.

The sinfulness of theft

To ascertain the degree of sinfulness of any particular theft one must consider three elements: (1) the value of the stolen goods, (2) the person against whom the theft is committed, and (3) the time over which the theft is spread. We shall analyze each of these three points in detail.

THE VALUE OF THE STOLEN GOODS

The value of the stolen goods may be either (1) absolutely grave, (2) relatively grave, or (3) slight.

1. By *absolutely grave value* is understood a value or amount so great as to constitute matter for a mortal sin regardless of the person from whom the goods are stolen. In order to protect the common welfare and the security of property in general, stealing

a considerable amount of another's goods must always be forbidden under pain of grave sin. In this case we are not concerned so much about whether the victim would be *greatly inconvenienced* by the loss of the stolen goods; the chief consideration here is rather the fact that unjustly taking from another an absolutely grave sum would constitute *a serious violation of public order*. If such thefts were only venially sinful, there would follow a constant, serious threat to peace and property rights, and the stimulus to acquire goods by honest means would be seriously lessened. As to how much money should be looked upon as the absolutely grave sum, an absolutely grave sum may be said to be the amount which is equivalent to the weekly wages received by a person of the middle class of society. Hence the exact sum necessary to constitute an absolutely grave sum usually will vary with different countries.

EXAMPLE. A man who steals two hundred dollars in a single theft from a millionaire commits a mortal sin of theft.

2. By *relatively grave value* is understood a value or amount so great that its theft would prove a notable loss to the particular owner in question. In this case we look to the inconvenience and damage that the theft would mean to the individual victim. If he is affected seriously by the theft, the injustice would be a mortal sin. Hence the stealing of goods below the absolutely grave amount would in many instances be grievously sinful because notable harm is thus inflicted on some particular individual.

Expressed in terms of money, a relatively grave sum is in general the average day's pay of the victim in question, or the sum needed to provide for one day both his family and himself with food, clothing, lodging, and the other necessities of life. This amount will vary, of course, with individuals, since one man may receive ten dollars a day, another thirty dollars, his wages depending on the country where he resides, on the nature of the work he does, on his ability, and so forth.

EXAMPLE. A maid in a hotel steals fifteen dollars from a guest who earns only fifty dollars a week. This would be a grave theft, for taking such a sum from this individual would cause him serious injury.

3. By *slight value* is understood a value or amount so small that its theft would be neither absolutely grave matter (a serious threat to public order) nor relatively grave matter (a serious loss

to the individual robbed). When the matter is slight, the sin of theft is venial.

THE PERSON AGAINST WHOM THE THEFT IS COMMITTED

We have already mentioned the general rule that the daily earnings of the person robbed determine the gravity of a theft committed against him. In addition we must consider the cases (1) of the very wealthy and (2) of one's own parents or immediate relatives.

1. The sinfulness of thefts from very wealthy individuals or from corporations should be computed according to the absolutely grave sum.

2. To steal from one's parents or close relatives is ordinarily not so great a sin as unjustly taking the same amount from a total stranger. The reason for this is that the evil of theft consists in taking *against his reasonable wishes* what belongs to another. Parents quite naturally would be less unwilling to be deprived of their possessions in favor of their own children than to have utter strangers seize these goods for themselves. Hence a child's thefts from his parents would not be grave unless they reached an amount much greater than that which would constitute a grave sin if it were stolen from a stranger in financial circumstances similar to those of the parents.

THE TIME OVER WHICH THE THEFT IS SPREAD

In addition to thefts of lump sums we have (1) thefts of small sums taken at intervals and amounting in the end to grave matter, (2) thefts of small sums begun with the intention of ultimately reaching a considerable sum, and (3) thefts of small sums that never amount to a serious sum.

1. If a sum of money is stolen at intervals, a little at a time, it does not ordinarily cause so much harm to the victim as would the taking of that same amount all at once. Hence in judging the sinfulness of such acts of injustice a distinction is made between a theft of one lump sum and a series of small thefts. In order to constitute grave matter a sum of money that is stolen at intervals would have to be much greater than that which would be a mortally sinful theft if taken at one time.

2. In some cases, however, the fact that the money or goods stolen is taken at intervals does not affect the gravity of the sin.

Even if the money is stolen at intervals, if one intends to steal a large sum of money (for example, three hundred dollars) little by little, there would be matter for grave sin regardless of how long it took one to carry out the theft. In this case these small thefts would coalesce or unite *through one's intention,* and no larger amount would be necessary to make up grave matter than would be required if he had stolen the three hundred dollars in a lump sum. Ordinarily, if one were to steal a fixed small amount habitually over a long period of time, he would have the intention of taking a large amount a little at a time. Hence his small thefts would coalesce through the intention either of stealing a certain grave sum or of stealing indefinitely from his victim.

> EXAMPLE. A clerk makes it a practice to steal ten dollars a week from his employer. He thinks that the loss of this amount will not be noticed, and he intends to continue these thefts indefinitely. The clerk sins gravely, for the thefts coalesce through his intention.

3. Small thefts that are repeated at long intervals, if not united through one's intention, do not coalesce.

> EXAMPLE. A salesgirl, without planning eventually to acquire a large sum of money, finds that over a period of five years she has stolen in small amounts a total of about twenty dollars a year from a large retail store. These thefts do not coalesce.

If these distinctions seem to be somewhat arbitrary, it should be recalled that moral theologians have the difficult task of determining what constitutes a serious violation of public order or serious inconvenience and damage to an individual. A line has to be drawn somewhere, and that drawn by moral theologians is based on a prudent judgment which takes all the factors into consideration. It is easy to make such distinctions an object of ridicule by reducing them to the difference of a few cents or a few days and asking with a shocked expression if theologians mean to say that a few cents or a few days would make the difference between saving my immortal soul or losing it. But if the line is not drawn, you can push it up penny by penny until you reach the obvious absurdity that the theft of a million dollars does not constitute a serious sin, or the equally absurd conclusion that the theft of one penny would make a person liable to eternal punishment. What is said here regarding questions of justice also applies to many other moral problems, such as the fulfillment of the obligation to attend Sunday Mass or the amount of food which constitutes a serious violation of the law of fasting. It is easy to ridicule, but ridicule does not solve the problem.

THE DANGERS OF PETTY THIEVERY

Though some, enticed by an apparently easy way of obtaining luxuries, may be tempted to indulge in small thefts because of the fact that the sinfulness is not grave, three considerations should halt any yielding to such allurements. First of all, a clear realization of the malice of venial sin, the greatest evil in the world except for mortal sin, should prevent all acts of injustice. Second, one should recall that, before God forgives sins of theft, the thief must promise to return the stolen goods insofar as he is able. Third, experience teaches that the vice of stealing is one that grows apace; and though a person begins in a small way and tries to persuade himself that he will stop there, it happens only too frequently that he soon finds himself entangled in very grave thefts and in a habit which is hard to shake off. Petty thievery also has a harmful effect on the whole personality because it leads to lying, secretiveness, and selfishness. It involves a false attitude toward life and encourages the tendency to shirk responsibility and to depend on others.

The rights of authors and inventors

Authors and inventors, according to the natural law, have full ownership over the fruits of their labor or genius. Hence writers and inventors enjoy a strict right to their manuscripts, plans, or designs, and others may not take, use, or publish them without the author's consent. If one does this and so cheats the author out of profits that should be his, restitution must be made. Authors and inventors should be advised to obtain copyrights or patent rights in order to protect their interests.

Taking another's goods in extreme need

The mere act of taking goods that belong to another is not sinful in itself. It is unjust only when the property is taken *without the owner's reasonable consent.* When, therefore, in a given set of circumstances, the owner's consent may be reasonably presumed, the act of taking his goods is justified and so should not be termed theft.

In extreme need one may licitly take of another's property what is necessary to relieve one's present necessity. Such extreme need exists when one is in very grave danger of losing one's life, health, liberty, reputation, or the equivalent, since these are surely of far more value than the goods seized. In these circumstances one's right to life and to the means necessary to preserve life, a connatural right, takes precedence over the owner's right to his property, an acquired right. If I am in extreme necessity, I may take what I need to tide me over that emergency. My action would be licit, even though the owner actually refuses to give up what is needed. The right of taking another's goods may also be exercised to relieve the extreme necessity of another. The one from whom I take the goods must not be placed in extreme need by my act, for then I would not be justified in taking his property but would be obliged to look elsewhere for help.

EXAMPLE 1. X, who is starving and unable to get work or help, secretly takes food from well-fed Z's home. X commits no sin.

EXAMPLE 2. A fisherman, sitting on a dock, hears a cry for help. He jumps into a rowboat not belonging to him and goes to the aid of a drowning person.

The needy person must take only what is absolutely necessary at the time. He is bound to restore later if able to do so. Thus, in Example 2 above, the fisherman would be obliged to return the rowboat of which he made use.

The civil law does not ordinarily recognize this right of taking another's goods when one is in extreme necessity. The reason is that the practice is open to grave abuse. The attitude of the state, however, does not change the morality of this manner of acting. Hence one could so act with a clear conscience, though, if apprehended by civil authorities, one might be punished. In some cases, however, civil law does recognize such a right. If a ship were disabled and the ordinary food supplies ran out, the crew and passengers could break into the cargo and use what they needed to survive without being liable to prosecution on criminal charges.

Occult compensation

At times one is unable to collect money that is due him in strict justice. It may be that the debtor is without a conscience and I cannot prove my claim in court, or it may be that it would be very inconvenient or injurious to me to bring suit for the recovery of the debt. In such circumstances occult compensation (secret appropriation) may be employed. This is a perfectly licit way of recovering one's property or of collecting from a debtor what is owed if the ordinary means of accomplishing this cannot be used. Before invoking this manner of exacting payment one must be sure that the following conditions are verified:

1. The debt is certain and is one of commutative justice. I may not use occult compensation just because gratitude should urge the other to give me a particular article or a sum of money, or because the other has promised it to me without the intention of binding himself in justice.

2. Other methods of collecting the debt would either be useless or would involve serious inconvenience. Legal justice forbids taking the law into one's own hands if this is not absolutely necessary. Thus, if a simple request or the threat of a lawsuit would result in the payment of the debt, such means must be used. Sometimes, however, one could not adopt the ordinary methods of collecting without creating scandal, incurring enmities, or causing great expense to oneself, and one would then have the clear right to employ occult compensation. In employing occult compensation under such conditions one must guard against unnecessary injury to the debtor (for example, by depriving him of what he needs for his work) or to a third party (for example, by directing suspicion toward him).

In general, one should be slow to use occult compensation, especially if one is not acting on the advice of some prudent, honest counselor (for example, his confessor). The danger is that in one's own case one will easily deceive oneself into believing that the necessary conditions are fulfilled when actually they are not present. One who feels that he has been treated unjustly can only too easily exaggerate the extent of the injustice, overlook essential details in the agreement that was made, fail to use available means of collecting the debt, and deceive himself into thinking that the payment of the debt has already been deferred in a manner unreasonable in itself and injurious to him.

Servants and other employees should be warned against concluding that the wages paid them are unjust and that they may therefore make use of occult compensation. Often enough one overrates his own worth and is thus led falsely to conclude that he is not receiving all that justice requires. Besides the conditions mentioned above, the following must in their case be verified before occult compensation may be used:

1. The wages that are being paid are certainly less than what strict justice requires.

2. The employer could pay more and still remain in business.

3. The employee's work is necessary or very useful; that is, he has not been hired out of charity.

THE OBLIGATION OF MAKING RESTITUTION

Making restitution means the restoring of things to their proper owner or the repairing of harm or injury which one has caused. The obligation to make restitution arises only when commutative justice has been violated. This duty necessitates reinstating the injured party in the same condition he enjoyed before the injury was inflicted. Since our neighbor may be harmed in either of two ways, (1) by another's unjust possession of his property or (2) by another's destroying or damaging his property, we shall study the restitution involved by an injustice committed in either of these two ways.

Restitution necessary because of unjust possession

One who has unjust possession of another's goods may possess them either (1) in good faith or (2) in bad faith.

POSSESSION IN GOOD FAITH

It may happen that I find that I have in my possession goods belonging to somebody else. These goods may have come into my hands in a perfectly legitimate way; for example, by gift, purchase, or inheritance. At the time I acquired them, I sincerely believed that they were justly becoming my property. Later, however, I learned that the one from whom I received the goods did not own them. Hence he was not able to give me a true title to ownership.

With regard to property thus acquired one of three things may be true: (1) The goods are still in one's possession. (2) They were consumed while the possessor thought they were really his property. (3) They were sold at a time when the possessor did not realize the goods belonged to another. These three cases must be treated separately because in each the obligation differs.

1. The first case is that in which the goods are still in the possession of the one who has no title to them. X, for example, a possessor in good faith, still has the goods (for example, a platinum wrist watch) when he learns that they do not really belong to him. What must he do? If X received the goods as a gift, he must see to it that they are restored to their true owner. Unless he does this, he is keeping in his possession the goods of another against the owner's reasonable wishes, and thus he is violating the owner's rights. If, however, X had bought the goods from a thief, he may return them to the thief and get the money back, provided the true owner does not appear and lay claim to the goods before X does this. (We here assume that X could not get his money back and at the same time safeguard the owner's property; for example, by having the thief arrested.) However, if the true owner claims the property before X returns it to the thief in order to get his money back, X must surrender it to the owner, even at the cost of a complete loss to himself.

2. The second case is that in which the goods have been consumed. Y, a possessor in good faith, has already consumed the goods (a case of Benedictine) when he learns that they really belonged to somebody else. What obligations has Y now as to making good the loss to the real owners? Y need make no restitution at all. In consuming the goods Y committed no sin, for he thought at the time when he was consuming them that they were his. Moreover, the goods themselves cannot be restored to the one who owned them, for they no longer exist.

If it happened that the goods were accidentally destroyed or lost while they were in Y's possession, Y likewise has no obligation to make restitution.

3. The third case is that in which the goods have been sold or given away. In this case the goods may have been consumed or destroyed, or they may still exist. Z, an unjust possessor in good faith, had already either sold or given away the goods before learning that he did not really own them, and the goods have been consumed or destroyed. Z is not held to restitution.

EXAMPLE. A sold B a diamond ring which A thought he really owned but which actually belonged to C. B's house burned down and the ring was lost. A need not make good C's loss.

If Z, the same unjust possessor in good faith, sells the goods to another and the property is discovered and claimed by the true owner, he must restore, upon demand of the purchaser, the money he received in payment for the goods.

EXAMPLE. A high-school boy buys a watch from a classmate and later sells it to one of his friends. Actually the watch had been stolen but neither of the buyers was aware of that fact. The real owner recognizes and retrieves his watch. The first buyer must restore the money to his friend even though he sold the watch in good faith.

THE QUESTION OF PROFITS AND EXPENSES

In the three cases of unjust possession in good faith which we have just treated, X, Y, and Z may retain any profits derived from the use of the goods while they were in their possession, provided such profits were due to their own industry. In the cases just discussed in which X and Z are held to restitution, they may exact from the true owner any expenses that were necessary in maintaining the article or useful in enhancing its original value.

EXAMPLE. X was given a Ford sedan. Since it needed overhauling, X had this done. Later the true owner appears. X must give him the Ford, but may exact payment for the overhauling.

POSSESSION IN BAD FAITH

If one knowingly and unjustly keeps in his possession another person's property, he is known as a possessor in bad faith. The obligations of such a possessor are quite simple and may be stated as follows:

1. If he has these goods on hand, he must restore them at once to their owner.

EXAMPLE. A burglar reforms and now finds that he has several stolen fur coats in his possession. He must arrange to have these coats restored to their owners.

2. If the possessor in bad faith has given away or destroyed or lost the goods, he must repair the damage to the true owner.

EXAMPLE. An impecunious lover of art stole a costly portrait and kept it in his house. The house through accident burned to the ground. He must restore to the true owner the full value of the painting.

POSSESSION IN DOUBTFUL FAITH

If one is doubtful as to whether he really owns an article in his possession, he must investigate the case. If he fails to investigate to the best of his ability, he becomes a possessor in bad faith.

If even after the investigation his doubt persists, he may licitly retain the article in question.

> EXAMPLE. An engaged man purchased a watch from a small jeweler. Later he discovers that this jeweler is in league with a group of thieves and disposes of some of their booty. He begins to wonder whether the watch he purchased had been stolen. His investigations do not clear up all his doubts. He is justified in retaining the watch.

DETERMINING THE AMOUNT TO BE RESTORED

In general, restitution of what has been consumed, lost, or destroyed may be made according to the value of the goods at the time they were stolen, despite the fact that the same article would cost more if purchased now.

Since the question of the obligation of making restitution is quite complicated, lay persons who must decide whether or not they are bound to make restitution are advised not to try to settle the problem themselves, but to go for guidance to their confessor, who has complete knowledge of this matter.

Circumstances excusing from restitution

There are some circumstances that may excuse one from making restitution for a debt clearly contracted. The following causes excuse from the obligation of repairing injury that has been inflicted through theft or unjust damage: (1) condonation of the debt by the creditor, (2) the debtor's inability to repay, and (3) bankruptcy.

CONDONATION BY THE CREDITOR

In cases of condonation the true owner freely gives up all claim to restitution.

> EXAMPLE. A boy decides to run away and takes one hundred dollars out of his uncle's wallet. He returns after spending the money. The uncle tells him not to worry about paying back the money.

THE DEBTOR'S INABILITY TO REPAY

Inability to make restitution may excuse the debtor for a time or forever. The exact length of time during which he is excused will depend on how long this inability endures. One is morally unable to restore when one cannot make restitution without suffering a serious loss in one of the following ways: (1) in goods justly acquired, or (2) in goods of a higher order, or (3) without being reduced to grave necessity.

EXAMPLE 1. X could not now repair the damage he has done without selling at a great loss some of his inherited books.

EXAMPLE 2. If Y makes restitution now, he will be suspected of being a thief and so will lose his good name.

EXAMPLE 3. Z owes one hundred dollars and is now out of work. If he pays S the money, he will have nothing on which to support himself and his family. Z is not bound to repay S right now.

BANKRUPTCY

A bankrupt is a person who has been declared, by judicial pronouncement, insolvent or unable to meet the just claims of his creditors. The civil law in the United States not only bars all legal action against an honest bankrupt for the recovery of debts but cancels the debts themselves. The purpose of this law is to allow the bankrupt to begin his business life anew, unhampered by the overwhelming handicap of such financial burdens. The United States Bankruptcy Law, revised in June 1938, reads in part as follows: "A discharge in bankruptcy shall release a bankrupt from all his provable debts, whether allowable in full or in part, except such as: (i) are due as a tax levied by the United States or any state or county . . . (ii) liabilities for obtaining money or property by false pretenses . . . or for alimony, and so forth."

The civil law also extinguishes such debts *in conscience* because the law is enacted for the common good and businessmen know the law and willingly assume the risk of losses because of the bankruptcy of those with whom they deal.

DISHONEST BANKRUPTCY

A culpable bankrupt must pay in full all his just debts. Even though one may deceive the civil court into declaring him legally bankrupt, he still has the same obligations regarding his debts as he had before the court decision.

UNJUST DAMAGE

One inflicts unjust damage when one causes harm to another with or without material benefit to oneself. For example, X destroys Y's overcoat by purposely splashing it with acid. The mere intention to inflict injury, though it is sinful, does not by itself create the obligation to make restitution. One who has inflicted unjust damage on another must repair the injury only if the following three conditions are verified:

1. The damage actually occurred. This condition is *not* verified in the following example:

> EXAMPLE. A factory worker who has been fired drops a wrench in a piece of expensive machinery. The wrench is accidentally discovered before the machine is started and no damage results.

2. His act must have caused the damage. For example, if a patient's illness is greatly prolonged because the wrong medicine was prescribed, it is not the druggist who caused the harm (for he merely filled the prescription), but rather the physician who prescribed the remedy.

3. His act must be done sinfully. Hence injury inflicted by one who is temporarily insane or by a person who is walking in his sleep involves no obligation of restitution, since in both cases sin is impossible because of lack of knowledge.

> EXAMPLE. A man who has become thoroughly intoxicated through no fault of his own takes his friend's jeweled watch and flings it into the river. He is not responsible for this damage.

Although a person may not be theologically guilty of unjust damages, he would have to pay for damages inflicted on another if civil authorities impose the obligation on him. If a man's car rolls down the street and bumps into another and the court determines that he is to pay for the damages, he must do so, even though he is convinced that he exercised all possible care in parking his car. It is essential for public order and the common good that the civil authorities should have this power and that citizens should have the obligation of obeying court decisions. The state cannot determine when a man is theologically guilty, and it would be impossible to try to settle damage suits if this condition had to be verified. This power of the state may sometimes work hardship for the individual, but in many cases the welfare of the individual must be subservient to the common good.

UNJUST COOPERATION

A particular type of unjust damage is that in which one does not actually perform the action which causes the damage, but cooperates with the one who does perform the action. Cooperation in these cases can be of various kinds: supplying another with the means; encouraging him; advising him how to go about it. It is obvious that such cooperation is immoral. The principles regarding the obligation of the cooperator to make restitution are very complicated. They are treated at some length in complete works on moral theology.

THE RIGHTS OF MINORS

A minor is a boy or girl under 21 years of age who is not emancipated. A minor may be emancipated by marriage, by entrance into a religious order, or by parental consent. The property rights of minors who are not emancipated pertain chiefly to (1) gifts and inheritances and (2) their earnings.

GIFTS AND INHERITANCES

All gifts and inheritances that minors receive become their own property and not that of the parents. Hence minors should be given both the capital and the interest or profits from all such possessions. The administration of the property of minors lies in the hands of the father.

EARNINGS

If a minor works in a place away from home and is not supported by his father, he has full ownership of all his earnings. If, however, his father supports him, he may use the minor's earnings to defray these expenses. Parental duty does not bind the father to do more than to see to it that the son's needs are provided for and ceases if the son is supporting himself.

Even though the minor is living at home, he has a right to his extraordinary earnings. This applies, for example, to child actors and musicians. The parent should permit the child to use an amount that is reasonable and should hold the remainder in trust until the child becomes of age.

ARTICLES FOUND

One who finds money, jewelry, or other articles may keep what he has found until the owner is located. Such articles do not become the property of the finder merely because he has found them, but he enjoys the right to retain them against the claims of everyone except the true owner. While the goods found are in his possession, he must use ordinary care in guarding them. Moreover, he must exercise reasonable diligence to discover the owner. The extent of the investigation to be made will vary according to the value of the article found. In the case of articles of moderate value (for example, a medium-priced watch), reading and advertising in the lost-and-found column of the daily newspaper for a few days would be sufficient. If, however, the article is of great value (for example, a costly gem), the civil law should be consulted as to what is required in the way of trying to discover the owner. The civil law is not the same in all the states of the Union. If after due investigation the owner cannot be identified, the finder may then regard the property as his own and may use it accordingly. Were the real owner to appear a year or so later, the finder would be obliged to surrender the article to him; but if he has wholly or partially consumed it or given it to the poor, he need not make good this loss to the owner.

THE OBLIGATIONS OF MERCHANTS

A merchant must reveal all substantial defects in an article to be sold. Substantial defects are those that make the article other than it appears or render it useless for the known purpose of the buyer. For example, if one sells synthetic wine for use at Mass, the purchase is substantially defective; for though the liquid tastes, smells, and looks like genuine grape wine, it is not valid matter for the holy sacrifice of the Mass.

The seller need not call attention to obvious defects of minor importance. If he is expressly questioned about them, he is obliged to mention them. Even though the customer in making the purchase overlooks the article's obvious defects, no injustice is done, provided the price is reduced accordingly.

EXAMPLE. A woman buys curtains a little torn at one corner. The salesman need not point out the tear if it is obvious.

If fraud or deceit is absent, it is not unjust:

1. To charge a high price for rare articles or for those that are merely luxuries.

EXAMPLE. I demand a large sum of money for a hat that belonged to George Washington or for a piece of bric-a-brac that is an antique.

2. To sell an article at the current price, even though I know for certain that the price will soon fall.

EXAMPLE. I sell a typewriter today for a hundred and ten dollars though I have secret information to the effect that the same machine will sell for ten dollars less within a week's time.

3. To demand an increase in price for an article very dear to me.

EXAMPLE. A collector wishes to purchase my family Bible to fill in a collection that he is making. Since this book was given to me years ago by my parents, I treasure it highly. I am justified in asking a large sum for it.

To raise the current price because of the buyer's special need is profiteering and is not just. The reason is that the purchaser's special need is not the property of the seller, and consequently he may not sell it.

THE DUTIES OF BUSINESSMEN

The businessman is engaged in work that is an asset to society. The fruits of other parts of the earth and the products of industrial centers far away are brought by merchants to a city or town for the benefit of its people. The businessman is making available for those dwelling in this district various commodities which they may need or find useful. He is providing them with the opportunity to purchase food, clothing, and equipment and appliances of many kinds. An occupation so worthy in itself should not be dishonored by unscrupulous practices.

THE CHRISTIAN ATTITUDE TOWARD BUSINESS

The machinery of business today is not always simple. It can become very complicated and involve many moral problems that are not easy to solve. Business must, of course, be conducted according to the principles of Christian morality. The explanations of the commandments of God, especially the Seventh, that are contained in MORAL GUIDANCE should, for the most part, make clear what obligations a businessman has. The chief difficulty arises from the attempt to apply to individual cases well-known principles of good conduct. Business involves competition, and often the competition is very great. In order to survive against this competition a man may indulge in ways of acting that he

214

would prefer to avoid. He may acquire the habit of judging the morality of his own actions by what his competitors practice. Before long he begins to feel that he is above reproach if he manages to escape the censure of better-business bureaus and the like. Too often this norm gradually becomes: "Make all the money you can in any way possible without becoming involved with the civil authorities." Does not the code of business ethics that is being acted upon today seem in the minds of some businessmen to come to this: "It is lawful if the other fellow is doing the same thing"? We can readily see how dangerous this practical standard of right conduct is when we recall who this "other fellow" is apt to be. He may be a pure atheist with little idea of morality. He may be one whose conscience has been dulled by an evil life. Catholics at times allow this greed for riches to undermine their faith and obscure their sense of justice.

The Catholic businessman, it should be remembered, is never excused from the observance of the ten commandments. A Catholic would not begin to believe that blasphemy or infanticide or adultery were permissible because of the commonness of these sins in the lives of those with whom he has business dealings. Why, then, does he not take the same unbending attitude toward the other teachings of the ten commandments? He must not allow himself to judge the goodness or badness of business practice by the actions of those whose only guiding light is expediency. Unless he keeps clearly in mind the teachings of justice, business will soon drag him down into its quagmire of dishonest dealings.

FORBIDDEN BUSINESS PRACTICES

It would be impossible to treat all abuses in business practice without writing a complete book, but a few of the more common ones which are clearly unjust should be mentioned. A contractor would be unjust to do work in such a way that extensive repairs would be necessary in a short time unless he makes it clear to the customer that such is the case and the customer insists that the work be done in that way. It would likewise be unjust to use materials inferior to those called for in the contract. It would be wrong for a contractor to give work to a subcontractor who is known for his unjust practices; if he cannot avoid giving the work to such a subcontractor, he must take means to protect the rights of his employer. It would also be unjust to charge for work which was not done—for instance, in repairing a plumbing system—or to charge for time which was not actually used on the job. It would be wrong to put in parts or do work which is unnecessary. It would not only be a lie but also an injustice to misrepresent one's product by claiming advantages which it does not possess or to lie about one's competitors or their products. It would be contrary to the Fifth Commandment and to justice to do work in such a way as to endanger the lives either of the workmen (because of poor equipment or lack of safety measures) or of others (because of faulty construction or defective material).

LIVING WAGE

Although we cannot enter into a great number of problems which involve economic facts, the problem of a just wage is so important that it cannot be omitted. Pope Leo XIII in *Rerum novarum* set forth the general principle that workers must be paid a living wage; that is, one which enables them to purchase the necessities of life and leaves them something for legitimate recreation and a certain amount of comfort according to their state in life. Pius XI made it more explicit that this wage was to be one which enables a man to raise a family. All moralists agree that the obligation to provide a family wage exists, but they do not agree as to who has the obligation. Ideally, the employer should pay a family wage, but it is impractical to demand that he do so when such a requirement would make it impossible for him to stay in business. This is especially true if one insists, as does Father Jeremiah Newman, that the family wage means an *absolute* family wage—one which is sufficient for a very large family.[1] It is much more realistic to hold that the paying of a family wage falls partially on the employer and partially on society in general. In the United States the government recognizes such an obligation by allowing tax exemptions for children. Private agencies such as unions also recognize the principle by establishing hospitals for the care of their members; obviously, a large family would profit more from such free care than an individual.

The obligation of the employer is to pay a family wage if possible in the present circumstances; if he cannot do so, then he

---

[1] See Jeremiah Newman, "The Just Wage." *Theology Digest* 5:120-26, Spring 1957.

must pay as much as is consistent with a reasonable profit. Since it will sometimes be impossible to pay a family wage to all employees, the employer should not be told that he has an obligation in strict justice to do so. This would mean that some employers are necessarily sinning by staying in business. If it is not possible to pay a family wage in the circumstances that exist, an employer has an obligation in social justice to work for a change in the conditions which prevent the paying of such a wage. The difference between what an employer can pay and what constitutes a family wage must be made up by society in general. This usually means that the state, which alone has sufficient authority to put into practice the necessary measures, must intervene either directly or indirectly.

A good norm for determining whether or not an employer is fulfilling his obligation is that given by the archbishops and bishops of the Civil Province of Quebec in their joint pastoral letter of 1950: "In the present labour conditions, the collective agreement, negotiated with a free union, may be considered as the normal means of deciding on the just wage; the means, however, would cease to be legitimate if the agreement were the result of undue pressure."[2] Two things should be noted in this statement. First, it is presupposed that labor unions are the ordinary means by which the workers bargain. Second, the wage agreed on should be considered just only if there is real freedom on both sides. This letter contains much excellent matter and should be read by anyone who wishes to understand the application of the general principles of the papal encyclicals to specific problems.

LABOR UNIONS

Attention has been called to the problems of labor unions by the long and often heated investigations of congressional committees. Unfortunately, these investigations have caused some Americans to suspect all union activity. A little knowledge of the history of labor in the past few centuries is sufficient to convince any open-minded person of the necessity of some form of protection for the workingman. Leo XIII saw the necessity of such protection and advocated it in his revolutionary *Rerum novarum* in

---

[2] *The Problem of the Worker in the Light of the Social Doctrine of the Church.* Montreal: Palm Publishers, 1950.

1891. So far no form of protection has proved feasible except labor unions. Attempts should be made to perfect, reform, or replace unions as circumstances demand, but the right of workingmen to organize cannot be questioned and employers have an obligation to respect this right. Even when an employer pays just wages and provides proper working conditions, the organization of workingmen is necessary to present demands and to govern relationships among the workingmen themselves.

Unions have a twofold function. First, they seek to protect the strict right of the workingman by obtaining just wages, reasonable hours, and proper working conditions. Second, they attempt to secure benefits which go beyond the strict right of the workingman but which can be legitimately sought by him. For example, they can bargain with employers for insurance or pension benefits. In addition to these two functions, which concern compensation for work, unions today recognize numerous other functions, such as setting up educational programs, providing medical assistance for members, and so forth.

Many rights and benefits are gained by ordinary bargaining. Moral theologians hold that the ordinary means of bargaining must be used before recourse is had to the drastic means of striking. In addition, they demand that any strike called must have reasonable hope of success and that the good effects sought must outweigh the evil effects of reduced income and production. The strike must be carried on by lawful and moral actions. Some hold that a strike can be called only to obtain what is owed to the worker in strict justice; others, however, would allow a strike even to obtain additional benefits because, unless the union could use this means, it would never be able to obtain such benefits from certain employers.

Workingmen have duties as well as rights. They are obliged in justice to do a reasonable day's work. In our complicated economy it is not always easy to determine what constitutes a reasonable day's work. It is regrettable that workingmen sometimes stretch out work in order to assure continued employment; but if we suppose a situation in which a man would not be employed for three or four months of the year if he worked at full capacity, there is certainly some argument for his working at a more moderate pace. In an economy which assures farmers a certain price for their products and rewards them for not planting more than a certain amount, we should not find such a practice shocking. Both farmers and unions should work to change social and economic conditions which make such practices necessary, but for the present it is difficult to see how they can be avoided.

BETTING, LOTTERIES, AND GAMBLING

Betting is a contract in which the parties involved agree to give a reward to whichever one correctly guesses a certain fact or future event. For example, one bets that a certain horse will win a race, that a certain baseball team will win the pennant, or that it was a certain author who wrote a book or a certain individual who won a prize.

THE LICITNESS OF BETTING

Betting is licit if the following conditions are verified:
1. The bet is not an inducement to committing a sinful act.

EXAMPLE. A passenger in a car bets the driver that he can't cover the next ten miles on a crowded and dangerous highway in a certain amount of time. In order to win the bet the driver would have to endanger his own life and the lives of others.

2. The betters are uncertain about the point in dispute.
3. The betters understand the terms and conditions of the bet in the same way.
4. Each intends to pay, and is able to pay, if he loses.

Though betting is licit under these conditions, it may happen that what is at first only an innocent pastime will gradually become an insatiable habit which carries one away to such an extent that one risks all on the outcome of the bet. Thus one may be placing in jeopardy what is necessary to satisfy one's just obligations. Hence one must be cautious in the matter, lest the habit of gambling gradually become enrooted. We read constantly of bookkeepers and other trusted employees who have embezzled thousands of dollars because they were "playing the races."

If one better is certain about the point in question and does not inform the other better of this certainty, the contract is invalid. An essential condition is lacking, and so the victor cannot in justice retain his winnings. If, however, he informed the other of his own certainty in the matter and the other insisted on betting anyway, he could keep his winnings, for in that case the other could be considered as consenting to making him a gift of the money that he won.

LOTTERIES

A lottery is a contract by which prizes are distributed by lot or chance among those who hold lottery tickets (for example, the Irish sweepstakes). A lottery is licit provided (1) there is no fraud and (2) the hope of winning is in fair proportion to the price of each ticket purchased. If, for example, "chances" on a Cadillac car are sold at five dollars each, the number of tickets should be so limited that those sponsoring the lottery make only a reasonable profit. Those who buy chances to help a good cause, however, are satisfied to have little hope of winning.

DEFINITION OF GAMBLING

Gambling is a contract in which the participants in a game of chance (for example, bingo, dice, poker) agree to give the winner a certain prize, sum of money, or something else of value. Playing billiards, golf, tennis, and other games for stakes is not strictly gambling, since the outcome depends on skill and not—or at least only partially—on chance.

THE LICITNESS OF GAMBLING

Gambling is licit provided that the following three conditions are verified:

1. The stakes belong to the one who gambles and may be disposed of by him. Hence a lawyer may not gamble with his client's money, nor may a man licitly stake money at poker that is necessary either for his family's support or for paying his just debts.

2. There is no fraud involved; as, for example, stacking the cards or loading the dice. It is not illicit to attempt to deceive one's opponents in a game by facial expression or tone of voice if such tricks are accepted as part of the game.

3. Equality of risk is observed; that is, there is for all participants an approximately equal hope of winning and equal danger of losing.

EXAMPLE. An expert poker player sits down to a game with an inexperienced player. Here there is no equality of risk at all and so the expert would not be acting honestly. If, however, the inexperienced player knows his opponent is an expert, realizes that he has little chance of winning, and still enters the game freely, he tacitly consents to waive the condition that is ordinarily necessary for lawful gambling. Hence the expert plays with him licitly.

PROFESSIONAL GAMBLING HOUSES

Professional gambling houses are establishments that make a business of gambling. Since the operators of these places depend for their livelihood on the profits of the games played there, they are very careful to see to it that the "house" wins regularly. In our country at the present time many evils are associated with professional gambling. The connection between gambling and gangsterism has been proved again and again. The existence of gambling houses is a constant temptation to many people to risk money which they need for themselves and their families. For these and other reasons they are forbidden in most states.

Granting that some individuals can frequent gambling houses and gamble within reason and that the state law is only a penal law, we can still question the morality of frequenting them. By so doing one is encouraging something harmful to the common good. When responsible members of society encourage gambling houses by their attendance, they make it more difficult for public authorities to control the evil effects and they give scandal to younger people and others who do not have the self-control to gamble rationally. Their actions are a violation of social justice because they encourage something harmful to the common good and of charity because they give scandal to some of their fellow men without a sufficient reason.

EFFECT OF THE ANTIGAMBLING LAW

If the civil law prohibits gambling and invalidates such contracts, the loser may in conscience refuse to pay to the winner the stakes lost in the game. In this case the winner cannot collect. On the other hand a winner in that same state, once he has possession of the prize, need not restore the winnings unless required by a court of law to do so.

THE STOCK MARKET

Playing the market is not in itself wrong. We need merely apply to this practice the rules given for licit gambling. Like gambling, however, it may easily lead one to squander large sums that are necessary for one's family expenses or for the payment of one's debts in the hope of becoming wealthy with little effort and without long delay.

Cases to be analyzed

1 A college student drops into a railroad-station restaurant. He orders his meal and then discovers on the counter money left by some previous customer in payment for his lunch. The student uses this money to pay the waitress for his meal.

2 Two boys make a bet as to which of them can eat more pancakes.

3 A man bets a rosary that his friend will use profane language before the day is over.

4 A pedestrian is stopped by a poorly dressed man who tells him that he is in grave need of money and that he is consequently willing to sell several costly rings and watches at a marvelously low price. The pedestrian recognizes the genuine value of this jewelry and, though he is a little suspicious that the man is a thief, he buys the articles without trying to learn how this stranger obtained possession of them.

5 A man sells for a charitable organization one hundred raffle tickets and neglects to turn in the stubs before the time set for the drawing for the prizes. He now realizes that his purchasers had no chance of winning.

6 A group of athletes are staying at a hotel and light a fire in the metal wastebasket in order to cause some excitement.

7 During the football banquet at a restaurant several of the players put silverware, ash trays, and other small articles in their pockets. "They'll never be missed," the players contend in defense of their action.

8 Two students pool their money to buy a student streetcar pass that is not transferable. Every day after one has boarded the car, he slips the pass out the car window to the other for his immediate use.

9 Louis stole a bicycle from Joe, a newsboy, and sold it to Tom for twenty dollars. Joe has spent about ten dollars in carfare since he had his bicycle stolen. Tom is willing to sell the bicycle back to Louis, who is now desirous of making restitution, but only at the increased price of twenty-five dollars. What obligations does Louis have in the matter?

10 An employee at a chain grocery store has been stealing canned goods from the store at the rate of a dollar's worth a month for the last six months. Worried now, he wonders whether he must make restitution.

11 A young man takes ten dollars of his brother's money without even presumed permission and runs it up to twenty-five dollars in a poker game. His brother demands the ten dollars, plus a share in the winnings.

12 The treasurer of a college union boasts to one of his friends: "In arranging dances and smokers I generally get my rake-off from the caterer I give the job to."

13 A football player makes up his mind to retain his football jersey. At the end of the season when all equipment is to be turned in he will simply

tell the manager that he lost his jersey. "Why shouldn't I keep it?" he argues with himself. "I earned it, didn't I?"

14 A pipe fitter discovers that the boiler he is installing is defective and apt to explode, thus endangering the lives of all in the building. Nevertheless he warns no one of this, but goes ahead with the work assigned to him.

15 "I am generally pretty lucky on Saturdays," says a cashier to her fellow cashier, "because that's the day I get lots of extra change that the customers forget about. It's easy. In making change for a five-dollar or a ten-dollar bill, all I do is hand over the silver change first, then pause a minute before giving out the dollar bills. In the Saturday rush a good many go off without waiting for those greenbacks."

16 Whenever any of her acquaintances purchase goods from her, a clerk in a department store gives them an unapproved discount or generously adds an extra article or two out of friendship.

17 A furniture dealer uses the installment plan to good advantage. If the customer has made several payments and then fails to pay an installment promptly, the dealer collects the furniture. Thus he finds that he can often sell the same piece several times.

18 A customer rarely leaves the department of an expert salesman without a purchase. "I make him buy," boasts the salesman. Often the customers do not need and cannot afford the articles he sells them.

19 "I'm doing a big job for the city now," a contractor remarks to his son, "so I can with a safe conscience get rid of the poor-quality materials that I wouldn't pass off on my private customers. With the city it's different. Nobody is going to know about it."

20 The proprietor of a radio repair shop explains his practice in billing customers as follows: "I repair the radios of those that come to me. If I see that they are not too well off, I charge them the ordinary price. If they are rich, I generally add to the bill the cost of a new tube and a few parts that I didn't put in."

21 A builder used so light a mixture of cement in the concrete work of a six-story building he erected that not long after the job was finished one wall crumbled and killed two men and a girl.

Topics for discussion[3]

1 Illustrate by examples the ordinary consequences of acquiring the habit of stealing little things.

2 Discuss the dictum that "honesty is always the best policy."

3 Why should our observance of the ten commandments be not merely according to the letter of the law but rather according to the spirit?

4 Proposed state laws that would make racing handbooks illegal are to be discouraged.

---

[3] Not all the assertions contained in the topics are true. The student is to judge the truth of any assertions made and to explain his decision.

5 Without the right to private ownership men in general would have little incentive to work.

6 One is never under the obligation of taking possession of lost articles.

Bibliography

Clune, G. *Christian Social Reorganisation.* Dublin: Browne and Nolan, 1940.

Connell, Francis J. *Morals in Politics and Professions.* Westminster: Newman Press, 1946.

Connery, John R. "Current Theology: Notes on Moral Theology." *Theological Studies* 15:616, December 1954 (on the family wage).

Corley, Francis J. "Why Federal Family Allowances?" *Social Order* 4:249-56, June 1954.

Cronin, John F. "Capitalism." In *Catholic Encyclopedia,* Supplement II, Vol. 18.

――― *Catholic Social Principles.* Milwaukee: Bruce Publishing Company, 1955.

――― *Social Principles and Economic Life.* Milwaukee: Bruce Publishing Company, 1959.

Davis, Henry. *Moral and Pastoral Theology,* seventh edition, edited by L. W. Geddes, Vol. 2, pp. 255-409. 4 vols. New York: Sheed and Ward, 1958.

Dempsey, Bernard W. *The Functional Economy.* Englewood Cliffs: Prentice-Hall, 1958.

Drummond, William F. *Social Justice.* Milwaukee: Bruce Publishing Company, 1955.

Duff, Edward. "The Living Wage: A Note." *Social Order* 5:294-99, September 1955.

――― "The Living Wage: A Further Note." *Social Order* 7:77-85, February 1957.

Ermecke, Gustave. "The State and Legalized Gambling." *Theology Digest* 2:94-97, Spring 1954.

Farrell, Walter and others. *The Natural Law and the Legal Profession.* Chicago: Catholic Lawyers Guild of Chicago, 1950.

Jone, Heribert. *Moral Theology,* pp. 161-247. Westminster: Newman Press, 1957.

Kelley, William J. "Labor Legislation." In *Catholic Encyclopedia,* Supplement II, Vol. 18.

Leo XIII. *The Condition of the Workingmen (Rerum novarum).* In Joseph Husslein, editor, *Social Wellsprings,* Vol. 1, pp. 167-204. 2 vols. Milwaukee: Bruce Publishing Company, 1940, 1942.

Lynch, John J. "Current Theology: Notes on Moral Theology." *Theological Studies* 18:223, June 1957 (on right to work laws).

Madden, James. "The Morality of Gambling." *Australasian Catholic Record* 35:222-26, July 1958.

Mitchell, James P. "The Christian Conscience in the Modern World." *Catholic Mind* 56:408-13, September-October 1958.

Newman, Jeremiah. "The Just Wage." *Theology Digest* 5:120-26, Spring 1957.

Pius XI. *Restoring the Christian Social Order (Quadragesimo anno).* In Joseph Husslein, editor, *Social Wellsprings,* Vol. 2, pp. 178-234. 2 vols. Milwaukee: Bruce Publishing Company, 1940, 1942.

Pius XII. *Summi pontificatus.* New York: America Press, 1939.

The Problem of the Worker in the Light of the Social Doctrine of the Church. Montreal: Palm Publishers, 1950.

Reh, Francis F. "The Morality of Gambling." In *Proceedings of the Sixth Annual Convention of the Catholic Theological Society of America,* pp. 112-14. New York: Catholic Theological Society of America, 1951.

Rondet, Henri. "A Theology of Work." *Theology Digest* 4:37-41, Winter 1956.

Shields, Leo W. *The History and Meaning of the Term Social Justice.* Notre Dame: University of Notre Dame Press, 1941.

Todoli, Jose. "The Theology of Work." *Theology Digest* 2:175-78, Autumn 1954.

Toner, J. *The Closed Shop.* Washington: American Council on Public Affairs, 1942.

CHAPTER XI

The

"Thou shalt not bear false witness against thy neighbor."
Exodus 20:16

eighth

commandment

CALUMNY, or the injuring of another's good name by lying, is directly forbidden by the Eighth Commandment. We will first consider injury to the neighbor's good name and then take up the question of lying which does not involve any injury to our neighbor's good name.

Respect for the natural right of man to his good name is essential if men are to live as they should in society. Without a good name it is difficult for a person to have friends; he is not trusted by those with whom he lives and works; he often suffers financial loss; he is deprived of the peace of soul necessary to serve God as he should. Loss of reputation often results in the warping of personality and in a bitterness toward society.

A man may be deprived of his good name justly or unjustly. A person would be justly deprived of his good name by the revelation of something that is true when such revelation is necessary for the common good, for the protection of another innocent party, or for the person's own ultimate good. In these cases the evil (loss of good name) can be allowed in order to assure a proportionate good. If I knew that the highly respected secretary of a criminal lawyer was using her position to get information for blackmailing, I could make this known in order to protect people whom she might otherwise victimize.

DETRACTION

A man may be deprived unjustly of his good name in two ways: first, by the revelation of something true without a sufficient reason; second, by attributing to him something which is not true. It may seem that it is not unjust to reveal something about another as long as it is true, but we must remember that we are never justified in doing harm to our neighbor unless a proportionate good is involved. By revealing something true but harmful to our neighbor we are inflicting evil on him; the fact that it is true does not give us the right to harm our neighbor. A little self-analysis will show that we would greatly resent the revelation of many things about ourselves and that we would consider their revelation an unjust evil. This type of unjust harm to a person's good name is called simple detraction.

If the accusation or imputation is false, it is called calumny. Obviously, calumny is always wrong because it is a lie and because it robs one of his good name unjustly. Since calumny is a form of detraction, we will use the one term "detraction" when speaking of principles which apply to both and "calumny" when speaking of what is peculiar to the harming of another's good name by lying.

Not only individuals, but moral persons, such as organizations, societies, and religious orders, have a right to their good name. The dead, too, still retain the right to the reputation they enjoyed while alive.

THE SINFULNESS OF DETRACTION

Detraction is a sin against justice. It robs one of something that is ordinarily deemed of greater value than riches, for one has a strict right to his reputation, whether this reputation be deserved or undeserved.

In order to evaluate the gravity of detraction in any particular case, we must consider the amount of harm caused to the other's good name. This harm is usually grave if a serious defect is revealed, slight if a venial fault is made known. In estimating the extent of the injury inflicted it is necessary to take into consideration, not only the defect that is revealed, but such circumstances as the following:

1. The person detracting. Is he one to whom credence will be given? Is he a known liar? An untrustworthy gossip? Has he the reputation of narrating rumors as though they were facts?

2. The person detracted. Is he a man of unblemished reputation? A man of honored dignity? A worthless individual? It would be but a slight sin of detraction to impute theft to a known bank robber, but grave detraction to charge a bishop of good repute with the habit of lying.

3. The audience. Would they readily believe the detractor? Would they pass over the detraction without much thought?

REPARATION FOR DETRACTION

Since detraction violates commutative justice, it involves the obligation of making reparation for the foreseen injury inflicted. Hence the detractor must try, not only to repair the harm done to the other's good name, but also to make up any foreseen temporal loss that resulted from the defamation (for example, loss of employment or of customers).

The manner in which reparation for calumny is to be effected differs somewhat from the manner of repairing an injury done by simple detraction. The calumniator has lied about his neighbor and must retract his false accusation. He may, for example, simply state: "I was mistaken about . . ." The simple detractor (that is, the detractor who is not also a calumniator), who has unjustly revealed true defects or crimes, cannot repair his wrongdoing by denying that the defect exists or that the crime was committed. He must, however, endeavor to restore the other's reputation by discreetly praising his victim, especially regarding the virtue attacked, or by making some such statement as "I was wrong in saying that about Mr. Killeen. . . ."

CIRCUMSTANCES EXCUSING FROM REPARATION

Any one of the following reasons would release either detractor or calumniator from the obligation of repairing the injury he inflicted on another's good name:

1. The injury no longer exists, either because the defamation has been completely forgotten or because the other's good name has been restored by a court decision, by a convincing defense of the victim by his friends, or in some other way.

2. The crime, which was revealed to a few, has since become public in a way that was independent of the detractor's action (for example, by a newspaper exposé).

3. Reparation is morally or physically impossible. This occurs if those in whose presence the detractor spoke are unknown or cannot be reached, or if they cannot now be influenced to change their opinion in the matter.

4. The one defamed excuses the detractor from the obligation of making restitution; for example, by stating that he prefers that no more be said about the matter. This condonation may be merely tacit.

5. Reparation would cause the calumniator a far greater injury than the one he inflicted. If, for example, his life would be endangered by repairing the calumny, he may omit the reparation while the danger exists.

If no one believed the detractor, no actual injury was inflicted and no reparation is necessary. It is not of course easy for a detractor to be certain that he was not believed.

LICIT REVELATION OF SINS AND DEFECTS

There are circumstances under which the sins or defects of another may licitly be revealed. There is no detraction in the following cases:

EXAMPLE 1. In order to bring about a boy's correction a friend of the family reveals to his father the fact that the boy has recently committed several thefts.

EXAMPLE 2. In order to obtain good advice about what I should do, I reveal to a prudent friend some hidden misdeeds of a member of the firm in which I work.

EXAMPLE 3. Seeking sympathy and advice, I manifest to one friend an injury done to me, revealing only what is required for this end.

EXAMPLE 4. That she may not be seduced, I warn a young girl that the man with whom she intends to spend the evening has often taken advantage of inexperienced girls.

EXAMPLE 5. In order to prevent harm to one of my friends, I warn him about a certain physician's lack of medical skill.

EXAMPLE 6. I describe the crimes of a certain juridically condemned criminal to those who otherwise would hear nothing of them.

Although it is licit to reveal the sins or faults of others to their superiors and parents, if one knows that the superior or parent will make the situation worse (for example, by cruel and excessive punishment), he ought not to make the revelation.

DETRACTION THAT IS VENIALLY SINFUL

The following are examples of revelations of defects or sins that are venially sinful:

EXAMPLE 1. Without sufficient reason a teacher reveals the natural defects or general propensities of one of his students, saying, for example, "He's lazy—peevish—proud."

EXAMPLE 2. I manifest a crime that is now hidden but will soon become public through other channels. If, however, my premature revelation would cause serious harm, I am bound under pain of grave sin to delay the manifestation.

DETRACTION THAT IS MORTALLY SINFUL

The following are examples of serious faults that may be committed by detraction:

EXAMPLE 1. To tell to several persons even one grave hidden sin of another; for example, that he committed adultery.

EXAMPLE 2. To imply in a veiled way that another committed a grave misdeed, though I do not name the sin; for example, "He'd never dare to hold up his head again if I told what I knew about him."

EXAMPLE 3. To say, "There is a nun in that convent who once committed perjury, but she covered it up so that no one knew of it." This would throw suspicion of grave sin on many in the community.

OBLIGATIONS OF NEWSPAPERS AND MAGAZINES

Newspapers and magazines may be said in general to be bound by the same principles in this matter as are private individuals. In addition to the rules that have already been given we may cite the following:

1. It is lawful to print accounts of public crimes, though these accounts should be sifted of what might induce others to sin.

2. It is allowable openly to criticize the public defects and mismanagement of public officials. Fear of such criticism acts as a wholesome restraining influence on these individuals.

LISTENING TO DETRACTION

Those who listen to detraction may participate in the sin of the detractor under the following circumstances:

1. If one deliberately provokes another to detraction, one sins in the same way as the person who is uttering the injurious remarks. For example, I deliberately bring someone's name up in conversation in order to get the latest gossip on him.

2. If one internally approves and rejoices over the slander to which one is listening, one sins; but since the sin is merely internal, there is no question of reparation.

3. If one merely refrains from trying to put a stop to the other's detraction, one's sin is ordinarily venial. Such a person acts thus through carelessness or human respect. Scrupulousness or real timidity would free his action from any guilt. A superior, however, could sin grievously against charity in this if the matter were of importance and concerned his subjects.

RASH JUDGMENT

A rash judgment is an undoubting assent that is given without sufficient reason concerning another's supposed sin. It violates another's right, since everyone has a right to the good esteem of others unless one has lost it by misconduct. A rash judgment, if it is deliberate and concerns what is gravely damaging to a particular and known individual, is a serious sin.

EXAMPLE. I notice that Jones has two quarts of whisky in his car, and that fact convinces me that he is a drunkard.

Rash suspicions or opinions of others are usually no more than venial sins, for they merely lessen and do not destroy another's reputation.

CONTUMELY

Contumely is the act of unjustly dishonoring another in his presence. Contumely sins against justice and charity, for it goes against one's right to the honor and external marks of respect that accord with his character and standing.

EXAMPLE. An ousted minor official meets his successor in a public restaurant and accuses him in a loud voice of being a liar and a crook.

Contumely is not merely the failure to pay honor due to a person but is a positive act of dishonor that expresses contempt. This may be accomplished in various ways; for example, by mimicry, lampoons, sardonic grins, caricatures, a slap in the face, burning in effigy. A slanderer or backbiter is like a thief who steals and tries to keep his misdeed concealed; one who commits contumely looks with contempt upon his enemy and shows it by insulting him to his face.

THE SINFULNESS OF CONTUMELY

Contumely is a grave sin if it does serious injury to another's honor; and since the sin is against justice, restitution is obligatory. If only slight injury is involved, the sin would be venial. For example, if a woman upbraids her neighbor with the words, "Vain creature!" "Gold digger!" the contumely is slight. In many such cases it is evident to all that the speaker does not really mean what she is saying.

LYING

Veracity is a moral virtue that inclines one fittingly to speak the truth. Belonging to this virtue are the virtues of (1) simplicity, which excludes all hypocrisy and double-dealing, and (2) fidelity, which inclines one faithfully to execute one's promises. "Wherefore, put away lying and speak truth each one with his neighbor, because we are members of one another" (Ephesians 4:25). After a summary of the traditional teaching on lying and mental reservation we will discuss (pages 238-39) certain modern objections to and qualifications of this position.

DEFINITION OF LYING

Lying is defined as speaking deliberately against one's mind. In order to understand well this important definition we must analyze it accurately.

1. By *speaking* is meant communicating ideas to another person. If one who is entirely alone talks to oneself, there is no sharing of ideas with another, and so there can be no lying involved, even though one is enunciating what he knows to be false. The same is true if one talks to his dog or horse, for there is no second person present to whom one is imparting his ideas.

If one tells falsehoods to a child who is wholly unable to perceive one's meaning, there is no lie involved, for one is equivalently talking to oneself.

2. By speaking *deliberately* is meant that the speaker must realize what he is saying. Hence if an individual in a fit of distraction says what he habitually knows to be false, though here and now he does not advert to the significance of his words, he is not telling a lie. He is merely guilty of a misstatement. In like manner, though one utters dozens of falsehoods in his sleep, one does not tell a lie.

3. When we say that lying consists in speaking deliberately *against one's mind* we mean that there must be real opposition between what one says and what one thinks. The speaking must be contrary to one's judgment in the matter. Therefore I lie if I actually speak the truth but think that my statement is false. On the other hand, I do not lie if I speak what is actually false, believing it to be true.

CIRCUMSTANCES THAT MODIFY THE MEANING

Speaking, which we use here in the broad sense of communicating ideas, is effected not only by means of words, enunciated or written, but also by gestures. A wave of the hand or a nod of the head could involve sufficient imparting of ideas to constitute a lie. Moreover, the meaning of the speaker's words is colored by the particular circumstances in which the words are pronounced. These various circumstances modify the meaning of what is said and are rightly considered as part of the speaking. Such circumstances include the time, the place, the manner of speaking, and the persons involved. The following cases exemplify the manner in which circumstances form part of the speaking and help to determine the meaning of what is said:

EXAMPLE 1. John, coming home from school, asks his sister Mary: "Have you seen Mother?" Mary replies: "No, I haven't." Mary, of course, had seen her mother a countless number of times, but the circumstances here modify the question, "Have you seen Mother?" to mean: "Have you seen her *recently?*"

EXAMPLE 2. A grocer has sold all his oranges except two dozen that he put aside for his family. A customer asks him: "Got any good oranges today?" He answers: "No, I'm all out of oranges." Here the customer's question in this setting means: "Have you any oranges *for sale?*" and so the grocer's reply is truthful.

EXAMPLE 3. At the end of a two-hour conference in which President R discussed many things, Vice-President G stalked through an aisle of newspaper men. Asked what he had talked about, G snapped: "I can't remember." In these circumstances G's reply simply meant: "I wish to

233

disclose nothing of our conversation for publication." Hence though he remembered very accurately all that was discussed, G was not guilty of lying to the reporters.

HYPERBOLES

Hyperboles are not necessarily lies. One man asks, "What kind of a fellow is Jones?" and the other answers, "Jones is the best man in the state." This is an exaggeration; and since it is easily understood as such, it is not a lie. It is merely another way of saying that Jones is a very fine fellow. A similar hyperbole is found in John 21:25, where it is said: "There are, however, many other things that Jesus did; but if every one of these should be written, not even the world itself, I think, could hold the books that would have to be written." This simply indicates how numerous were the noteworthy actions of the Redeemer.

IRONY

Ironical expressions are not necessarily lies. After several members of his class have failed to answer a question on matter just taught, a teacher tells them that he is very pleased to have such an alert class. His impatience may not be praiseworthy, but his meaning is clear.

FICTION

Fictitious narratives presented as such are not lies. "It was 4 o'clock on Wednesday, July 16, 1891, when John Swinson, the young lawyer, walked up the steps of the White House." The author may know nothing about what happened in Washington that day. He is merely telling a story accepted as fictitious.

JOKES

Jokes are not lies if their jocose nature is evident. "I went to the City Art College today and drew my breath." The evident attempt at humor, the twinkle of the eye, the smile, the manner of saying a thing—these are circumstances that may brand remarks as fiction and not fact.

THE MALICE OF LYING

A lie is intrinsically evil because it involves using a natural faculty in a way that is directly contrary to its natural end or purpose. The primary purpose of the faculty of speech is to manifest to others one's thoughts and judgments. Since we are by nature obviously destined to live, not each in utter seclusion, but with other human beings, God evidently intended us to exchange ideas with them, and the means given us for this is the faculty of speech. The right use of this faculty is to reveal to others the thoughts of one's mind. To employ this faculty in order to manifest as the thought of one's mind what is not the thought of one's mind is contrary to the primary end of speech. The intention to deceive does not pertain to the essence of lying, and a lie is properly defined as "speaking against one's mind."

THE GRAVITY OF THE SIN OF LYING

A lie *in itself* is never more than a venial sin. The gravity of the malice of lying is measured by the seriousness of the disturbance of the order of nature, and this disturbance is not great. Jocose lies (that is, those which are uttered merely to amuse) and lies of excuse (sometimes called "white lies") are likewise venially sinful. A jocose lie differs from a joke in this, that the jocose nature of the speaker's words is not evident to his hearers and that as a consequence what he is saying contradicts what he is thinking.

At times because of other circumstances a lie may involve grave guilt. These other circumstances would introduce an additional fault joined to the violation of veracity. In the following examples lies involve other serious sins:

EXAMPLE 1. A witness tells a lie while under oath to tell nothing but the truth. Here we have a grave sin of perjury.

EXAMPLE 2. A salesman tells a lie that brings serious loss of business to one of his competitors. Here we find a grave sin of injustice.

EXAMPLE 3. A Catholic, when justly questioned by public authorities about his religion, states that he is not a Catholic. Here is a grave sin of denial of the faith.

MENTAL RESERVATION

One is never justified in telling a lie. Still at times one is obliged in conscience to veil the truth, for there are secrets to be guarded and detractions to be avoided. Sometimes silence will not suffice to maintain the secret which one is trying to guard. In fact, it may happen that silence would betray the secret. Hence there must be some licit means of concealing the truth when necessary. This licit means is the broad mental reservation.

Mental reservation consists in limiting the common and obvious sense of one's words to a particular meaning. Mental reservations are of two kinds: (1) the strict mental reservation and (2) the broad mental reservation.

1. A *strict* mental reservation is one that limits the meaning and gives no clue to the particular sense intended. This type of mental reservation is a lie, and so is never allowed. For example, A asks B: "Are you going to New York this summer?" B answers "Yes," and he means that he is going there merely in imagination. This is a lie, for no clue is given to the sense intended.

2. A *broad* mental reservation is one that limits the meaning and contains some clue to the sense intended. Here there is no lie involved, for what is said has two meanings. These two meanings are present either by reason of the words themselves or by reason of the circumstances attending their utterance. One who employs a broad mental reservation actually expresses what one thinks, and uses words according to the meaning that they really have. The words, however, have another meaning also, and the speaker foresees that it is in this other meaning that the one spoken to will probably understand them. For a sufficient reason we may thus permit others to deceive themselves by taking the wrong meaning out of what is said, and this remains true though the listener because of his ignorance does not know that there is another meaning to the word that is employed.

EXAMPLE 1. "Mrs. Smith is not at home now." Custom has given this phrase two meanings: (1) She is not now in the house. (2) She is not receiving visitors at this time. If Jones, being told that Mrs. Smith is not at home, concludes that she is not in the house, he may be deceived. The butler has not lied, even though Mrs. Smith is in the next room listening to the visitor's inquiries.

EXAMPLE 2. A murderer in court pleads "Not guilty." To the ordinary meaning of the phrase the qualification "not *juridically* guilty" is added by the circumstances.

EXAMPLE 3. A priest, asked if a parishioner committed a murder, may (and must) answer, "I don't know," though the parishioner has just confessed the murder to him. The circumstance of his priesthood colors his answer, so that it means, "I have no communicable knowledge on that subject." The same holds true for lawyers, doctors, nurses, and others who give answers bearing on knowledge acquired in the fulfillment of their duties. Even if the questioner does not know that he is addressing a priest, doctor, or lawyer, it is permissible for the speaker to deny possessing the information sought, for the other's ignorance does not make this additional circumstance (his professional position) less real. It is actually there in spite of the fact that the other does not know of it, and it could be learned upon inquiry.

EXAMPLE 4. If somebody we cannot trust asks us to lend him a hundred dollars, we would be justified in saying, "I haven't any money," meaning "any money that I wish to lend you."

EXAMPLE 5. If in answer to an invitation to some social gathering one writes, "I accept with pleasure" or "I am happy to be invited," there is no question of a lie, even though one really feels just the opposite about the invitation. These formulas are merely conventional replies and are not intended to indicate the writer's genuine sentiments in the matter. The same is true of phrases addressed to an elderly woman that praise her youth and beauty. This is mere urbanity.

EXAMPLE 6. If a suspicious husband asks his wife whether or not she has committed adultery, she may licitly answer, "No," even though she has actually sinned thus many times. Her answer really means: "No, I have committed no crime of adultery that I must reveal." The question is rightly aimed only at knowledge that is not secret, and so the wife may reply accordingly.

THE LICITNESS OF BROAD MENTAL RESERVATION

Unless one has a good reason for concealing some fact, one may not licitly use a broad mental reservation. If broad mental reservations could be employed without some justifying reason, there would result general loss of security and confidence in our social relations. Thus there would be engendered widespread mistrust and suspicion. We would not accept the word of others at its face value, but would constantly be obliged to try to uncover some hidden meaning.

A sufficient reason for using a broad mental reservation is genuine utility for oneself or others, and this is graded according to the degree of importance of concealing the truth of which there is question.

While under oath in a court of law one may use broad mental reservations, though he must have a very good reason for doing so. One who acts on this teaching does not violate his obligation as a witness "to tell the truth, the whole truth, and nothing but the truth," for to the words of the oath is attached the tacit limitation "insofar as the law obliges me to reveal it." Hence the defendant may use broad mental reservations to avoid incriminating himself, since he need not give proof of his own guilt.

Not all modern moral theologians are satisfied with the explanation of lying and mental reservation just given. Objection is made to it on the grounds that the use of mental reservation is too difficult for the ordinary person and that it is a mere fiction to say that a person deceives himself. It is suggested that we need a new terminology to express what all recognize as legitimate ways of speaking. One way of putting the question is to ask if a false statement is always a lie. Some theologians answer in the negative. When a child tells a caller that mother is not home, he makes a statement which is objectively false and speaks contrary to what he knows to be true, yet no one would accuse him of lying. Sometimes it is necessary to make a false statement in order to protect secret knowledge. Silence or the use of mental reservation is not sufficient; the only way to protect the secret is to make a statement contrary to what you know to be true. To call such a statement a broad mental reservation is stretching the meaning of speech and only leads to confusion. Therefore, it is contended, we ought not to define lying as speaking deliberately against one's mind. Vermeersch suggests the use of the term "formal speech," by which is meant speech made in such circumstances that the speaker can be reasonably thought to be communicating his mind. In other circumstances he may use a false statement. A lie would consist in formal speech contrary to one's mind. Others suggest similar definitions, such as "the denial of communicable truth."

The Reverend Martin E. Gounley, C.SS.R., uses a slightly different approach based on the purpose of the faculty of speech. The faculty of speech is ordered *per se* to the representation of one's knowledge or belief in words or other signs; more radically, however, it is ordered to the maintenance of peaceful, helpful intercourse. *Per accidens* it can be used to deceive, as in time of war or when one must protect secret knowledge.

Whether one follows the traditional position or accepts the opinion of these modern theologians, his answer to practical cases will usually be the same. Advocates of the newer explanations claim that they do not have recourse to unrealistic distinctions and definitions and that they give a clearer justification for practices recognized by all as legitimate. The defenders of the traditional position object to any attempt to change the definition of lying, on the grounds that it will lead to laxity and open the way to abuses of the faculty of speech. Whether or not their contention is correct cannot easily be determined, because few of those who support the newer theory have worked it out completely by applying it to a large number of cases.

CHEATING IN EXAMINATIONS

Cheating is usually treated under the Eighth Commandment as a form of lying. It is considered to be a lie because one who cheats implies that the paper which he turns in contains answers based on what he knew and not on what he was able to obtain from books, notes, or others who were taking the same examination. We will discuss some cases of cheating and then consider the harmful effects of the practice of cheating even if it could not be shown to be sinful.

If a student cheats in an ordinary classroom examination but does not in any way deprive others of their rightful grades or of any other honor or reward, he would commit a venial sin of lying according to the opinion of most theologians. A few theologians would deny that cheating is a lie. In addition to the venial sin of lying, most cheating would also involve injustice because teachers usually grade on a relative basis and those who take the examination honestly receive a lower grade than they would if others had not cheated.

If a student cheats in an examination and thereby deprives someone else of a scholarship, a medal, or an honor of any type, he has been unjust. If the cheating did not actually affect the outcome, the injustice is only in the internal act. If it did affect the outcome, he has deprived someone of a thing to which he had a right and must make restitution. It may be that because he did not realize the seriousness of his action there was no serious sin, but the duty of restitution would remain. In some cases he might be excused from restitution.

A more difficult case is that in which a student gains admittance to a medical school of limited enrollment by repeated cheating. It might be impossible to discover who would have been admitted in his place, but he may have deprived someone of admission to the school. It might have been, however, that he would have been admitted anyway, in which case it could not be said that he unjustly deprived someone of admission; but, as was said in connection with scholarships and other prizes, he was guilty of an internal sin of injustice.

There are other aspects of cheating which make it illicit. Most schools have severe penalties, even expulsion, for those who are found cheating. One who is discovered suffers a notable loss of reputation which at times is very embarrassing both to him and his family. To expose oneself to this loss of reputation is contrary to the charity due to oneself and to any others who would be embarrassed. It may also involve injustice toward one's parents, who have supported a boy or girl in school and now find that their money has been wasted because he or she was dismissed and cannot gain admittance to other schools. In most cases failure involves disobedience because of a refusal to study and a wasting of the money which was paid for tuition.

Moral theologians are concerned about the habit of cheating. Their concern arises from their own experience with students and from the testimony which they have heard from experienced teachers. Constant cheaters tend to distrust others, to become suspicious, and to try to rationalize their practice by arguing that others would do the same thing if they were not afraid. They frequently lie in order to defend themselves when accused. They also develop the habit of taking the easy way out and try to get more important things by trickery or doubtful means. A good test of the seriousness with which teachers view constant cheating is to ask them if they would recommend a constant cheater for a job which required integrity and dependability.

It would not be fitting to treat only the negative aspects of lying and cheating. The virtue of honesty is one of the most attractive qualities of youth. A boy or girl who refuses to lie and is willing to accept the consequences of his actions attracts and wins the admiration of old and young alike. One of the most pleasant aspects of the life of teaching is the association with so many young men and women who are completely honest even when honesty results in an apparent or real temporary loss. A student who tells a teacher that he failed to get his work done because of carelessness or because he had something more interesting to do wins real respect. One who fails an examination honestly may be the one who would be most trusted and recommended for positions which demand integrity. This may seem naive to the sophisticated, but even hardheaded businessmen take a keen interest in the honesty of applicants. We are not saying that honesty should be practiced simply because it is, in most cases, the best policy. It should be practiced because it develops characteristics which make one a trusted friend, a reliable employee, and a valuable member of society. More important, it should be practiced because it is most pleasing to God. Christ chose twelve apostles. All of them had serious faults (overconfidence, ambition, cowardice, stubbornness) but they were all honest men except the one who betrayed Him, and the one whom He chose to be head of His Church seems to have won the heart of Christ because he was absolutely honest.

SECRETS

A secret is hidden knowledge which may not be revealed unless some higher right intervenes. It may be an invention (for example, television) or some incident (for example, a murder or a clandestine marriage). There are three types of secret:

1. The *natural* secret is one which the natural law itself binds its possessor to keep hidden.

> EXAMPLE. A woman knows that her brother did some very shameful things in his youth. He has now settled down and is highly respected by his family and by friends who are unaware of his past life.

2. The *promised* secret is one which must be kept hidden because of a promise made after one already knows the secret.

> EXAMPLE. A businessman discovers that one of his employees has been dishonest. He calls him in and is convinced that the man is sorry and will not repeat the offense. In order to assure the employee of his confidence, he promises to tell no one of his dishonesty.

3. The *entrusted* secret is one which is confided to another on the condition that it be kept hidden. The agreement to maintain secrecy may be explicit or only implicit.

> EXAMPLE. A physician, while examining a patient, discovers that he has a venereal disease. The physician is bound to guard this knowledge as an entrusted secret. By virtue of his office the doctor enters into at least a tacit contract with his patients not to reveal what was discovered during the course of professional services if such a revelation would in any way be damaging to the patient.

241

The same obligation of secrecy applies to others in similar offices; for example, lawyers, nurses, and student counselors.

Every person has a strict right to his secret. This right is founded either on the ownership that each one has over the fruits of his own thoughts, industry, and talent or on the right that each one has to his good name. A secret belongs, then, to its owner, and one may not steal that secret. Hence we may not do the following in order to learn the secrets of others:

1. Eavesdrop.

2. Bribe servants to communicate to us secret knowledge of family affairs.

3. Try to trick others into betraying secrets.

4. Open the letters of others and read the contents.

THE OBLIGATION OF RESPECTING SECRETS

In the various types of secrets there is a difference regarding the binding force of the obligation imposed on those who share a secret.

1. A *natural* secret obliges its possessor, under pain of grave sin, to keep the matter hidden if it is of grave importance. Justice would be violated if the unlawful revelation of the secret would cause damage to the party concerned.

> EXAMPLE 1. An employee knows of a secret crime of one of his fellow workers and reveals it to the employer without a justifying reason. As a result his fellow worker is discharged and finds it very difficult to get another job.
> EXAMPLE 2. A woman discovers that the couple who live next door are not validly married. She discloses this to several friends at a meeting.

Charity only is violated if the unlawful revelation of the secret merely causes sadness or embarrassment.

> EXAMPLE. Without a justifying reason I reveal to a boy's mother the secret fact that he on one occasion became drunk, though not through his own fault.

2. A *promised* secret obliges according to the wish of the one making the promise. Hence promised secrets may bind under pain of venial or mortal sin and either from justice or from fidelity only, the nature of the obligation depending upon what the promiser intended. If the matter in question is also a natural secret, it binds

in justice, and the obligation is grave or slight according to the seriousness of the matter. If the matter does not bind under natural secrecy, the secret binds in fidelity and would not ordinarily be a serious obligation. There might be exceptional cases, however, in which a person, because of the importance of the matter, would intend to bind himself seriously.

3. An *entrusted* secret always obliges in justice and the obligation in matters of grave importance is serious.

WHEN SECRETS IN GENERAL MAY BE REVEALED

In general, the obligation of any type of secret is ended:

1. If the guarded knowledge has already become public property. This holds good even though the manner in which the secret was disclosed was illicit.

EXAMPLE. A secret crime is discovered and published in a local newspaper. One who knew about the crime can now talk about it, but should be careful not to reveal additional details which might further contribute to the loss of good name.

2. If one may justly presume the permission of the party concerned to reveal the secret. One must be careful, however, not to presume permission without a sufficient reason, especially if he has the knowledge as an entrusted secret.

It is lawful to discuss the above-mentioned secrets with anybody else who possesses the same secret knowledge. In case of a sacramental secret, however, this is not allowed.

EXAMPLE. A physician learns from examination and consultation that his patient has a disease whose revelation would be embarrassing. He may discuss it with the patient's uncle, who already knows about it.

WHEN NATURAL AND PROMISED SECRETS MAY BE REVEALED

With regard to natural or promised secrets, the obligation of secrecy ceases when keeping the knowledge hidden would involve grave inconvenience:

1. To the one who owns the secret knowledge.

EXAMPLE. I learn by chance that a young man is nearly going out of his mind with secret worries, and I inform his father about it so that he may help his son to get rid of these anxieties.

2. To the one who shares the secret.

EXAMPLE. A college student tells one of his friends about something he did which makes him liable to expulsion. The friend himself is accused of the misdeed, and the only way he can protect himself is to tell who was actually guilty.

3. To an innocent third party.

EXAMPLE. A woman learns that one of her friends intends to marry a man who secretly married another woman in a different part of the country. She may inform her friend of the secret marriage.

4. To the state or community.

EXAMPLE. A father knows that his son is subject to sudden blackouts. The son applies for a job as a bus driver and refuses to tell the company about the blackouts. Although the father had promised not to say anything about them, he now thinks his obligation to the community obliges him to give the knowledge to the bus-company officials.

If the guarding of a secret will not result in injury to a third person, and if I expressly promised to guard the secret even at the cost of grave inconvenience to myself alone, I am then bound to do so.

WHEN ENTRUSTED SECRETS MAY BE REVEALED

One should be very careful about the revelation of secrets in any case, but especially if the secret revealed is an entrusted one. It is essential for the common good that people be able to talk to professional men and women with perfect confidence that what they say will be kept secret. Public trust in professional men is easily disturbed, and they should therefore take pains to see that clients are not even given grounds for suspecting that their confidence has been violated. One incident of the violation of entrusted secrecy can do untold harm to a community. It does not necessarily follow that there may not be circumstances in which professional men have the right, or even the duty, of revealing what they know in their professional capacity. Great prudence, however, is needed in making a decision to reveal such secrets. The harm to be averted would have to be much greater for the revelation of such secrets than for the revelation of natural or promised secrets. We are not obliged to prevent all evil. The decision to be made must be based on the relative harm which would result from my keeping the secret and from my revealing the secret. If I can prudently judge that my revelation of a secret would not be considered by ordinary people a violation of confidence and that the harm prevented by the revelation is sufficient to risk unreasonable loss of faith in professional men, I may reveal even a promised secret; but

244

because the common good is involved, it would seem to be better to keep the secret unless the opposite course is clearly obligatory. The Church has ruled that no reason is sufficient for the revelation of matter revealed in the sacrament of penance. Professional men are not bound to the same degree, but they can learn from this law of the Church the importance which the Church attaches to the obligation of secrecy. The examples which follow are cases in which the right to reveal entrusted secrets seems certain. Entrusted secrets may be revealed to avert great harm:

1. From the state or community. Here the common good takes precedence over the good of the individual.

> EXAMPLE. In examining a patient a doctor finds that he is afflicted with a very contagious disease, though to the ordinary observer he appears to be in good health. Learning that the patient intends to take passage on a large ocean liner sailing the next day and that he refuses to disclose his condition to the boat officials, the doctor sends them word of the grave danger.

2. From an innocent third party.

> EXAMPLE. A lawyer learns from talking to one of his clients about his family affairs that the man is very upset and that he is thinking of murdering his wife. He may inform the wife or take other means for the protection of her life.

3. From the one to whom the secret is entrusted or from the one whose secret it is.

These secrets need not be maintained at such a price, for if the obligation continued even in such circumstances as these, then most persons, including doctors, lawyers, and other professional men, would refuse to accept such secrets and this refusal to receive confidences from anyone would redound to the detriment of the common welfare.

> EXAMPLE. A doctor is accused of malpractice by one of his clients and would have to pay a large amount of money for damages and also lose a large part of his clientele if he did not defend himself. He may do so even though his defense involves the use of secrets entrusted to him by the client making the accusation.

REVEALING AN ENTRUSTED SECRET TO ONE PERSON

I may reveal an entrusted secret of importance to a prudent individual who will keep the matter hidden, provided I have a good reason. Such a reason would be real need of advice as to the course of action that should be pursued. When a secret is revealed to such a person there is no danger that it will become public. If, however, I have no justifying reason for my action, I am guilty of venial sin.

READING THE LETTERS OF OTHERS

Opening and reading others' letters and reading their private notes or diaries is sinful unless (1) one has or can reasonably presume the permission of the owner of the letters, notes, or diaries or (2) such an action is thought necessary for averting grave harm from the state, from an innocent third party, or from oneself. A nation may censor mail in time of war. A mother may read a child's letters when she thinks it is necessary for the child's good. Anyone may read another's letters when he has adequate reason for believing that this is required for protecting the state, another, or himself against serious injury. The degree of sinfulness which is involved in reading without permission another's letters, notes, diaries, and other similar material will depend on the importance of the secret information that the reader foresees he will unjustly acquire.

Cases to be analyzed

1 A member of the president's Cabinet, approached by a reporter, said: "I am of no use to the newspapers right now; my answer to all your questions, whatever they may be, is no."

2 A stranger approached John Smith and asked: "Do you come home along this street on Mondays?" Smith, fearing to be waylaid, replied, "No," though that was the way he went home every weekday.

3 Whenever she receives invitations over the telephone, a teen-age girl makes use of any reasonable falsehood that comes to mind; for example, she falsely asserts that she expects an out-of-town friend to come on a visit but that she will not know for certain until the next day whether the friend will keep her promise. This enables her to decide at her leisure the desirability of accepting the invitation.

4 Peterson has just asked Dr. Jones, Smith's physician, whether Smith has a hidden disease. Dr. Jones, because he knows that Peterson is unaware of the fact that he is a doctor, hesitates to guard his secret knowledge of Smith's disease by using the answer, "No, Smith has no hidden disease that I know of."

5 A man whose friends all know that he likes a drink is offered a glass of whisky by an acquaintance. "No, thanks; I never use it," he says while reaching for the glass.

6 I overhear two men on a day coach discussing a secret plan they have by which they hope to make a fortune. Acting at once, I use this method of theirs and make thousands of dollars.

7 By chance I hear two women across the aisle on a streetcar reveal the secret fact that Jones, my grocer, is an ex-convict. I believe what they say and refuse to trade with him any longer.

8 A father tells his daughter's fiancé that she was an adopted child; as a result the fiancé refuses to go through with the marriage.

9 Four gangsters torture and threaten to kill a night-club employee unless he reveals the combination of the vault. He finally tells them.

10 A man tells several lies to amuse a sick friend. He feels that jocose lies may be permitted for a good reason.

11 A girl, spending the night at the home of her friend, notices a letter on the dresser. Moved by curiosity, she reads the letter.

12 A man disguises his voice when he goes to confession to his pastor. He would find it somewhat embarrassing to be recognized.

13 A soldier is captured by the enemy. Known to possess secret knowledge regarding his country's troop movements, he is threatened with death unless he divulges this information. He feels that under such circumstances his obligation to keep the secret would cease.

14 Harry, 15 years old, is asked by the pastor why he did not attend school the day before. The boy excuses himself by resorting to a direct lie. His companion tells him that he is guilty of a mortal sin because he lied to a priest.

15 The postmaster in a small town reads all the post cards that pass through his hands and thus acquires much personal information about the people of the town.

16 Several gamblers approach a college basketball player and offer to pay him a large sum of money to see that his team does not win their next game by more than five points.

17 Because he finds it rather difficult to refuse his friend, a student lends him his written class assignment.

18 A girl softly picks up the receiver of the extension telephone at home and listens to her brother's conversation with his fiancée.

Topics for discussion[1]

1 Only a jocose lie is ever permissible. One who tells a jocose lie seeks only to amuse.

2 It is allowable to tell a lie whenever you wish to conceal a secret.

3 A physician may not disclose professional secrets about a patient except to members of the patient's family or to other doctors.

4 Discuss the possible bad effects which might follow from a change in the definition of lying.

---

[1] Not all the assertions contained in the topics are true. The student is to judge the truth of any assertions made and to explain his decision.

5 The essence of lying does not consist in the speaker's intention to deceive the hearer.

6 One may licitly make use of a broad mental reservation in order to avoid hurting another's feelings.

7 Indicate the exact words that you would use in order to protect your brother's reputation if asked about a secret crime that you knew your brother had committed. Justify your answer.

8 May a soldier who is a military policeman disguise himself as a chaplain in order to obtain from an erring fellow soldier information by which he can convict him?

9 Give two examples of cases where a newspaper would be permitted to publish secret knowledge in the interests of the common good.

10 What is to be said of the morality of a husband's revealing to his wife certain secret defects of his son?

Bibliography

Connery, John R. "Current Theology: Notes on Moral Theology." *Theological Studies* 19:557-58, December 1958 (on self-accusation in court).

Davis, Henry. *Moral and Pastoral Theology,* seventh edition, edited by L. W. Geddes, Vol. 2, pp. 410-26. 4 vols. New York: Sheed and Ward, 1958.

Di Marino, A. "Why Is Lying Forbidden?" *Theology Digest* 4:9-12, Winter 1956.

Fisher, J. Harding. "The Malice of a Lie." In J. F. Leibell, editor, *Readings in Ethics,* pp. 528-33. Chicago: Loyola University Press, 1926.

Gounley, Martin E. "Praise or Blame—Which Shall It Be?" *The Priest* 3:824-29, November 1947.

Jone, Heribert. *Moral Theology,* pp. 248-60. Westminster: Newman Press, 1957.

Lynch, John J. "Current Theology: Notes on Moral Theology." *Theological Studies* 19:187-92, June 1958 (on the Fifth Amendment).

CHAPTER XII

The laws
of fast
and abstinence

T HE general law of the Church which treats of fast and abstinence is found in Canon 1252. This law prescribes for some days
fasting only, for other days abstinence only, and for still other
days both fast and abstinence. The following norms have been
approved by the American hierarchy for their dioceses in the
United States. Since, however, in some places there are differences in the matter, the local diocesan regulations, usually published immediately before Lent in the diocesan newspaper, should
be consulted.

WHEN FASTING ONLY IS PRESCRIBED

Fasting only is prescribed for all the weekdays of Lent except
those that are days of both fast and abstinence (that is, all the
Fridays, Ash Wednesday, Ember Wednesday, Ember Saturday,
and Holy Saturday).

Neither Sundays nor holydays of obligation are ever days
either of fast or abstinence. When Christmas, for example, or the

Feast of All Saints, or any other holyday of obligation falls on a Friday, meat may be eaten on that day.

WHEN BOTH FAST AND ABSTINENCE ARE PRESCRIBED

A distinction must be made between days of complete abstinence and days of partial abstinence. On days of *complete* abstinence no meat may be taken. On days of *partial* abstinence meat may be eaten once, at the principal meal only. Whether one is fasting or not, he must observe both the complete and the partial abstinence.

Fast and *complete* abstinence are prescribed:

1. For the vigil of the Immaculate Conception.

2. For either December 23 or December 24, at the option of the individual, according to the decree of December 3, 1959.

3. For Ash Wednesday and the Fridays of Lent.

4. For Ember Fridays. The ember days, which occur four times a year, are the Wednesday, Friday, and Saturday that follow (a) the first Sunday of Lent, (b) September 14, (c) December 13, and (d) the Feast of Pentecost.

Fast and *partial* abstinence are prescribed:

1. For Ember Wednesdays and Saturdays.

2. For the vigil of Pentecost.[1]

WHEN ABSTINENCE ONLY IS PRESCRIBED

Abstinence only is prescribed for all Fridays which are not included among the days mentioned above.

REGULATIONS CONCERNING FASTING

Canon 1251, §1 reads: "The law of fasting prescribes that only one full meal a day be taken, but does not forbid a small amount of food in the morning and in the evening." Fasting, then, consists essentially in taking only one full meal. Because today it would be very difficult to limit oneself to a single repast, though a hearty one, the Church permits taking a little food at breakfast and a light meal (that is, a collation) later on in the day.

When fasting is prescribed for a day that is not also a day of abstinence, meat may be eaten only at the principal meal by one

---

[1] The bishops of the United States have dispensed the faithful from fast and partial abstinence on the vigil of All Saints.

who is fasting. Those who are not fasting (because exempt, excused, or dispensed from the obligation) may eat meat on such days as often as they wish.

EXAMPLE. One not yet 21 years old may eat meat on a Monday of Lent as often as one wishes. Because of his age he is not obliged to fast, and a Monday of Lent is a day of fast only.

THE QUANTITY PERMITTED TO THOSE FASTING

The quantity permitted varies for (1) the full meal and (2) the collation and breakfast.

1. The quantity of food that is allowed for the *full meal* is in no way limited. This meal must be morally continuous; that is, it must not be broken in upon by an interruption of an hour or longer. Such an interruption would, in a moral sense, make two meals of that session of eating.

A slight interruption, even without a good reason, is permitted and does not involve sin. An interruption is looked upon as slight if it is less than a half hour long. Hence one still preserves one's fast if shortly after leaving the dining room one eats, for example, candy, nuts, or cakes.

The full meal may be interrupted by more than an hour by one who is unexpectedly called upon to attend to some business of moment. If a physician, for example, who has begun his full meal is summoned to attend someone injured in an accident, he may continue his meal after an interruption of two hours or more. The reason is, as explained by moralists, that the Church does not wish to make the law of fasting so strict that one is deprived of sufficient food under circumstances such as these.

2. In the United States one may use the *relative norm* in computing the quantity of food to be taken at breakfast and at the collation unless other regulations have been established for the diocese. The collation is either lunch or supper. The amount of food which is permitted according to the relative norm depends upon the needs of the individual. Persons vary in their needs; for some are much stronger than others and some engage in work which is more fatiguing than that of others. The *relative norm* makes allowance for these and other differences; it permits the individual to eat at breakfast and at the collation as much as he sincerely judges necessary to enable him to perform his daily duties without notable inconvenience or hardship. At the begin-

ning of Lent one should make a moral estimate of how much food he requires at breakfast and at lunch (or supper) and without scruple follow that judgment. The amounts of food of these two meals, when added together, must be less than that of one full meal. Meat, moreover, may not be taken either at breakfast or at the collation.

The "full meal" to which reference has been made is not the meal actually eaten at dinner on some particular day; in other words, an individual is not obliged to reduce the amount eaten at breakfast and lunch because he foresees that he will eat a very light dinner on that day. A full meal for anyone is a dinner which he can honestly tell himself he would consider reasonable under ordinary circumstances. What is needed is a conscientious estimate rather than an attempt to settle the matter in terms of pounds and ounces.

THE TIME OF THE FULL MEAL AND THE COLLATION

One may take the full meal during any time of the day from about 11 A.M. To eat the principal meal before 11 A.M. would be venially sinful unless one has a good reason for thus anticipating; for example, if he must catch a train that does not carry a diner. It is permissible to take the collation (lunch) either at noon or in the evening.

One who out of forgetfulness takes a hearty breakfast (more than he would usually take but not a full meal) is bound to observe the fast that day. He has not violated the fast substantially, and so it is still possible to observe the law's requirements.

WHAT CONSTITUTES A VIOLATION OF THE FAST

Outside these three meals (breakfast, dinner, and collation) no food is allowed. Drinking liquids does not break the fast and so is allowed, no matter how great the quantity. Hence tea, coffee, beer, ginger ale, fruit juices, vegetable juices, and wine do not break the fast. The hierarchy, moreover, have declared that in the United States ordinary whole milk may be regarded as a drink that is permitted without restriction at all times. Malted milk, on the contrary, as well as frappés, "frosts," and milk shakes are classified as food and are therefore forbidden between meals. Ice cream, honey, soup, and the like are also placed in the category of food.

A substantial violation of the law of fasting involves grave fault. A substantial violation is committed if one exceeds the amount allowed by more than a third of a full meal. This circumstance would be verified if one took that extra quantity of food outside mealtimes or if, at breakfast or at the collation, he exceeded by that amount what is permitted to him.

REGULATIONS CONCERNING ABSTINENCE

The law of abstinence forbids the use of meat on certain days. By the word "meat" is meant the flesh of all warm-blooded animals. The term includes the flesh of all mammals and birds, even aquatic birds. Meat soups, broths, and gravy are also forbidden.

The law of abstinence allows the eating of frogs, turtles, and other sea food (for example, crabs, lobsters). Gelatin too is allowed. Lard and the fat of any animal may be used in cooking, or as a seasoning or flavoring.

WHAT CONSTITUTES A VIOLATION OF ABSTINENCE

To eat about two or more ounces of meat is ordinarily considered a grave violation of this law. A less amount would constitute slight matter.

Some have the erroneous idea that, if the law of abstinence has once been violated on a certain day, it is permissible to eat meat as often as is desired during the remainder of that day. It is true that one who eats meat out of forgetfulness on a day of abstinence commits no sin. As soon, however, as the abstinence obligation is remembered, one must abstain from meat for the rest of that day. The law binds us to abstain from forbidden food during every moment of the day and so, though one unwittingly violated the law before the end of the day, one can (and must) fulfill the requirements of the law for the period of the obligation that still remains.

WHO ARE OBLIGED TO FAST?

Those Catholics who are not yet twenty-one years of age or who have reached their fifty-ninth birthday are not bound by this ecclesiastical law. All others are obliged to fast on the days prescribed by the Church unless they are either excused from the obligation by a grave reason or are dispensed by the proper ecclesiastical authority.

THOSE EXCUSED FROM FASTING

Since a grave reason excuses from this obligation, the following are not bound to fast:

1. the sick or the convalescent;
2. those whose health would be notably impaired if they attempted to fast;
3. nursing mothers; women with child;
4. hard manual laborers (for example, men who load freight cars, baggage trucks);
5. those engaged in useful occupations if fasting would interfere with the proper performance of their duty.

Students are not excused from fasting because of their occupation. Some students, however, will have sufficient reason for asking for a dispensation. In case of doubt one should consult his pastor or confessor.

Traveling does not of itself excuse one from fasting. If one has to make a long journey on foot or in circumstances that entail grave inconvenience, this fact would excuse from the obligation.

Those who have an excusing cause need not consult a priest. If one is in doubt, he should ask whether he has a truly excusing cause or request a dispensation.

WHO ARE OBLIGED TO ABSTAIN?

All Catholics who have completed their seventh year of age and who have the use of reason are bound by the law of abstinence. This obligation continues up to the time of their death.

THOSE EXCUSED FROM ABSTAINING

The sick who need meat for their recovery are excused from this obligation. The same is true of all those, whether men or women, who are engaged in what would be considered hard labor and who really need meat to maintain their strength.

DISPENSATIONS FROM FAST AND ABSTINENCE

It may happen that one who is not excused from the obligation either of fast or abstinence has nevertheless a just reason for wishing to be released from the obligation. If his reason is not sufficient to excuse from the law but is a good one, he may ask for a dispensation. Dispensations from the laws of fast and abstinence may be requested either from one's bishop or from one's pastor. The assistant pastors also often possess the power to dispense their parishioners.

Cases to be analyzed

1 A 23-year-old bank clerk observes the lenten fast very faithfully. He limits his lunch to about eight ounces of food, but as a result he usually has a headache all afternoon. Since in spite of the headache he can perform his work with his customary efficiency, he does not feel free to take a larger lunch.

2 A girl is attending a football game on an Ember Saturday in September. Between the halves she buys a hamburger and eats it before recalling that it is a day of partial abstinence. "Oh, well," she exclaims, "there's no sin in what I did. Besides, now I can eat meat for dinner tonight."

3 A Catholic college girl is taking lunch with her friend who is also a Catholic. She remembers that it is Friday and so orders an abstinence meal. Her friend, however, completely forgetting what day of the week it is, orders a chicken sandwich. The college girl is now worried about whether or not she must remind her friend that it is Friday.

4 A 23-year-old Catholic girl sometimes takes a chocolate soda in the afternoon during Lent. "I won't take any dessert for this evening's dinner," she explains. "This soda will take the place of my dessert, and so, you see, I am not breaking my fast."

5 A Catholic man, in looking over the menu of the restaurant where he is taking his lenten lunch, notices that the dish of the day is whale steak. He is eager to try this new food but he is doubtful whether it could be classified as fish.

6 A Catholic woman generally takes a large glass of chocolate milk at ten o'clock in the morning and again at four o'clock in the afternoon. Sometimes, too, she takes a small cookie with this drink. Her husband insists that she cannot continue this practice if she intends to fast.

7 Taking her lunch on Friday in a restaurant near the college, a girl orders baked beans. When the dish is served she notices that the beans have been baked with pork. Carefully separating the meat from the rest, she eats only the beans.

8 A Catholic sits down to dinner at the home of a non-Catholic friend. It is Friday and the Catholic finds that a delicious steak is being served. What is he to do?

9 A woman, dining in a restaurant with a friend, suddenly exclaimed: "Look! Do you see that soldier at the next table? I saw him in our church this morning, but he can't be much of a Catholic. Look at that delicious steak he is eating and today is Friday." "It seems to me," her

companion observed, "that soldiers and sailors have some kind of privilege regarding the law of abstinence."

10 A Catholic is attending a dance on an Ember Friday. Late in the evening a lunch is served and he partakes of it. "This light meal," he says, "does not break my fast substantially, and so it is all right to take it."

11 A girl, seeing her older sister take a large bowl of soup at lunch on Ash Wednesday, warns her: "You know you can't eat much more than that soup for your collation. That must weigh about five or six ounces."

12 A Catholic woman is on an automobile trip across the country. Though she realizes it is Friday, she orders a meat dinner. "We don't have to abstain today," she explains to her companion; "we're traveling."

Topics for discussion[2]

1 Would it not be preferable for the Church to do away with the obligation to abstain on Fridays?

2 A Catholic mother should not allow her young children, who are not yet seven years old, to eat meat on Fridays.

3 Protestants, if they have been baptized, are bound by the Church's laws of fast and abstinence.

4 Observing the lenten fast not infrequently injures one's health.

5 Outline the history of the laws of the Church regarding fasting.

6 Are all countries bound by the same laws of fast and abstinence as the United States? Explain.

Bibliography

Davis, Henry. *Moral and Pastoral Theology*, seventh edition, edited by L. W. Geddes, Vol. 2, pp. 429-40. 4 vols. New York: Sheed and Ward, 1958.

Jone, Heribert. *Moral Theology*, pp. 261-66. Westminster: Newman Press, 1957.

---

[2] Not all the assertions contained in the topics are true. The student is to judge the truth of any assertions made and to explain his decision.

CHAPTER XIII

Forbidden
books

A LTHOUGH all law is to some extent a limitation of freedom, as the word is used by most people, because it forbids me to do something which I may wish to do or requires me to do something which I may dislike, the exercise of censorship seems to be the occasion of more than ordinary resistance. All true law, however, has as its ultimate purpose the freeing of man to be himself in the most perfect way possible. The ten commandments place certain restrictions on activity, but it would be absurd to object to the restriction on murder on the grounds that it was an unjust limitation of human freedom. Traffic laws restrict the speed which I may travel in order to make it possible for men to travel safely; no reasonable person objects to them as a limitation on his freedom. The same is true of censorship which is exercised prudently. We are referring here to censorship in the strict sense; that is, censorship exercised by an authority over its own subjects. For the present we will not treat censorship in the wider sense; that is, moral persuasion exercised by an individual or a group over those who are not their subjects or over their subjects but without the imposition of an obligation in the strict sense. Both the state and the Church can and do exercise censorship in the strict sense.

One of the reasons for the somewhat violent reaction to censorship is that there is an inherent danger in it which is not found in many other laws. We have plenty of examples of the evil effects which unjust censorship can have. Whole nations have been deprived by dictators of knowledge to which they have a right. We have reason to study any form of censorship very carefully and to consider, not merely its immediate effects, but the pattern which it establishes and the possible evils which it will occasion.

Nevertheless there are legitimate exercises of censorship for the common good. The state has always placed some limitation on the dissemination of knowledge or opinion, especially in time of war. The Church does so by her laws in regard to the publication, possession, or reading of certain books. In each case the authority in question has made a judgment that the limitation on freedom is necessary for the common good and for the protection of higher and more precious freedoms.

Reading may be fruitful of good or of evil, for printed words may lead along the path of virtue or of vice. Not infrequently a piece of literature contains both good and bad parts. Blasphemous and obscene literature is at times written with appealing charm of style. Because our spiritual health should be our chief concern, we may not rashly run the risk of sullying our souls just to improve ourselves literarily or scientifically. Hence all men—Catholic, Protestant, and Jew—are forbidden to indulge in certain reading, and this prohibition arises from the natural law. Catholics have in this matter not only the teaching of the natural law to look to, but also the positive legislation of their Church. The Catholic Church, ever alert to protect her members from the evils of the day, singles out certain literature as dangerous to faith or morals and forbids any Catholic to read such writings.

WHY CERTAIN READING IS ILLICIT

The reading of certain books, periodicals, or newspapers may therefore be prohibited for either (or both) of two reasons: (1) because the natural law forbids it or (2) because the Church forbids it. A prohibition imposed by the Church binds all Catholics; a prohibition arising from the natural law affects only those for whom the material would be dangerous.

READING FORBIDDEN BY THE NATURAL LAW

The natural law forbids me to read whatever would be a proximate occasion of sin for me.

EXAMPLE 1. Someone writes me a long letter that is a clever, insidious attack on the Catholic Church. The church law against certain writings is not concerned about such documents as letters in manuscript form. Therefore if I read this letter, I violate no church law; but if reading the letter would weaken or endanger my faith, I am prohibited by the natural law from reading it.

EXAMPLE 2. A certain novel is intentionally lascivious. One man can read such a book with no danger at all, for he is old and unemotional. Another, young and warm-blooded, knows that such books lead him to grave sin. The natural law would allow the former to read the novel but would forbid it to the latter.

READING FORBIDDEN BY CHURCH LAW

The Catholic Church brands certain books, periodicals, and newspapers as dangerous to faith or morals for the generality of mankind, and so forbids all her members to read such publications. This prohibition of the Church binds each individual Catholic with regard to all the condemned writings, even though this particular person may be so different from the generality of mankind that he could read some of them without taking harm.

THE CHURCH LAW CONCERNING READING

In the following paragraphs we shall discuss only those writings that are forbidden by church law. What is prohibited in this matter by the natural law should be clear from our explanation of the occasions of sin, pages 52-56.

The church law concerning forbidden books is included under two divisions:

1. Certain individual writings. The Church singles out specific authors and their works and forbids her members to use them. This list of individually prohibited writings is called *The Roman Index of Forbidden Books*. Forbidden, for example, are Voltaire's *History of the Crusaders* and Gibbon's *Decline and Fall of the Roman Empire*.

2. Certain classes of writings. The Code of Canon Law (Canon 1399) gives twelve different classes of writings that Catholics may not read; for example, books of heretics that promote heresy, Bibles edited by non-Catholics.

EXPLANATION OF THE ROMAN INDEX

The *Roman Index* includes the names of many authors whose works have been judged dangerous to faith or morals. (This list, however, indicates but a small part of the works which Catholics are prohibited to read.) In most cases the extent of the prohibition is clear, because the author and his condemned books are explicitly named. In other cases, however, no individual book is named, but the author is put under the general condemnation *"opera omnia*—all his works." Thus, for example, we find on the *Roman Index* David Hume and we observe that "all his works" are condemned. This would, at first, seem to be an all-embracing prohibition that forbids reading any work of Hume. That, however, is not the case, for this term *opera omnia* has a technical meaning that needs interpretation.

The stigma *opera omnia* simply condemns an author's works *as a group*. It may be that one or another of his writings is not bad, but as a group his works are bad. Just as one might say that the books in a certain library are bad, though actually some few good books are to be found there, so here the Church says: "Hume's works are a bad lot and we condemn them." The Church does not condemn any good book to be found among the author's bad ones. If there is a good book among those written by an author so condemned, that book is not forbidden. Hence the stigma *opera omnia* means that all the works of an author are as a whole under suspicion; but they are individually forbidden only if one of the following conditions is verified:

1. The work falls into one of the classes of forbidden books. Canon 1399 enumerates these classes.

2. The work has been condemned by name in a special decree of a pope or of a Roman congregation.

3. The book professedly deals with religion and is written by a non-Catholic.

If none of these three conditions is verified with regard to a particular work of an author who bears the *opera omnia* condemnation, then the reading of that particular book is not forbidden by church law. The following are examples of cases in which certain works of an author may be read even though all the works of the author *(opera omnia)* have been condemned:

Author	Prohibition	Not prohibited
Anatole France	*Opera omnia*	*The Crime of Sylvester Bonnard*
Emile Zola	*Opera omnia*	*The Dream, The Debacle*

Another phrase of general condemnation that we find in the *Roman Index* is "*omnes fabulae amatoriae*—all love stories." We rightly interpret this stigma in exactly the same way as *opera omnia*. Moreover, this condemnation does not include dramas or comedies. As an illustration of this interpretation we may give the following example:

Author	Prohibition	Not prohibited
A. Dumas (father)	*Omnes fabulae amatoriae*	*The Three Musketeers*

CLASSES OF BOOKS THAT ARE FORBIDDEN

So much for the first division of prohibited books: "certain individual writings." Now we shall investigate the second division: "certain classes of writings."

The important classes of writings expressly forbidden by church law (Canon 1399) may be summed up as follows:

1. Books against the faith, among which are included the following classes of books:

a) Books promoting heresy or schism; for example, Cornelius Jansen's *Augustinus.*

b) Books attacking the foundations of the faith (for example, the existence of God, the immortality of the soul), the Catholic Church or any point of Catholic belief (for example, the Immaculate Conception of the Blessed Virgin), ecclesiastical discipline (for example, the law of clerical celibacy), the hierarchy as such, or the clerical or religious state as such.

c) Books by non-Catholics on religion, unless they are plainly in accord with Catholic teaching. This prohibition would not apply to books which simply explain the teachings of a certain religious group.

2. Books against morals, among which are included:

a) Books professedly treating of the lewd or obscene.

b) Books attacking sound morals (for example, advocating birth control or defending suicide, feticide, mercy killing, dueling, divorce).

c) Books favoring spiritism, fortunetelling, divination, superstition, and the like.

The Church's prohibition of certain classes of books in general
or of certain books in particular must be understood and applied
in the light of the following principles:

1. The term "books" means not only books but also magazines,
newspapers, pamphlets, and other publications. It does not include manuscripts or mimeographed notes that have not been put
on general sale.

2. Picture magazines, though they contain a few lines explaining the various illustrations, are not prohibited by church law.

3. Plays or motion pictures that are based on forbidden books
are not included in the church prohibition; for example, the motion picture *Les Miserables.*

4 Church law does not forbid reading any part of the Douay
version of the Bible.

5. The prohibition of a certain publication makes it unlawful
to read or retain that work in whatsoever language it appears; for
example, *Les Miserables* of Victor Hugo, though translated into
English, is still forbidden.

6. Lewd or obscene writings are those which treat of the subject matter of the Sixth Commandment and do so in a way that
would notably arouse venereal pleasure in the normal reader.
What would be accounted obscene for the young would not necessarily be so for the married. Moreover, purely scientific works
(for example, books on anatomy or surgery) are not prohibited,
since they are not obscene.

There are some books which Catholics are forbidden to read
merely because they lack the *imprimatur* or stamp of ecclesiastical
approval. The following are the only books that Catholics are prohibited from reading simply because they lack the *imprimatur:*

1. Books of Holy Scripture, whether edited by Catholics or
non-Catholics.

2. Books of commentaries on Holy Scripture.

3. Books or pamphlets (a) that record new apparitions, revelations, prophecies, or miracles or (b) that foster new devotions.

Reading Catholic books promoting old and approved devotions is not prohibited for the reason that they lack the *imprimatur*. A certain book, for example, on *The Seven Dolors of the Blessed Virgin* bears no *imprimatur*. If its teaching is orthodox, a Catholic may read it without scruple.

WHAT IS FORBIDDEN BY THE PROHIBITION

If a book falls under the church prohibition either because it is in one of the classes of books forbidden by Canon 1399 or because it is individually singled out by the *Roman Index*, Catholics are not allowed to read that book, to retain it, or to communicate it to another. To *read* means that I read it and understand what I am doing. Letting my eyes wander over the pages of a book written in Japanese could not be considered reading if I am wholly unacquainted with the language of Japan. To *retain* means that I may not keep it in my possession or have another keep it for me. To keep a set of forbidden books in a storage house violates the church law. To *communicate* means that I may not lend it or read it to another. Thus a physician may not place forbidden books in his waiting room for his patients.

The prohibition ceases if the part that gave rise to the prohibition is torn out or made illegible by gluing the pages together or smearing them with ink.

THE SINFULNESS OF DISREGARDING THE PROHIBITION

How much of a forbidden book must be read in order to constitute matter for grave sin? The answer is: The amount that would create for the normal individual the proximate danger of sinning gravely. How many pages of a particular book this would be depends on the type of book that is under consideration. If the book is very lascivious or an insidious, convincing attack on the Church, fewer pages would constitute matter for grave sin than if the book is not especially bad.

ENCYCLOPEDIAS

An encyclopedia is prohibited only in case either of the following conditions is verified:

1. If of set purpose it attacks faith or morals.
2. If, written by non-Catholics, its main subject matter is religion and it contains doctrine contrary to the Catholic faith.

If neither of these conditions is verified, the general use of the encyclopedia is not forbidden to Catholics, even though one or another article is condemned.

ANTHOLOGIES

If the anthology contains *harmless* excerpts from forbidden books, it is permissible to read and retain it. An anthology, for example, which contains no selections from any book that has been condemned other than harmless readings from *Les Miserables* would not be forbidden. If, however, the excerpts practically constitute the same work as the one forbidden, then one may not read nor retain the anthology. It falls under the same prohibition as the original book.

COMPENDIA

If a compendium is made of a prohibited book, the compendium is not the same as the original book. Its goodness or badness is to be judged as it is now without reference to its source. This applies to synopses of books in the *Reader's Digest* and other similar publications.

FORBIDDEN MAGAZINES AND NEWSPAPERS

Reading or retaining "evil" newspapers or magazines is forbidden by church law. How may one judge whether or not such a publication is to be characterized as evil according to the meaning of the church legislation? We may take as the measure for judging the editorial policy of the magazine or newspaper. If the articles of the periodical are in general moral, though an occasional article favors artificial birth control, divorce, or some other forbidden practice, the publication is not evil in the technical sense. Evil periodicals in the technical sense are those that *normally* go counter to any of the parts of Canon 1399. Examples of such periodicals are the now-defunct *Menace* and atheistic propaganda sheets.

It is considered *grave matter* (1) to read "evil" magazines or (2) to read even in a single copy a lengthy article that is directly against faith or morals.

It is considered *venial matter* to read wholly harmless parts of such publications (for example, death notices, weather reports, advertisements). Though such parts of the publication may be in themselves harmless, reading them in that setting would usually involve some danger.

If one has a good reason for reading or keeping a prohibited book, he may obtain permission from his bishop to do so. He may write to the chancery, stating his reasons for wishing the dispensation and listing the names of the books that he wishes to read or retain.

In addition to the obligation not to read forbidden books without proper authorization Catholics have the positive obligation of encouraging good books and discouraging those which are harmful to morals or the common good. As members of a society they ought to work to provide the best conditions for the moral and spiritual good of the whole society, especially for the young and impressionable. In trying to prevent the publication or dissemination of books, magazines, or motion pictures which are harmful to morality they are exercising censorship in the wider sense of the word.

Great prudence is required in exercising such censorship. First of all, there should be solid reasons for believing that it will be successful; if its failure seems certain, it should not be attempted. Second, other effects that may result from the attempt to exercise censorship should be studied. Even if successful, censorship might do more harm than good because it gave people the impression that the Church was using her power of numbers to impose her standards on others. This evil effect might be allowed in some cases for a sufficient reason, but in many cases it would outweigh the good effects. Third, we should not depend upon censorship to accomplish what ought to be done by proper training. Whether we like it or not, Catholics in the modern world are going to come into contact with many things which are occasions of sin. It is much more important that they be taught proper principles and be trained to make mature judgments than that they be partially protected from evil influences. Fourth, those who attempt such censorship should have the proper background. Parents can and should exercise a certain censorship over their children, but that does not mean that they have the ability to act as censors for society in general. Censorship in the latter case should be done only by those who have a wide knowledge of history, theology, and the arts and who are outstanding for their prudence. Anyone else treading on this dangerous ground will only do more harm than good.

Topics for discussion[1]

1 Show the wisdom of the Church's laws regarding the reading of books and periodicals.
2 Non-Catholic scholars have an advantage over Catholic scholars because they may read whatever they wish.
3 Many books explicitly forbidden by the *Roman Index* are not nearly as bad as some that receive no mention.
4 The prohibitions of the *Roman Index* make things rather difficult for Catholic students at non-Catholic colleges.
5 Does a Catholic have an obligation to memorize the names of all the books that the *Index* forbids?

Bibliography

American Hierarchy. "Censorship." *Catholic Mind* 56:180-86, March-April 1958.

Connery, John R. "Prudent Censorship." *Catholic Mind* 56:500-13, November-December 1958.

Davis, Henry. *Moral and Pastoral Theology*, seventh edition, edited by L. W. Geddes, Vol. 2, pp. 441-55. 4 vols. New York: Sheed and Ward, 1958.

Gardiner, Harold C. *Catholic Viewpoint on Censorship.* Garden City: Doubleday and Company, 1958.

Goffi, Tullo. "Forbidden Books: The Index and Moral Law." *Theology Digest* 7:99-102, Spring 1959.

Jone, Heribert. *Moral Theology*, pp. 269-74. Westminster: Newman Press, 1957.

Murray, John C. "Literature and Censorship." *Catholic Mind* 54:665-77, December 1956.

Reed, John J. "Permission To Read Forbidden Books." *Theological Studies* 19:586-95, December 1958.

---

[1] Not all the assertions contained in the topics are true. The student is to judge the truth of any assertions made and to explain his decision.

CHAPTER XIV

The
duties
of doctors

GRADUATES of many medical schools take the so-called oath of Hippocrates, which runs as follows: "I solemnly swear that I will treat the sick only with a view to helping them and never in order to inflict injury. I will not give anyone a deadly poison, even if requested to do so, nor will I suggest such a way of acting. I will lead a pure and holy life and practice my art in a manner that is above reproach. Into whatsoever house I enter, I shall go to help the sick insofar as I am able. I will abstain from all evil and particularly from seducing others into wrongdoing. Whatever I see or hear, professionally or otherwise, if it should not be made known, I shall be careful to guard as a secret."

We note how clearly and correctly this oath outlines the conduct that should be followed by every conscientious physician or surgeon. This solemn promise strikes one as being the more remarkable when one realizes that it comes down to us from a pagan era, for it had its origin in Greece several centuries before Christ. Perhaps this may help us to understand the fact that the moral code for medical men which is found in Catholic authors is no more than an explanation of the obligations of the natural law. It does not bind members of the Catholic Church only. It is for all alike, for it is not uniquely Catholic doctrine. This is part of the universal morality that the author of nature imposes equally on all—Catholic and Protestant, Jew and gentile.

THE PHYSICIAN'S OBLIGATION IN GENERAL

The physician's obligations toward patients vary according to circumstances. They may bind him to care for the patient either in justice, in charity only, or in both.

TO WHAT THE PHYSICIAN IS BOUND IN JUSTICE

Under certain circumstances the obligation of a physician to care for a patient is one that binds in justice.

1. If the physician is under contract to the patient (for example, paid an annual fee), he must in justice:

a) Go to his patient's aid at any hour of the day or night, even at the cost of grave inconvenience unless he knows that his delay will cause no harm to the patient.

b) Care for the patient even though the latter is afflicted with a contagious disease.

2. If a physician has already begun the care of a patient, a tacit contract is thus entered into and so he must in justice:

a) Cure the patient as best he can.

b) Not desert the patient even though the disease turns out to be contagious unless he makes satisfactory provision for the care of the patient elsewhere (for example, in the isolation ward of a hospital).

TO WHAT THE PHYSICIAN IS BOUND IN CHARITY

The physician is bound in charity only in cases that do not come under the above-mentioned circumstances. If he refused to aid the gravely ill, he would sin seriously against the virtue of charity only when the two following circumstances are verified:

1. He is the only doctor available.

2. He could offer his help without grave inconvenience to himself. If, however, the patient is in *extreme* need, the doctor is obliged to go to his assistance even at the cost of grave incon-

venience to himself. When we say that a patient is in extreme need we mean that he is in a dying condition or that some very grave physical harm will follow, such as complete loss of sight.

THE OBLIGATION OF CAREFUL TREATMENT

In treating all cases the physician must use at least ordinary care. The fact that the patient is a mental defective or is being administered to out of charity does not justify the doctor in being overly hasty or slipshod in his treatment. He must always use the safer remedy. If there is a sure remedy available, he may not try uncertain ones on his patient with the danger of causing his death or serious injury to his health, even though the patient has given him permission to do so. The patient cannot give him permission for such experiments, since he is not master of his own life. The doctor may not argue that such a remedy, if once proved effective, would undoubtedly save many others and that the sacrifice of one or two individuals during the experiments would result in benefit to a large number afterward. This way of arguing would be to advocate committing evil actions in order to accomplish some good—a principle that must be condemned as immoral. (See Romans 3:8.) If there is no safer remedy available, the doctor may, in cases where death would otherwise result, employ such uncertain remedies, for then he is doing all that he possibly can to save the patient. He is here using this means only as a last resort.

AVOIDANCE OF NEEDLESS EXPENSE

The physician may not impose useless visits upon his patients, for this would be demanding payment for what is valueless. Though of no value physically, however, visits may be quite helpful to the patient psychologically, as happens in the case of some slowly dying patients who are beyond the aid of doctors but who would be greatly worried if the physician did not visit them and prescribe medicine for them. The physician may call on such patients, listen to what they have to say, prescribe harmless pills, and charge for this service.

A doctor may not call in other medical men for consultation at the expense of the patient unless there is real need for such professional assistance. On the other hand, a physician sins if in difficult cases he refuses to allow other doctors to be called in for advice or if in calling such a consultation he looks to friendship in preference to competency.

The physician's fees should not exceed those charged by others in his section of the country unless he makes it clear to the patient in advance what his fee is to be. This price will vary according to whether one is a specialist or a family doctor. The physician may demand higher fees from the wealthy and thus reimburse himself for the service he renders for a minimum fee to those in moderate circumstances.

OBLIGATIONS TO THE POOR

The doctor is not obliged to seek out the sick among the poor. He need attend only those who ask his help. If those who seek his aid are unable to reimburse him at all, the physician's obligations are those of charity and may be summarized as follows:

1. If the patient is in extreme need of medical attention, the doctor has the grave obligation to aid him even though he finds it seriously inconvenient to do so.

2. If the patient is in serious need, the doctor is not obliged to help him if he would find it gravely inconvenient to do so.

3. If the patient is in ordinary need, the doctor is obliged to give him only the time he has free after his regular work is done. Moreover, his obligation to do this is slight.

The obligation of service should be fulfilled prudently. A physician should not regularly deprive himself of needed sleep and recreation necessary to keep himself in good health and to insure efficient performance.

CONDUCT IN REGARD TO OPERATIONS

A surgeon may not advise or perform any operation that is not required for the health of the body (for example, he may not suggest an appendectomy when he knows that there is no necessity for it). He may never under any circumstances advise or actually perform sinful operations such as abortion, craniotomy, and unnecessary vasectomy or ovariotomy. He should scrupulously avoid all such immoral practices.

270

A Catholic doctor is not forbidden under absolutely all circumstances to assist at such operations. At times (for example, during internship at a state or city hospital) Catholic doctors are practically forced to help in operations that are obviously sinful. Doctors may never, of course, cooperate formally in any sinful operation. They may, however, cooperate materially, provided they have a sufficiently serious reason for doing so (for example, if to refrain from so acting would cause them very grave inconvenience). Hence in some cases the doctor may assist as a material cooperator at sinful operations (for example, abortion) in the following and similar ways. He may:

1. Prepare the body for the operation.

2. Administer the anesthetic.

3. Hand the necessary instruments to the surgeon who is performing the operation.

4. Sew up and bandage the wound.

THE USE OF DRUGS

It is allowable to use drugs in order to prevent, alleviate, or end pain or disease. If the sickness or pain is severe, drugs may in general be administered even though loss of consciousness results. Strong drugs, especially those which deprive the patient of consciousness, should not be used for the relief of minor illnesses.

EXAMPLE. A physician gives a strong dose of opium to his patient for a slight headache.

To administer drugs to a dying man so that he will die in the state of unconsciousness and thus escape the agony that usually accompanies death is illicit under any one of three conditions:

1. If the drug would notably accelerate the patient's death. (This would be against the Fifth Commandment.)

2. If there is reason for believing that the patient is not in the state of grace, for then this action would deprive him of the opportunity of making his peace with God.

3. If, even when the patient is in the state of grace, the pain is not severe, for this would be depriving him of a valuable occasion for meriting.

The administration of drugs to a dying man so that he will die in the state of unconsciousness is licit (1) if so far as can be known the patient is in the state of grace, or at least if there is no evidence indicating that he is probably not in the state of grace; (2) if the patient is suffering acute pain; and (3) if the patient gives his consent to the act, at least implicitly.

TWILIGHT SLEEP

In cases of ordinary childbirth "twilight sleep" should not be used, for it generally creates some danger of harming the off-spring. This danger is slight, however, and so such use without good reason would not constitute more than a venial sin. Twilight sleep may be resorted to without any sin at all in order to alleviate pains that are extreme or for some other sufficient reason (for example, to facilitate the handling of a difficult parturition).

WARNING PATIENTS OF IMPENDING DEATH

The physician is obliged in charity to warn the patient or his near relatives of the danger of death, so that the dying person may arrange his spiritual and temporal affairs. This duty (which is one of charity) would cease if the doctor could not give the warning without grave inconvenience.

With regard to newborn babies, the doctor should see to it that they are baptized if they are in immediate danger of death. He himself may perform the ceremony if no priest is available. Even if the child is born of infidel parents who are bitterly opposed to baptism, charity enjoins the doctor to baptize the dying infant in spite of the parents' stand, for they are clearly in the wrong if they interfere with the rights of the dying. The doctor in many cases will find it possible to baptize the child secretly. If secrecy is impossible and if the doctor foresees that by baptizing the child he will cause the parents to complain loudly and to spread among others hostility to the Church, he should refrain from baptizing the child.

BIRTH CONTROL

A doctor may under no circumstances recommend artificial birth control nor even hint at its necessity or advisability. To do so would be to encourage others to perform an intrinsically evil act. Moreover, he is not allowed to give patients information as to the best methods of artificial birth prevention, nor to purchase for them or insert contraceptive devices.

With regard to the "rhythm" theory, or natural birth control, Catholic doctors may give their assistance and advice whenever asked to do so. They may even suggest this method when the circumstances of a particular case seem to warrant it.

THE OBSERVANCE OF SECRETS

The secret that exists between the physician and his patient is called an entrusted secret. A patient in consulting a doctor may either expressly exact from him the promise that any knowledge obtained from the patient will be guarded as a secret, or he may merely take it for granted that the doctor will keep all such information to himself. This latter is usually the case, and it should be noted that the physician's obligation in this event binds to secrecy just as strictly as in the former. Ordinarily the physician experiences little difficulty with regard to keeping such knowledge secret. Very extraordinary conditions may arise, however, that create a conflict between the rights of the patient and those of others. Hence a doctor should bear in mind that privileged secrets always bind except in the following cases:

1. The one who entrusted the secret now consents to its revelation. This consent may be either explicit or implicit.

2. The secret has become generally known.

3. It is necessary to reveal the secret in order to avert grave harm from the state.

EXAMPLE. A man has a disease that may infect many in the community if he is not isolated, but he refuses to refrain from associating with others. One who knows this, even under entrusted secrecy, may divulge the secret for the common good.

4. The right of an innocent third party may be endangered by guarding the secret.

EXAMPLE. If a man who is about to marry a healthy girl is found to be infected with a venereal disease in its active state, the doctor should urge him to inform the girl of this disease or else postpone the marriage until a complete cure can be effected. If the patient refuses and insists on going ahead with the marriage, the physician may warn the girl of the impending danger to her health. He need not warn her if to do so would entail grave inconvenience for himself, since his obligation would cease in such a case.

5. The revelation of a privileged secret is necessary in order to avert grave harm from the one communicating or from the one receiving the secret.

EXAMPLE. Y tells X (as an entrusted secret) where he (Y) was on October 10. X, by revealing this, can prevent Y's being shot by Z. X may make known this fact in order to save Y.

A doctor must, according to the law of certain states, report individuals who come to him with gun or knife wounds. Though the doctor is not bound in conscience to disclose this information, he may do so in order to avert grave harm that might otherwise be visited on him. If he failed to report, he would be liable to fine and perhaps imprisonment as accessory to a crime.

One of the best summaries of the moral principles of medical practice is found in the *Ethical and Religious Directives for Catholic Hospitals* of the Catholic Hospital Association of the United States and Canada. We reprint it here for the benefit of those who wish to go further into problems of medical practice.

Ethical and Religious Directives for Catholic Hospitals[1]

INTRODUCTION

RESPONSIBILITY OF HOSPITAL AUTHORITIES

1. Catholic hospitals exist to render medical and spiritual care to the sick. The patient adequately considered, and inclusive of his spiritual status and his claim to the helps of the Catholic religion, is the primary concern of those entrusted with the management of Catholic hospitals. Trustees and administrators of Catholic hospitals understand that this responsibility extends to every patient and that it is seriously binding in conscience. A partial statement of this basic obligation is contained in these Ethical and Religious Directives. All who associate themselves with a Catholic hospital, and particularly the members of the medical and nursing staffs, must understand the moral and religious obligations binding on those responsible for the management and operation of the hospital and must realize that they are allowed to perform only such acts and to carry out only such procedures as will enable the owners and administrators to fulfill their obligations.

VITALITY OF DIRECTIVES

2. The principles underlying or expressed in these Directives are not subject to change. But in the application of principles the Directives can and

---

[1] With permission of the Catholic Hospital Association of the United States and Canada.

should grow and change as theological investigation and the progress of medical science open up new problems or throw new light on old ones.

EXTENT OF PROHIBITIONS

3. As now formulated, the Directives prohibit only those procedures which, according to present knowledge of facts, seem certainly wrong. In questions legitimately debated by theologians, liberty is left to physicians to follow the opinions which seem to them more in conformity with the principles of sound medicine.

SOLUTIONS OF MORAL DOUBTS

4. Cases can arise in which the morality of some procedure is doubtful, either because the Directives do not seem to cover the case or because their application is not clear. In such cases, consultation is obligatory, if possible; and the hospital reserves the right to insist on this and to choose or to approve the consultants. In urgent cases that allow no time for consultation, the physician in charge should do what seems most proper to his own conscience. Having done what he honestly judges best in such an emergency, the physician has no just cause for anxiety of conscience; but he should refer the matter to the hospital authorities to obtain guidance for future emergencies of the same nature.

SECTION I: ETHICAL DIRECTIVES

GENERAL

5. These Ethical Directives concern all patients, regardless of religion, and they must be observed by all physicians, nurses, and others who work in the hospital.

6. Even the procedures listed in this section as permissible require the consent, at least reasonably presumed, of the patient or his guardians. This condition is to be understood in all cases.

7. Everyone has the right and the duty to prepare for the solemn moment of death. Unless it is clear, therefore, that a dying patient is already well-prepared for death as regards both temporal and spiritual affairs, it is the physician's duty to inform him of his critical condition or to have some other responsible person impart this information.

8. Adequate consultation is required, not only when there is doubt concerning the morality of some procedure (as stated in n. 4), but also with regard to all procedures involving serious consequences, even though such procedures are listed here as permissible. The hospital reserves the right to insist on such consultation.

9. The physician is required to state definitely to the supervisor of the department concerned the nature of the operation he intends to perform or of the treatment he intends to give in the hospital.

10. All structures or parts of organs removed from patients must be sent at once and in their entirety to the pathologist for his examination and re-

port. If the physician requests it, the specimens will be returned to him after examination.

(Note: In the event of an operation for the removal of a diseased organ containing a living fetus, the fetus should be extracted and baptized before the excised organ is sent to the pathologist.)

11. The obligation of professional secrecy must be carefully fulfilled not only as regards the information on the patients' charts and records but also as regards confidential matters learned in the exercise of professional duties. Moreover, the charts and records must be duly safeguarded against inspection by those who have no right to see them.

DIRECTIVES CONCERNING SPECIFIC PROCEDURES

I. *Procedures Involving Serious Risk to, or Destruction of, Life*

Principles

12. The direct killing of any innocent person, even at his own request, is always morally wrong. Any procedure whose sole immediate effect is the death of a human being is a direct killing.

13. Risk to life and even the indirect taking of life are morally justifiable for proportionate reasons. Life is taken indirectly when death is the unavoidable accompaniment or result of a procedure which is immediately directed to the attainment of some other purpose, for example, to the removal of a diseased organ.

14. Every unborn child must be regarded as a human person, with all the rights of a human person, from the moment of conception.

Particular Applications

15. Direct abortion is never permitted, even when the ultimate purpose is to save the life of the mother. No condition of pregnancy constitutes an exception to this prohibition. Every procedure whose sole immediate effect is the termination of pregnancy before viability is a direct abortion.

16. Operations, treatments, and medications during pregnancy which have for their immediate purpose the cure of a proportionately serious pathological condition of the mother are permitted when they cannot be safely postponed until the fetus is viable, even though they indirectly cause an abortion.

17. Regarding the treatment of hemorrhage during pregnancy and before the fetus is viable: Procedures that are primarily designed to empty the uterus of a living fetus still attached to the mother are not permitted; procedures primarily designed to stop hemorrhage (as distinguished from those designed precisely to expel the living and attached fetus) are permitted insofar as necessary, even to the extent of risking an abortion. In this case the abortion would be indirect.

18. Cesarean section for the removal of a viable fetus is permitted, even with some risk to the life of the mother, when necessary for successful delivery. It is likewise permitted, even with some risk for the child, when necessary for the safety of the mother.

276

19. Cranial and other operations for the destruction of fetal life are forbidden. Procedures designed to preserve fetal life (for example, aspiration for hydrocephalus) are permitted even before delivery when such procedures are medically indicated.

20. In extrauterine pregnancy the affected part of the mother (for example, an ovary or fallopian tube) may be removed, even though the life of the fetus is thus indirectly terminated, provided the operation cannot be postponed without notably increasing the danger to the mother.

21. Euthanasia ("mercy killing") in all its forms is forbidden.

22. The failure to supply the ordinary means of preserving life is equivalent to euthanasia.

23. It is not euthanasia to give a dying person sedatives merely for the alleviation of pain, even to the extent of depriving the patient of the use of sense and reason, when this extreme measure is judged necessary. Such sedatives should not be given before the patient is properly prepared for death . . . nor should they be given to patients who are able and willing to endure their sufferings for spiritual motives.

24. Hysterectomy, in the presence of pregnancy and even before viability, is permitted when directed to the removal of maternal pathology which is distinct from the pregnancy and which is of such a serious nature that the operation cannot be safely postponed until the fetus is viable.

25. Post-mortem examinations must not be begun until real death is morally certain.

(Note: The main point here is that the physician should be reasonably certain that the subject is not merely apparently dead before he starts the post-mortem. . . . Theologians usually allow the following intervals for the conditional administration of the sacraments: one-half hour to one hour, in the case of death after a lingering illness; and two or even more hours, in the case of sudden death.)

26. For a very serious reason labor may be induced immediately after the fetus is viable. In a properly equipped hospital the fetus may sometimes be considered viable after 26 weeks (6 calendar months); otherwise, 28 weeks are required.

27. In all cases in which the presence of pregnancy would render some procedure illicit (for example, curettage), the physician must make use of such pregnancy tests and consultation as may be needed in order to be reasonably certain that the patient is not pregnant.

28. Radiation therapy of the mother's reproductive organs is permitted during pregnancy only when necessary to suppress a dangerous pathological condition.

II. *Procedures Involving Reproductive Organs and Functions*

(Note: The subsequent Ethical Directives suppose that there is no special risk to life, either for the patient or—in the case of a pregnant woman—for a fetus; otherwise the principles previously given must be applied.)

Principles

29. The unnatural use of the sex faculty (for example, masturbation) is never permitted, even for a laudable purpose.

30. Continence, either periodic or continuous, is the only form of birth control not in itself morally objectionable.

31. Procedures that induce sterility, whether permanent or temporary, are permitted when (a) they are immediately directed to the cure, diminution, or prevention of a serious pathological condition; (b) a simpler treatment is not reasonably available; and (c) the sterility itself is an unintended and, in the circumstances, an unavoidable effect.

Particular Applications

32. Castration, surgical or otherwise, is permitted when required for the removal or diminution of a serious pathological condition, even in other organs. Hence: oophorectomy or irradiation of the ovaries may be allowed in treating carcinoma of the breast and metastasis therefrom; and orchidectomy is permitted in the treatment of carcinoma of the prostate. In all cases the procedure least harmful to the reproductive organs should be used, if equally effective with other procedures.

33. All operations, treatments, and devices designed to render conception impossible are morally objectionable. Advising or otherwise encouraging contraceptive practices is not permitted.

(Note: Continence is not contraception. A physician is entitled to . . . explain the practice of periodic continence to those who have need of such knowledge.)

34. Hysterectomy is permitted when it is sincerely judged to be the only effective remedy for prolapse of the uterus, or when it is a necessary means of removing some other serious pathology.

35. Hysterectomy is not permitted as a routine procedure after any definite number of cesarean sections. In these cases the pathology of each patient must be considered individually; and care must be had that hysterectomy is not performed as a merely contraceptive measure.

36. Even after the childbearing function has ceased, hysterectomy is still a mutilation, and it must not be performed unless sound medical reasons call for it.

37. If procedures designed to correct uterine malpositions induce sterility, the conditions given in n. 31 must be fulfilled; if they do not induce sterility the principle of proportionate good, as stated in n. 40, is to be applied.

38. Sterility tests involving the procurement of the male specimen by masturbation or unnatural intercourse are morally objectionable.

39. The use of artificial means to enable the natural marital act to be fertile (for example, the cervical spoon) is permitted. No other form of artificial insemination is in accord with the divine plan for human procreation. Especially objectionable are donor insemination and unnatural methods of obtaining semen.

III. Other Procedures

Principle

40. Any procedure harmful to the patient is morally justified only insofar as it is designed to produce a proportionate good.

Ordinarily the "proportionate good" that justifies a directly mutilating procedure must be the welfare of the patient himself. However, such things as blood transfusions and skin grafts are permitted for the good of others. Whether this principle of "helping the neighbor" can justify organic transplantation is now a matter of discussion. Physicians are asked to present practical cases for solution, if such cases exist.

Particular Applications

41. The removal of an apparently healthy appendix while the abdomen is open for some other reason may be allowed at the discretion of the physician.

42. Experimentation on patients without due consent and not for the benefit of the patients themselves is morally objectionable. Even when experimentation is for the genuine good of the patient, the physician must have the consent, at least reasonably presumed, of the patient or his legitimate guardian.

43. Ghost surgery, which implies the calculated deception of the patient as to the identity of the operating surgeon, is morally objectionable.

44. Lobotomy and similar operations are morally justifiable when medically indicated as the proper treatment of serious mental illness or of intractable pain. In each case the welfare of the patient himself, considered as a person, must be the determining factor. These operations are not justifiable when less extreme remedies are reasonably available or in cases in which the probability of harm to the patient outweighs the hope of benefit for him.

45. The use of narcosis or hypnosis for the cure of mental illness is permissible with the consent at least reasonably presumed of the patient, provided due precautions are taken to protect the patient and the hospital from harmful effects, and provided the patient's right to secrecy is duly safeguarded.

46. There is no objection on principle and in general to psychoanalysis or any other form of psychotherapy. The psychiatrists and psychotherapists, however, must observe the cautions dictated by sound morality, such as: avoiding the error of pan-sexualism; never counseling even material sin; respecting secrets that the patient is not permitted to reveal; avoiding the disproportionate risk of moral dangers.

47. Shock-therapy is permitted when medically indicated.

48. Unnecessary procedures, whether diagnostic or therapeutic, are morally objectionable. A procedure is unnecessary when no proportionate reason requires it for the welfare of the patient; *a fortiori* unnecessary is any procedure that is contraindicated by sound medical standards. This directive applies especially, but not exclusively, to unnecessary surgery.

SECTION II: THE RELIGIOUS CARE OF PATIENTS

I. BAPTISM

49. Except in cases of emergency (that is, danger of death), all requests for baptism made by adults or for infants should be referred to the

chaplain of the hospital, who will see that the prescriptions of canon law are observed.

50. Even cases of emergency should be referred to the chaplain or to some other priest if one is available. If a priest is not available, anyone having the use of reason can and should baptize.

51. The ordinary method of conferring emergency baptism is as follows: Water is poured on the head in such a way that it will flow on the skin, and not merely on the hair; and while the water is being poured these words are pronounced: *I baptize you in the Name of the Father, and of the Son, and of the Holy Ghost.* The water will more easily flow on the skin if it is poured on the forehead. The same person who pours the water should pronounce the words.

52. When emergency baptism is conferred, the fact should be noted on the patient's chart, and the chaplain should be notified as soon as possible so that he can properly record it.

II. OTHER SACRAMENTS

53. It is the mind of the Church that the sick should have the widest possible liberty to receive the sacraments frequently. The generous cooperation of the entire hospital staff and personnel is requested for this purpose.

54. While providing the sick abundant opportunity to receive Holy Communion, there should be no interference with the perfect freedom of the faithful according to the mind of the Church to communicate or not to communicate; and moreover there should be no pressure exerted that might lead to sacrilegious Communions.

55. Those in danger of death are not obliged to keep the Eucharistic fast. Others must observe the modified legislation as given in the Appendix.

56. Sufficient privacy should be provided for confession in wards and semi-private rooms, or the patient moved elsewhere for confession, if this is possible.

57. When possible, one who is critically ill should receive Holy Viaticum and extreme unction while in full possession of his rational faculties. The chaplain must, therefore, be notified as soon as an illness is diagnosed as critical.

III. SPIRITUAL CARE OF NON-CATHOLICS

58. While avoiding odious proselytism, we must not be indifferent to the spiritual needs and desires of non-Catholics; and everything consonant with our principles must be done for them. In particular, when a non-Catholic patient asks to have his minister or rabbi called this request should be honored.

IV. DISPOSAL OF AMPUTATED MEMBERS

59. Major parts of the body should be buried in a cemetery when it is reasonably possible to do so. Moreover, the members of Catholics should, if possible, be buried in blessed ground. When burial is not reasonably possible, the burning of such members is permissible.

V. DISPOSAL OF DEAD FETUS

60. The normal manner of disposing of a dead fetus, regardless of the degree of maturity, is suitable burial. A fetus may be burned only if sanitation or some similarly serious reason requires it. In exceptional cases, there is no objection to retaining a fetus for laboratory study and observation; but it should not be preserved in its membranes unless it is so obviously dead that baptism would certainly be of no avail.

(Note: It is imperative that all who are concerned with the disposal of a fetus should know and observe pertinent prescriptions of civil law. If there seems to be a conflict between the provisions of civil law and the instructions given here the matter should be referred to the hospital authorities for clarification.)

Cases to be analyzed

1 A physician sometimes performs unnecessary operations on wealthy patients who are convinced that an operation is necessary. He uses the money to finance some important research.

2 "I never ask a priest about the morality of certain operations," says a certain physician. "I am not certain that they are wrong, so I just go ahead with them."

3 The parents of a five-year-old child refuse to allow blood transfusions even though the physician in charge says they are the only hope for the child. He gives the blood transfusions anyway.

4 A famous surgeon accepts many patients but allows his assistants to perform many of his operations. His patients are not aware that they were operated on by the assistants.

5 An intern at a state hospital remarks: "An intern must do many things that he knows are not morally justifiable. He need not worry about this, though, because he is simply carrying out the orders of his superiors."

Topics for discussion[2]

1 A physician performs abortions only when called for by the teaching of medical books.

2 What principles are involved in the paragraph entitled "Birth Control" (pages 272-73)? Explain.

3 A Catholic doctor urges non-Catholics to practice birth control if necessary, for the Church's prohibition does not bind them.

4 A physician cannot always follow in practice what Catholic authors contend is the only right way of acting.

5 The life of a mother of a family is more important than that of a baby just entering the world, and so where both lives cannot be saved, the doctor may take the life of the baby in order to preserve the life of the mother.

---

[2] Not all the assertions contained in the topics are true. The student is to judge the truth of any assertions made and to explain his decision.

6 What should a surgeon do in an emergency case where in his opinion he will probably be doing wrong if he operates and probably be doing wrong if he does not operate? He must do one or the other at once.

7 A physician has the obligation of giving advice on moral questions and therefore has the obligation of acquainting himself with the moral teachings of the Church.

8 If a patient is doing something which is morally wrong but which he thinks to be all right, it is better for the physician to say nothing.

9 In dealing with certain types of mental patients it is very useful to record interviews. A physician can do this without the consent of the patient because it is for the patient's good.

Bibliography

Healy, Edwin F. *Medical Ethics*. Chicago: Loyola University Press, 1956.

Kelly, Gerald. *Medico-Moral Problems*. St. Louis: Catholic Hospital Association, 1958.

CHAPTER XV

The
duties
of nurses

Nursing is clearly a noble profession, for its object is the practice of the corporal work of mercy of caring for the sick. Its objectives of lessening human suffering and of saving human life raise this profession high above many others with less spiritual aims. The nurse is called upon to attend to human needs from cradle to deathbed. In the performance of her services she has it in her power to be a great influence for good. By her sympathy and kindness she can win many souls to God. By her help in bringing the sacraments to the sick and the dying she can be a real apostle. In order to perform her sublime offices with the proper devotion and prudence and in order properly to utilize her golden opportunities for gaining merit, the nurse should regard all her patients as children of God and administer to them as to His children. She should make use of the countless occasions she has for practicing self-discipline and self-sacrifice, for growing steadily in virtue. Her long hours of solicitous watching, her ever-amiable attitude toward the many types of individual with whom she has to deal, her inspiring calmness in the midst of trying circumstances—all this requires extraordinary patience. The many unpleasant menial tasks that she is called upon to perform will lead her to humility. She can quickly advance too in generosity, in meekness, and in compassion. One can, then, readily see the precious opportunities that a nurse has to develop in herself the full-blown beauty of soul of the truly Christian woman.

A good nurse is one who fulfills all the essential requirements of her calling, and in order to do this she must be a person of strong, sterling character. A person who begins this profession should, then, make a careful analysis of her various qualities in order to ascertain what needs strengthening and what needs rectifying. Let her determine, with the aid perhaps of a sincere friend, what her defects are; whether, for example, she is self-centered, irritable, lazy, vain, austere, pessimistic, flighty, too talkative, too taciturn, and so forth. By reinforcing her virtues and by correcting her defects she will not only make herself a more efficient instrument in her high calling, but she will ennoble and beautify her whole person through growth in holiness, to her own benefit and that of her patients and of her profession.

Today the field of nursing is very wide. There are nurses who are attached to Catholic hospitals, to public hospitals, to small private hospitals, to factories, to schools, and to doctors' offices. There are public-service nurses, United States Army nurses, missionary nurses, and local visiting nurses. Each of these groups has its own peculiar problems. We shall limit ourselves to the consideration of a few general points that more particularly concern all those of the nursing profession. Since many of the principles that have been explained under "The Duties of Doctors" apply in some degree to nurses also, it would be well to review the material in the preceding chapter.

REMAINING ON A CASE

If a nurse takes over a case, this act of hers creates between the patient and herself a contract. This contract binds the patient to remunerate the nurse according to the fee agreed upon. It also imposes on the nurse the duty of giving the patient the ordinary care and attention looked for in one of her profession. She may not abandon the case at will unless she provides or gives the patient time to provide a capable substitute, or unless she has a reason that justifies her dropping the case. A justifying reason would be one which would cancel the contract made with the patient because of the latter's violation of the terms of the agreement, as would happen, for example, if a patient suddenly decided to move to a distant city and demanded that his nurse come there to care for him.

THE NURSE'S NEED OF RESERVE

The nurse must be solicitous for her patient's wants and sympathetic in her dealings with those under her care, but this involves the danger of lowering barriers that would ordinarily serve as a restraint against improper conduct. Male patients who receive the conscientious administrations of an alert nurse will deeply appreciate the services rendered and will be drawn to her by feelings of natural affection. In that uncustomary atmosphere where he enjoys so much leisure and such constant attention, the male patient is apt to allow his emotions to influence him unduly, and as a consequence he may forget the rules of conduct which guide him in the surroundings of his everyday life. There is danger here, and the nurse by her strictly professional attitude must help to protect the patient against himself. She can do much to prevent occurrences that would later be a source of deep regret both to herself and to the patient.

Because of the subject matter of part of her studies and because of her intimate care of the bodies of the patients, there may follow for the nurse a slight lessening of that modest reserve that is one of the safeguards of virtue. This may manifest itself in the careless way in which she chats about sexual matters or recounts off-color jokes and stories, and so forth. This manner of acting, although perhaps sinless, may quite easily prepare the way for sin, especially if such loose talk is indulged in with those of the opposite sex; for example, with orderlies, interns, or male nurses. Moreover, others at times use such conversation as a starting point for trying to engage in undue familiarities.

A woman nurse will, of course, be called upon to attend both male and female patients. In administering to the wants of male patients delicate situations may arise, and these the nurse should accept in a purely professional way. She may, without scruple, satisfy the requirements of necessity. She is simply fulfilling the demands of her duty, and she may permit any temptations that thus arise either for herself or for the patient. She does not want them there, nor does she encourage them in any way. She merely tolerates their presence.

RESPECTING SECRETS

The nurse often finds herself in circumstances where she shares in the secrets of her patients. It may be that she cannot but overhear the confidential matters that the patient discusses with members of the family, with physicians, or with others. It may happen that she hears the patient revealing secrets in his sleep or while coming out of the anesthetic. These secrets she is bound to respect. She may not divulge their contents to others (for example, fellow nurses). She should be governed by the rules laid down regarding secrets on pages 241-46.

Secrets that the nurse has learned from her patients may not be disclosed, even to the attending physician or to the other nurses who are working on the same case or to members of the patient's family. The secret has been entrusted to the nurse alone, and she has no right to pass it on to others, even though she tell them under secrecy. Attempting unjustly to worm secrets from patients who are coming out of the anesthetic is of course sinful. This is forcing the patient to reveal his secret knowledge to one who has no right to it.

This duty of maintaining secrecy with regard to confidential communications does not end once the nurse finishes the case where she learned these secrets. The nurse may never reveal such secrets, whether they were entrusted to her or whether she learned them in performing her professional services (for example, if while caring for the patient she discovers a hidden, disgraceful disease).

AVOIDANCE OF LIES

It is never necessary, in order to be a good nurse, that one should be able to tell lies without betraying oneself, for one is never under any circumstances permitted to tell a lie. All lies, even "white lies," are sinful. Lying should have no place in the life of a conscientious nurse, whether the lies providing a way out of a difficulty are told to the patient, relatives of the sick man, attending physicians, or hospital authorities. Lying would not be justified even if it were done at the bidding of the physician handling the case or of hospital authorities.

Is it not actually impossible to carry on the work of a nurse and not be obliged to tell lies, at least occasionally; for example, in order to save the patient from a severe and injurious shock? No, it is not at all impossible. No one is ever under the obligation of sinning, even for a good cause. Hence if there were to be a choice between telling a lie and allowing the patient to suffer a grave injury, the physical injury must be preferred to the offense against God.

Though it is never permitted to tell a lie, still a nurse must in many instances hide the truth. She may not, for example, disclose secrets; she must at times prevent the patient from learning his true condition; and she must find some means of keeping worrisome reports from nervous, anxious relatives. What is the nurse to do when it is imperative that the truth be hidden from certain persons? The answer is simple. She must use either evasion or a broad mental reservation. She may evade giving the information sought by answering the question asked with another question. If, for example, a visitor asks the nurse: "Is it true that your patient has cancer?" the nurse may try to evade giving an answer either by referring the inquirer to the doctor in charge of the case (the ordinary way), or by remarking: "What a ridiculous question!" or "My patient told me the funniest joke yesterday," and she recounts the story in detail in order to change the subject from the patient's malady.

Evasion, however, is not always possible or preferable. The only resort left may be the use of a mental reservation. In treating this matter before, we stressed the fact that not only the words used by the speaker convey meaning, but also the circumstances in which the words are spoken. Hence the phrase, "Circumstances speak." This must be kept in mind when we apply the doctrine of mental reservation to cases where the nurse would be called upon to use this means of concealing the truth. Because of the practical value for nurses of the proper understanding of this doctrine, we here give some examples showing the difference between mental reservations and lies.

1. A dying patient asks the nurse: "Nurse, is there any hope of my getting well?"

If the nurse answers: "Of course there is. Don't worry. You will be all right," she has used a mental reservation, although actually there is no hope in her mind that the patient will recover. If, however, the nurse says: "I was talking to the famous Dr. Jones about your case yesterday and he thinks you will recover," and if the nurse in reality has said nothing to Dr. Jones about the case, she is guilty of a lie. Such a statement is positively false, and there are no circumstances present that could give it a second meaning.

The first answer is a mental reservation because circumstances give such phrases as these a meaning different from the bare words themselves. They are general formulas used with the sick to keep them from brooding over their condition and to hide the real state of affairs in hospital phrases that mean very little. The sick man, if prudent, will recognize them as such and will not accept them in their literal meaning. Such phrases, then, as the following may be used without scruple, even though the patient actually shows no improvement: "You're looking much better today" or "You are improving right along."

2. A relative of a patient when visiting a hospital asks a nurse how the patient is getting along. Actually the patient is much worse today. If in this case the nurse answers: "Mary is getting along nicely" or "She is doing as well as can be expected," she has used a mental reservation. These are merely stock answers which the prudent man recognizes as hospital formulas. They are known to mean no more than this: "I can give you no information about the condition of the patient. She is here at the hospital. That is all I can say." If on the other hand the nurse says: "Mary ate a hearty breakfast this morning," when actually Mary had taken no breakfast at all, she is guilty of a lie. Here the nurse pronounces as true a statement that she knows to be false and there are no circumstances present that modify the meaning of the statement.

Falsifying the chart of a patient has the same malice as lying. It is, in fact, a written lie, for the nurse puts down on the record a statement with regard, for example, to medicine, temperature, or treatment that does not coincide with what she knows to be the truth. Moreover, such false reports could result in harm to the patient whom the nurse is under contract to help. Hence such a nurse is not only guilty of the venial sin of lying, but she may also be responsible for causing injury to another.

HELPING IN ILLICIT OPERATIONS

Eugenic sterilization, feticide, abortion, and similar operations are against the natural law, and so may never be performed without sin. The surgeon who perpetrates these crimes is violating the Fifth Commandment. May a nurse ever assist at illicit operations such as these? To answer this question accurately we must distinguish between the various meanings of the term "assist at."

1. A nurse may never participate in the actual operation or in the performing of the evil act. This type of assistance means taking active part in the unlawful act itself, and so is of its very nature evil. Hence it would always be forbidden under pain of sin. A nurse would rarely be asked to cooperate in this manner, for she has not been trained to do so.

2. May a nurse ever be present at illicit operations in order, for example, to attend to the requirements of the operating surgeon? May she hand him the instruments necessary in an operation for criminal abortion and the like? The nurse should, if possible, avoid being present at such operations. At times, however, she may find it very difficult to refuse to be present. In general, then, a nurse may assist at illicit operations by proffering instruments to the surgeon, by assisting in moving the patient, and in other similar ways, provided two conditions are verified: (a) she must in no way desire this illicit operation to take place; (b) she has a weighty reason for being present.

She must in no way desire the illicit operation, for if she does so she desires that God's law be violated, that sin be committed. Hence she would be guilty of formal cooperation in thus desiring and helping on this illicit operation. Formal cooperation in evil is always sinful.

If the nurse in no way desires the illicit operation to occur and is only offering her material cooperation because she has an excusing reason, she commits no sin. An excusing reason for such material cooperation would be any one of the following:

1. The nurse would lose her position if she refused to assist in this way (that is, by material cooperation), and she could not

get another position without much difficulty; or she would have to leave her present training school and attend, at much inconvenience to herself, one located in a distant city.

2. She would lose her position here at this hospital were she to refuse to assist at such operations. She could get a position at other hospitals, but she could not get the special courses and training which she gets here in her present position.

3. She would lose her present position, though she could easily get another position elsewhere, but her present position enables her to provide spiritual help for many who otherwise would receive no spiritual attention.

> EXAMPLE. If Ann leaves this state hospital, she could find work at St. Joseph's Sanitarium; but at this state hospital she is doing much spiritual good in summoning the priest for Catholic patients, in helping the dying to make their peace with God, in baptizing dying babies, and in other ways. If she is replaced at this hospital by a non-Catholic, this good will not be done.

In brief, then, a nurse may assist at (cooperate materially in) illicit operations, provided two conditions are fulfilled. These two conditions are: (1) She does not wish the surgeon to perform this sinful operation. She would prevent it if she could. (2) She has a weighty reason for lending her material cooperation.

The assistance that the nurse may render under these conditions refers to such actions as the following: (1) preparing the patient's body for the operation, (2) bringing the patient to the operating room, (3) administering the anesthetic (local or general), (4) handing the instruments to the operating surgeon.

ADMINISTERING BAPTISM

A nonviable fetus, no matter how prematurely it is born, should be baptized at once. Moreover, stillborn infants should be baptized unless it is certain that they are dead. The only absolutely certain sign of death which medical authorities recognize is putrefaction.

The nurse should see to it that she is familiar with the proper way to baptize, and also with the further precautions which are necessary with regard to the baptism of the immature fetus. At times, too, she will find it her duty to administer the sacrament of baptism even during the child's birth; namely, when there is grave danger that death will overtake it before it is fully born. The way to administer baptism is to *pour* water on the child's head and pronounce *at the same time* the words: "I baptize thee in the name of the Father, and of the Son, and of the Holy Spirit." It is permissible to soak a piece of cotton batting in water and squeeze it over the child's head so that the water flows on the head.

BAPTISM OF DYING INFANTS

If an unbaptized infant for whom the nurse is caring is in a dying condition, the obligations of the nurse as regards the administration of baptism are conditioned by the religion of the parents. We must distinguish as follows:

1. If the mother or father of the child is a Catholic, there is ordinarily no difficulty. The nurse should at once summon a priest in order that he may administer the sacrament. If, however, no priest is available and there is immediate danger of death, she herself may and should baptize the dying child.

2. If the parents are non-Catholics, the nurse may baptize the child unless more harm than good would result from her act. "More harm than good" would result if the nurse were to baptize such a child openly and despite the non-Catholic parents' prohibition, for her act would redound to the harm of the Catholic Church. It would generally create bitterness and resentful attacks against the Church, and so it would go counter to the common spiritual good. Hence if the parents object to the dying baby's baptism, the nurse should not baptize it unless she can administer the baptism altogether secretly.

BAPTISM OF THE DYING INSANE

The insane who are dying may be dealt with in the same way as dying infants.

BAPTISM OF DYING ADULTS

As regards dying adults who are not baptized, we must distinguish here between the various cases that might occur:

1. If the dying adult is conscious, he may not be baptized unless his consent is given and unless he receives, if possible, instruction in the essential mysteries of the faith (that is, God's existence, His rewarding with heaven and His punishing with hell, the Trinity, the Incarnation).

291

2. If the dying adult is unconscious and will probably remain so until death, he may be baptized conditionally in all cases even if he is totally unknown.

THE LAST SACRAMENTS

If a nurse is caring for a Catholic patient, she should notify the priest, at least when her patient becomes dangerously ill, so that he may administer the last sacraments. Moreover, even though her patient has apparently died the priest should be summoned immediately if the patient has not received the last sacraments. Why summon the priest after the patient is, to all appearances, dead? The reason is that the stopping of respiration and circulation does not indicate for certain that death has come. Life may still be present, though it is so weak that it is not manifested externally. The only certain sign of death is general putrefaction, and so, unless this sign is there, the sacraments may be administered conditionally.

How long after the patient's pulse has stopped is he to be considered as still probably alive? If death is the result of a long illness, the patient is probably still alive for at least an hour after all external signs of life have disappeared; if death is sudden, life probably remains for about four hours after apparent death. The sacraments may therefore be administered conditionally an hour to four hours after apparent death, the time depending on the individual case; and so the nurse should summon a priest in order that her patient may have the benefit of the last sacraments.

INDULGENCED PRAYERS

A nurse would do well to provide herself with (1) a happy-death crucifix and (2) a Stations of the Cross crucifix.

A happy-death crucifix is one to which has been attached the plenary indulgence at the hour of death. Since the use of this crucifix is not limited to its owner, any dying Catholic can gain this plenary indulgence by kissing or at least touching it and recalling with love the name of Jesus. The dying person must also accept with resignation his suffering and death. By her prudent use of such a crucifix the nurse could greatly help many Catholic patients in their last agony.

292

A Stations of the Cross crucifix is one to which have been attached the indulgences of the Stations of the Cross. With this crucifix a Catholic who is confined to a hospital room or who is unable without much inconvenience to make the Stations of the Cross in a church in the ordinary way may gain all the indulgences granted to those who make the Stations of the Cross. To do this the sick person should hold the crucifix in his hand (or if that is too inconvenient, he must at least have it on his person) and recite with contrite heart twenty Our Fathers, twenty Hail Marys, and twenty Glorias for the following intentions: fourteen Our Fathers, Hail Marys, and Glorias in honor of the fourteen Stations of the Cross; five in honor of the five wounds of our Lord; and one for the intentions of the pope.

The nurse herself (or anybody else) who is unable to leave the sickroom and go to the chapel or church may gain the Stations of the Cross indulgences in the same way in which the patient can. If the nurse (or anyone else) recites these prayers with the patient, both gain all these indulgences (provided of course that both fulfill the requirement of being unable to go to the chapel). If these prayers are said in common, only one person need hold the indulgenced crucifix. These Stations of the Cross indulgences may be gained as often as the above conditions are fulfilled, even many times on the same day.

Moreover, in case the sick person is unable even to recite the prescribed prayers (that is, twenty Our Fathers, Hail Marys, and Glorias), he may gain the indulgences if with contrite heart he kisses or looks upon the Stations of the Cross crucifix as it is held before him and he recites some prayer (for example, "Sweet Heart of Jesus, be my love") in memory of our Lord's passion and death. Both indulgences, the happy-death and the Stations of the Cross, may be attached to the same crucifix. Many priests belonging to religious orders enjoy the faculty of putting on crucifixes both these indulgences.

HOSPITAL REGULATIONS

Rules that are prescribed for nurses by hospital authorities do not ordinarily bind under pain of sin. This applies to regulations forbidding smoking while on duty, informing patients of their temperature, eating with patients, or going out of the hospital without permission. These regulations are in themselves merely penal laws. If the nurse is caught violating them, she must be ready to suffer the penalty imposed.

Though they do not bind in conscience, these rules should nevertheless be obeyed because they help in the general management of the hospital and contribute to the welfare of the patients. In certain circumstances, moreover, a nurse might be bound by the natural law to do what is prescribed by hospital regulations. For example, if telling the patient his temperature would be harmful to him, charity would require that she refrain from telling the patient what his temperature is.

Topics for discussion[1]

1 Should the Catholic nurse try to convert her non-Catholic parents?
2 What books would you recommend to a non-Catholic who desires to become acquainted with Catholic teaching (1) if the non-Catholic is an uneducated adult, (2) if she is a college student, (3) if she is a girl of 15 years?
3 A good nurse must be able to tell lies discreetly.
4 What reasons should prompt the nurse to give self-sacrificing and devoted care to her patient?
5 No nurse may advise the practice of artificial birth control.

Bibliography

Gounley, Martin E. *Digest of Ethics for Nurses.* Paterson: St. Anthony Guild Press, 1949.

Hayes, Edward J.; Paul J. Hayes; and Dorothy E. Kelly. *Moral Handbook of Nursing.* New York: The Macmillan Company, 1956.

Johnson, Brian D. *The Catholic Nurse.* London: Burns, Oates and Washbourne, 1950.

La Rochelle, Stanislas and C. T. Fink. *Handbook of Medical Ethics for Nurses, Physicians and Priests,* eighth edition, translated by M. E. Poupore, A. Carter, and R. M. H. Power. Westminster: Newman Press, 1949.

Lennon, Sister Mary Isidore. *Professional Adjustments.* St. Louis: C. V. Mosby Company, 1946.

McAllister, Joseph B. *Ethics, with Special Application to the Nursing Profession.* Philadelphia: W. B. Saunders Company, 1947.

McFadden, Charles J. *Medical Ethics for Nurses.* Philadelphia: F. A. Davis Company, 1946.

---

[1] Not all the assertions contained in the topics are true. The student is to judge the truth of any assertions made and to explain his decision.

Index

Astrology, 80-84
Atomic bombs, 161-62
Attack, defense against unjust, 154-56
Attention required at Mass, 116
Authors, rights of, 203

Babies, baptism of, 272, 279-80, 290-91
Bad faith, possession in, 208
Badness of an act, 9
Bankruptcy, 210
Baptism
    of dying adults, 279-80, 291-92
    of dying infants, 272, 279-80, 290-91
    of dying insane, 291
    of nonviable fetus, 290
    of stillborn infants, 290
Benediction, attendance at, 118
Best man, at Protestant wedding, 71
Betrothed, duties of, 183-84
Betting, 219-22
Bible
    Protestant and the Index, 262
    use of in taking oath, 107
Birth control, obligations of doctors concerning, 272-73
Bishop
    duties of faithful toward, 136-37
    power of to dispense from fast and abstinence, 254-55
    power of to grant permission to read forbidden books, 265
    power of to prohibit dancing, 187
Blasphemy, 101-02
Body, duty of caring for, 147-53
Bombs, atomic and hydrogen, 161-62
Books
    censorship of, 265-66
    forbidden. See Forbidden books
Borrowing with presumed consent, 199
Bridesmaid, at Protestant wedding, 71
Broad mental reservation, 236-38
Buchman, Frank, 72
Businessmen
    Christian attitude in, 214-15
    duties of, 214-19
    forbidden practices of, 215-16

payment of living wage by, 216-17
Byzantine rite, hearing Mass in, 117

Calumny, 226-27. See also Detraction
Capital punishment, 153-54
Careless driving, 152-53
Caricatures, 232
Catholic Hospital Association of the United States and Canada, code of ethics of, 274-81
Catholic hospitals, ethical and religious directives for, 274-81
Catholic schools, parents' obligation of sending children to, 131-33
Cemetery, sacrilege against, 93
Censorship
    in general, 257-58
    of books, 265-66
Certain conscience, 25
Chain prayer, 92-93
Chalice, sacrilege against, 93
Chapel, sacrilege against, 93
Charge accounts, 199
Charity
    and the obligations of doctors, 268-69
    toward God, 44
    toward the neighbor, 44-45
    virtue of, 43-45
Charms, 91
Charts, falsification of by nurses, 288-89
Chastity
    beauty and merit of, 189-91
    determining guilt in temptations against, 178
    means of overcoming temptations against, 191-93
    sources of danger to, 179-88
Cheating in examinations, 239-41
Children, duties of, 126-30. See also Parents
Choir, singing in during Mass, 116
Christ, spirit of love in law of, 3
Church, sacrilege against, 93
Circumstances of human act, 8-9
Citizens, duties of, 135
Civil law, 23
Civil occupations on Sunday, 121
Civil rulers, duties to, 135

Revelation of secrets, 241-46,
273-74, 286
Revelations, describing fictitious, 73
Revenge, 163-64
Ridicule, 231-32
Right, 36
Rite, hearing Mass in any approved,
117
Roman Index of Forbidden Books.
See Forbidden books
Rosary, purchasing an indulgenced,
95
Rulers, duties to civil, 135

Sabbath, worship on transferred to
Sunday, 112
Sacramental secret, 245
Sacraments, sacrilegious reception
of, 93
Sacred objects, blasphemous ridicule
of, 101
Sacrifice as form of worship, 66-67
Sacrilege, 93-94
Saints
blasphemous ridicule of, 101
irreverent use of names of, 100
recovering relics of from
pawnbroker, 95
Satan, appeal to, 74-75
Scandal, 49-52
Scandalum pusillorum, 50
Schools, prohibition against attend-
ing non-Catholic, 131-33
Scripture. *See* Holy Scripture
Seances, spiritistic, 87-89
Second Commandment, 99-111
Secret, 241-46, 273-74, 286
Self, indirect killing of, 141-42
Self-abuse, 188
Self-defense, 154-56
Servile work on Sunday, 121-23
Seventh Commandment, 196-225
Sex
Catholic principles concerning,
173-74
incorrect attitudes toward, 172-73
purpose of, 171-72
Sex urge, 172-73
Ship, breaking into cargo of
disabled, 204
Simony, 95-96
Simple vincible ignorance, 10

Sin
degrees of gravity in mortal, 59
degrees of gravity in venial, 59-60
degrees of guilt in, 56-60
distinguishing between mortal
and venial, 58
formal, 57
indeliberate venial, 60
licit revelation of, 229-30
material, 57
mortal, 57-59
occasions of, 52-56
promise to commit, 106
requisites for mortal, 58-59
venial, 58-60
See also Conscience; Double
effect; Imputability; Law
Sinning for a good cause, 21-22
Situation ethics, 27-28
Sixth Commandment, 171-95
Slander, 227-31
Slight fear, 13
Sobriety, 149-52
Social justice, 37-39
Sovereign pontiff, duties to, 135-36
Speed-up in factories, 134
Spiritism, 87-89
Spiritual evil, calling down of on
others, 102-03
Spiritual necessity, 45
Spiritual needs of children, 131
State of life, choice of by children,
130
Stations of the Cross crucifix, 293
Statues of the nude, 180
Steady dating, 184-85
Stealing, 198-206
Sterilization, 143-47
Stillborn infants, baptism of, 290
Stipends for Mass, 95-96
Stock market, playing the, 221-22
Strict mental reservation, 236
Strikes, 135
Strip-tease dancers, 180
Substantial badness or goodness of
an act, 9
Suggestion, cures effected by, 90
Suicide, 141-42
Sunday, obligation of hearing Mass
on. *See* Mass
Sunday observance, 112-13, 118-23.
See also Mass